Beauty In Every Form

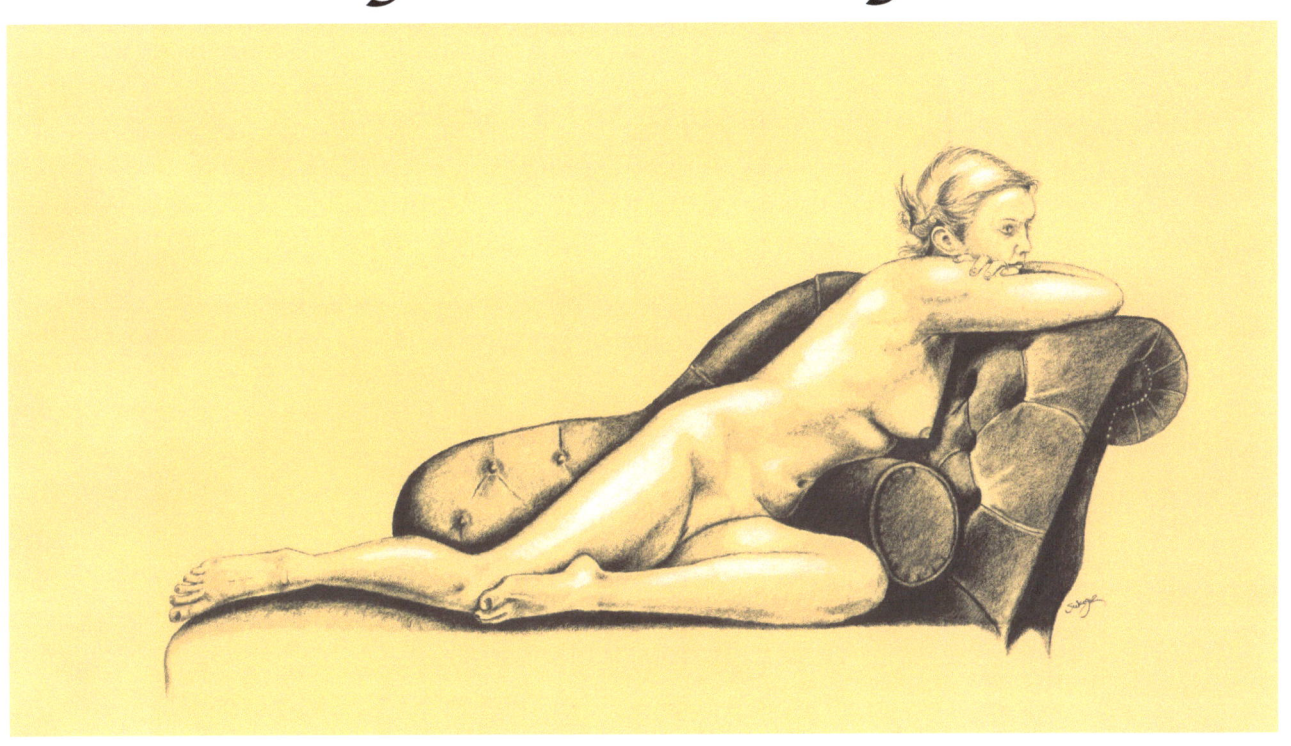

By
Richard J. Savage

ISBN 9781914301339

Copyright 2013 Richard Savage

Illustration Copyright 2013 Richard Savage
All rights reserved.
No part of this book may be used or reproduced
in any manner whatsoever without written permission,
except in the case of brief quotations embodied in
critical articles or reviews.

Published 2013 by Savage Publications
together with BVS Publishing Company
in the United States of America

All world wide rights reserved

Savage Publications

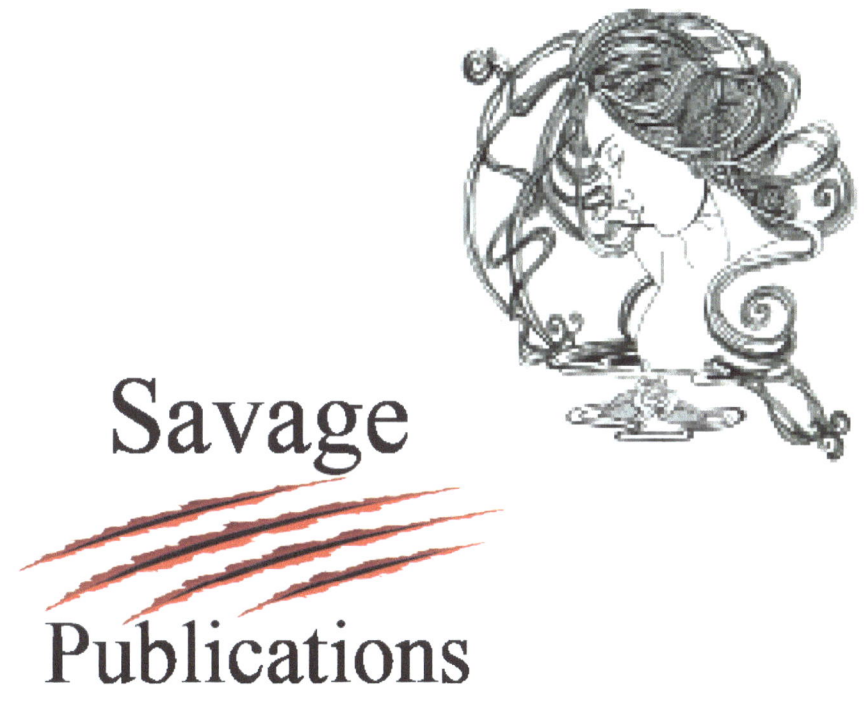

In Association With

Black Velvet Seductions

Beauty In Every Form

By
Richard J. Savage

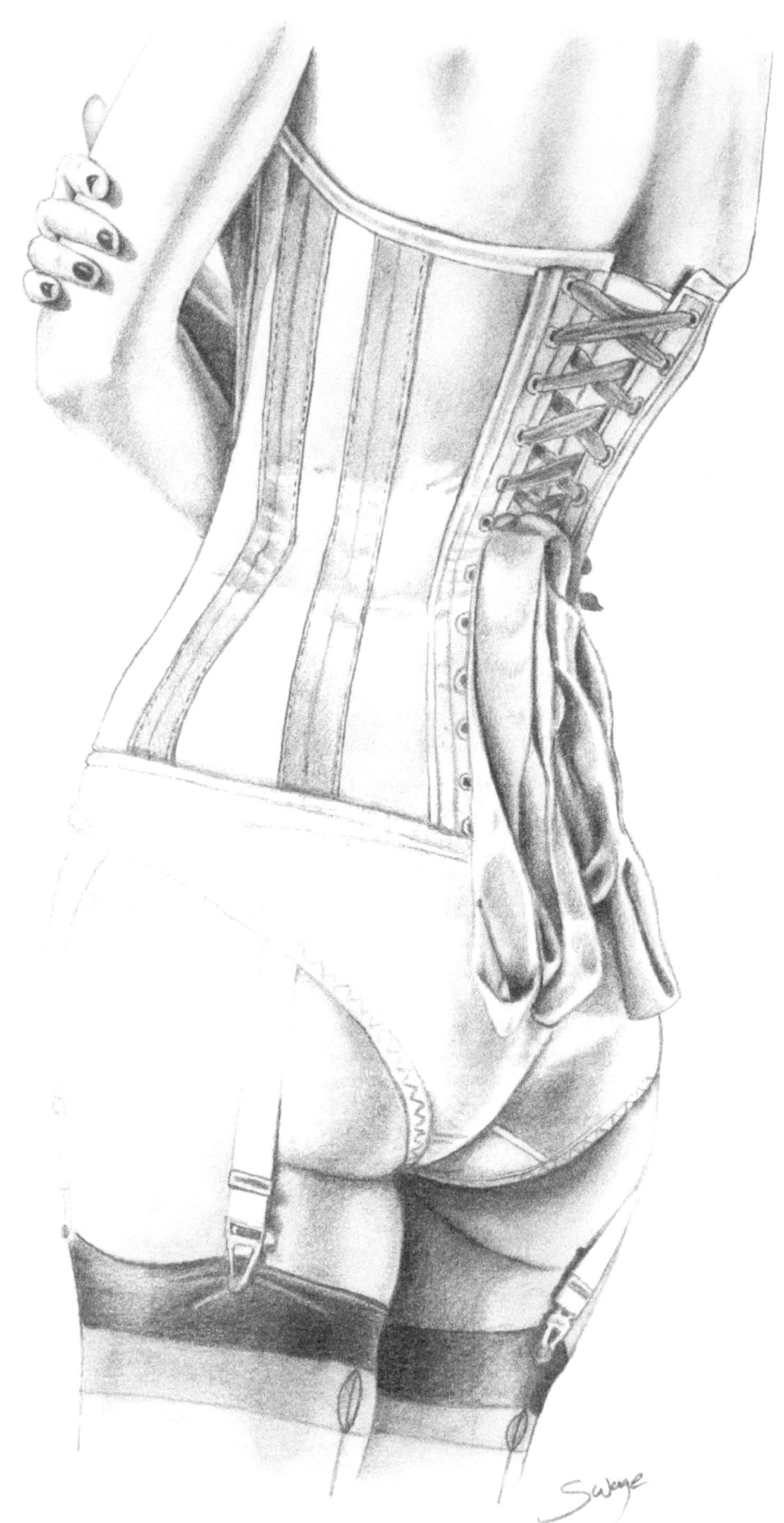

I would like to dedicate this book to all the truly beautiful people I have met in my life. Especially my wife without whose unending patience I would not be able to pursue my dreams.

I would like to thank all the beautiful people who have taken the time and trouble to help me and have believed in this, without whom there would not be this book.

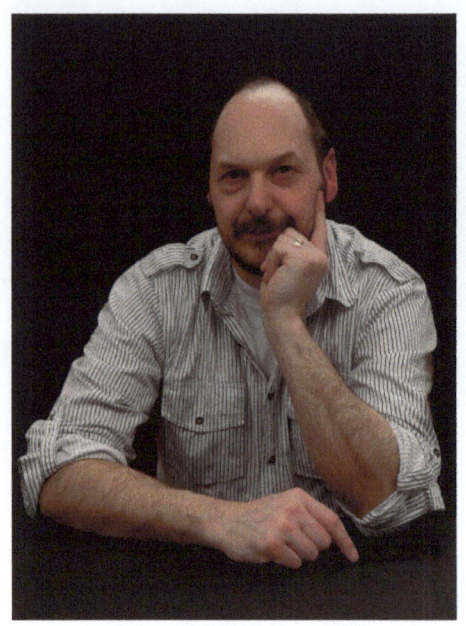
Photograph by Rob Morris 2009

I was born in the north of England, just outside Sheffield, in 1962. My family are very down to earth people. My father was a no nonsense guy, a civil engineer, who encouraged and supported my various endeavors. From my mother I inherited my joy of life, sense of humor and, unfortunately, my dreadful sense of direction. My wife, Kath, is steadfast behind me. Without her hard work I would not be able to explore my creative projects as I do.

I left school at eighteen, forming my first company as a freelance entertainer. Between the ages of eighteen and twenty-five I had a series of interesting jobs, most of which ran concurrently. I was a professional DJ and MC. I served as program controller for a rather busy hospital's radio and TV stations and I had five glorious years as a presenter on pirate radio. Even while working in this creative world, there was one thing that was always a driving force in my life, my artwork.

I have always worked obsessively. At twenty-five I bought a pub in rural Cambridgeshire which my wife and I expanded to incorporate a restaurant. We have run this business successfully for the last twenty- five years.

In the early days, I aspired to be an illustrator of children's stories but this was not an ambition I realized until a couple of years ago. Along with children's illustrations, artistically, I have always been inspired by the human form. I have been a figurative artist for over twenty years. During that time I have always strived to make my art work challenging and thought provoking. I have tried to cover as many diverse topics as I can, trying to capture something of the celebration of life in all its varied and wonderful shades.

I currently work from my Cambridgeshire studio where I teach and have my weekly life drawing class. Many of the life studies in this book were drawn during that class. For many years I worked mainly in acrylics. A lot of my early work was in shades of gray but commercial pressures moved me into color. Over the past year I have worked more in oils. I like the richness of oils and plan to do a lot more of my work in that medium. I am also happy working in pastels, line and wash, watercolor and mixed media.

I draw my inspiration from many sources which include the classical artists, Rembrandt and Rubens, and the Pre-Raphaelites, as well as contemporary artists. I have a high regard for Boris Vallejo and Jack Vettriano. I admire Vettriano's dark, sexy, atmospheric work. There is another artist who inspired me in the early days, Ian Gibson, a great figurative illustrator in my opinion. I am a massive fan of his overtly sexual figurative style from 2000 AD comic.

Foreword By
Dr. Tuppy Owens

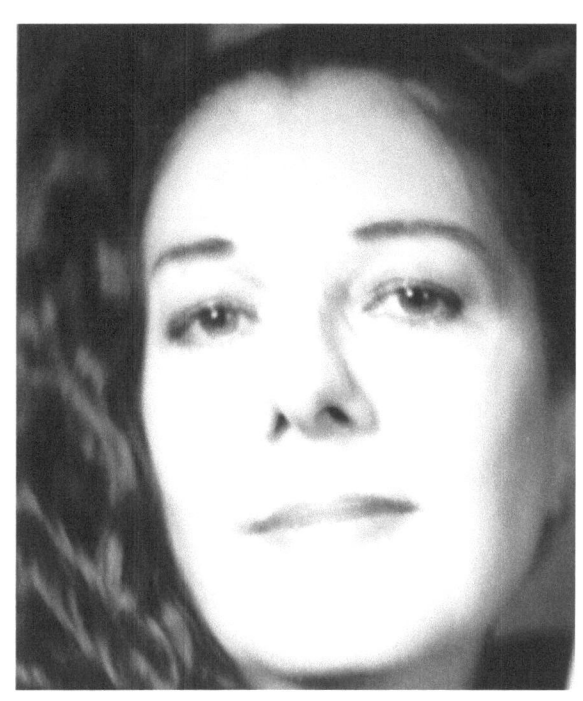

Tuppy Owens is a sex therapist, consultant, campaigner, and writer. She is the author of more than thirty publications. Outsiders, an organization that Tuppy started, seeks to break down barriers between disabilities and sex, relationships and pleasure.

Beauty in Every Form is a triumph of a book, providing a collection of personal feelings from the hearts of many human beings, feelings that are often silenced and considered unfashionable but even so need to be heard.

Considering we are all judged by our appearances, we all have a duty to ourselves to ensure that, as far as possible, our appearances reflect our personalities and we have worked towards making our appearances as delightful as possible *because we are worth it.*

I've been running Outsiders since I founded the club in 1979. It's a club where people with physical and social disabilities can find partners. I think of Outsiders as a microcosm of acceptance in a cruel world. I wish the whole world was like us but it is not.

I entered the sex industry by accident in the 60's and have observed many models and actors go through their own personal journeys of acceptance. I've witnessed how the camera and the paintbrush facilitated those journeys. People who never considered themselves beautiful suddenly blossomed.

The same thing happens to disabled people when they choose to be photographed or painted, a choice normally made to raise their self-esteem. They feel like the lens or the paintbrush is making love to them. Nobody may have looked at them as objects of beauty or even as being worth viewing at all, apart from out of pity.

It's great news that physical attraction between humans is not from looks but through "smelling" a different set of immune system genes. That's good for evolution and good for people who are not conventionally attractive. However, stigma and prejudice still tend to rule. People should learn to trust their noses, and trust their hearts.

This book should help us trust our hearts.

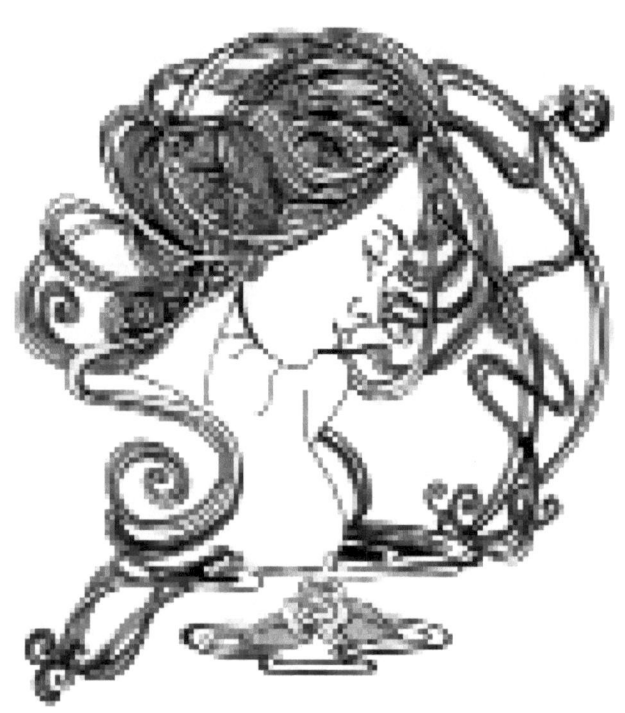

So what is this book about?
Beauty?
What exactly is beauty?

I suspect this book will raise more questions than it answers and I feel that this is good because the answers are within you rather than within me. I am happy if this book simply opens this topic for debate.

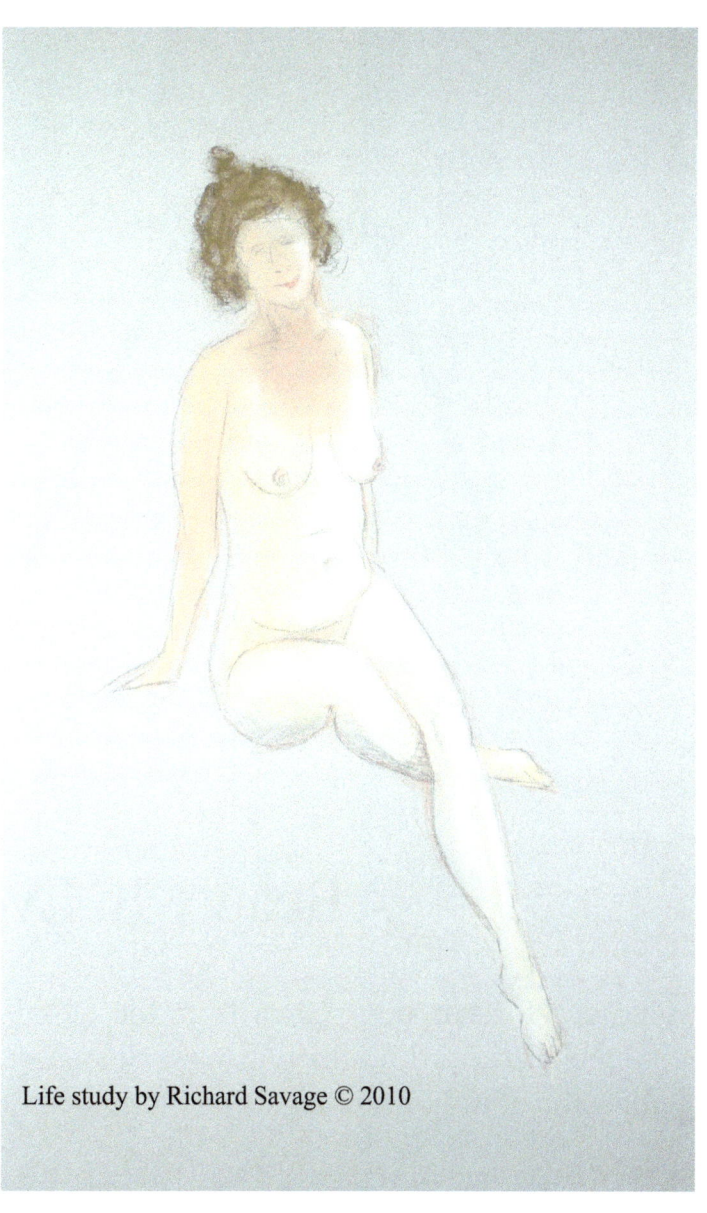

Is everybody beautiful
in their own way?

Is beauty in the eye of the beholder?

Is beauty merely skin deep?

Can an inner beauty shine out?

Is it only the young

who can be beautiful?

And just who gets to say?

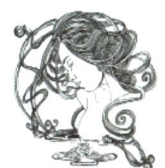

Life study by Richard Savage © 2010

Beauty, for me, is a very subjective term and I do not feel that there is any place for absolutes. In essence, I hope this book will be a celebration of the human form in all its wondrous shapes and sizes, a myriad of unique diversity and fascinating individuality.

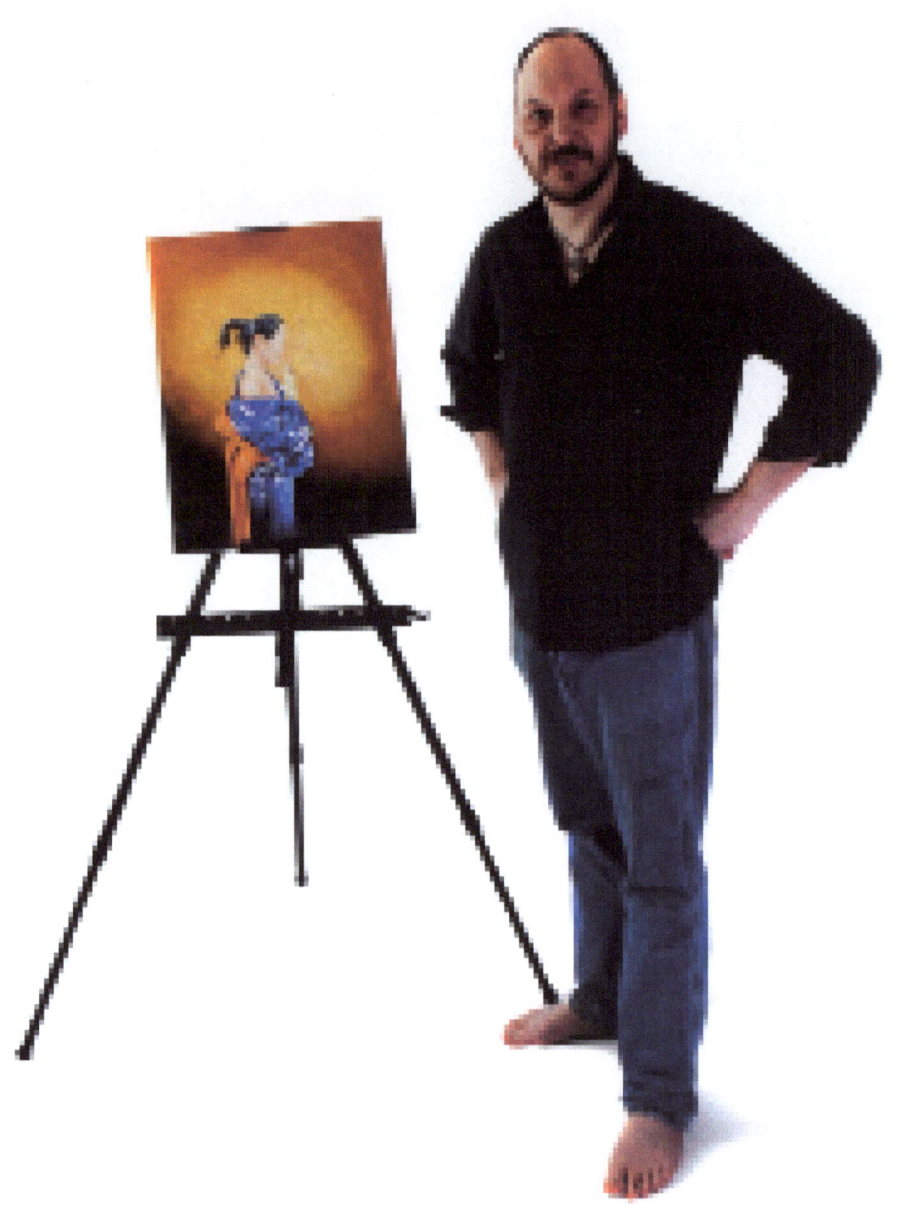

Photograph by Rob Morris 2009

Beauty In Every Form

The idea for this book came from the culmination of several years of life drawing, comments heard while chatting to art clients, artists, photographers and models, together with some of my own thoughts on the subjects of art and beauty.

Art and beauty are both subjects that I am passionate about though I do not profess to be an expert on either.

When I started out as a professional artist many years ago, I had a view of beauty, and that view has not changed. I see beauty everywhere.

Beauty And My Reason For Putting This Book Together

Beauty is a subject I feel passionately about. This book has been swimming around in my mind for several years in one form or another. Originally this was going to be a simple book, showing some of my art, with a running narrative from me, basically saying it is fine to look as you do. I mentioned this idea to my publisher, Laurie Sanders from Black Velvet Seductions. From the outset she was very keen on the idea, but as we talked about our own life experiences and discussed things we had heard from other people on the subject of self-esteem and the judgmental views of others the scope of the project changed.

I don't think many people can say that they have never had low self-esteem. Over the last few years I have felt increasingly more frustrated by some of the judgmental views on body shape. You only have to look at the media in general to see that what seems to be promoted is pencil thin models that are shown in print, every blemish meticulously airbrushed out. These retouched models are there to sell the product and that is fine, but what I resent is the way in which everyday people are made to feel inadequate if they don't live up to this perceived standard. I don't dispute that these models are beautiful, but I believe beauty to be a much broader concept than that.

The media influenced my thinking for this book, positively and negatively. You only have to look in glossy fashion magazines and you see the airbrushed ideals that women, and men for that matter, are supposed to live up to. The positive side was seeing a series of programs on UK TV on this topic. Channel 4's *How to Look Good Naked,* presented by Gok Wan was influential, as was *What Not To Wear,* presented by Trinny and Susannah. In the USA, Oprah Winfrey's shows have dealt with the subject of body image and self-esteem and have been influential as well.

Another factor driving me was working for a guy in the States who perpetually said, "But you are going to paint them pretty aren't you?" My gut reaction was to say, "No, I was planning to paint them butt ugly…. Of course, I plan to make them look beautiful." I was painting the models as they looked to me. To me they looked beautiful. I thought maybe it was me, maybe my lack of ability as an artist, and maybe it was, but it was also clear that beauty really is in the eye of the beholder.

I mentioned these experiences and thoughts on the book to one of my life models during one of my teaching sessions. Within seconds my studio was alive with anecdotes and discussions on what beauty meant to the members of my class. I mentioned it to others and got similar reactions. So it seemed to me that many people had a take on this subject. I went back to Laurie and floated ideas to her and during the conversation we discussed broadening the book to incorporate the ideas of others. The result is this book.

Contributors

It has been fascinating compiling this book and hearing the life experiences of the individuals who have contributed. I sincerely thank all those who have been so open.

Many people have contributed to this book, both directly and indirectly. I have tried to get a diverse range of opinions. The contributors to this book are from all of walks of life and from many backgrounds with a rich variety of life experiences. Featured are: academics, artists, models, dieticians, therapists, photographers, writers, health workers, designers, people with disabilities and people from alternative life-styles. Some contributors are named and their contributions appear in a dedicated section and others are mentioned in sound bites throughout the book. Where possible I have wanted to put a face to a name, but a few contributors have wanted to remain anonymous and I have respected their privacy. Some of the entries are not much more than sound bites, some are more serious, some are funny, some are downright quirky, some are deeply moving and inspirational, some take a view not in sync with mine, but all are equally valid and valued contributions and I thank them all.

Making a living as a figurative artist, I have drawn, painted and sculpted people of all shapes and sizes. It has been a privilege to work with each and every one of them to capture the beauty in each natural curve, the beauty in every form.

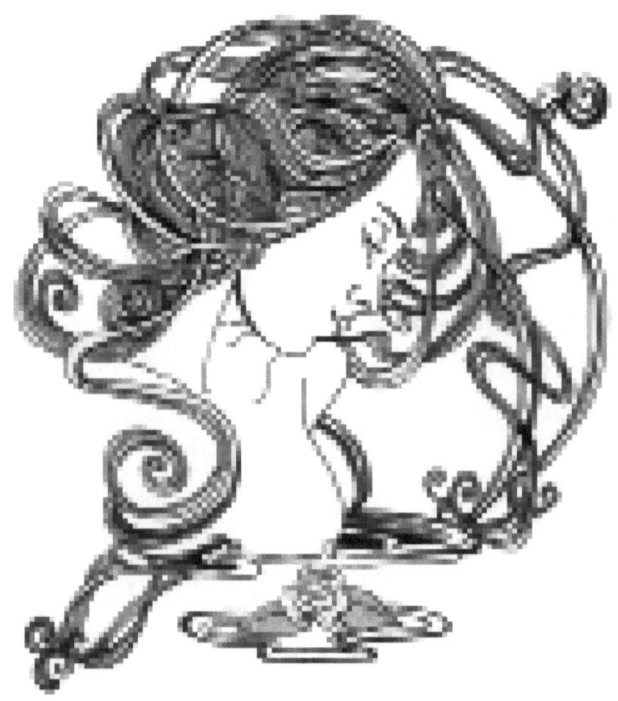

A Special Mention Of Contributors

I would like to mention some of the people who have helped throughout this book and who have provided inspiration during the dark times when I was not sure I would ever see the light at the end of the tunnel.

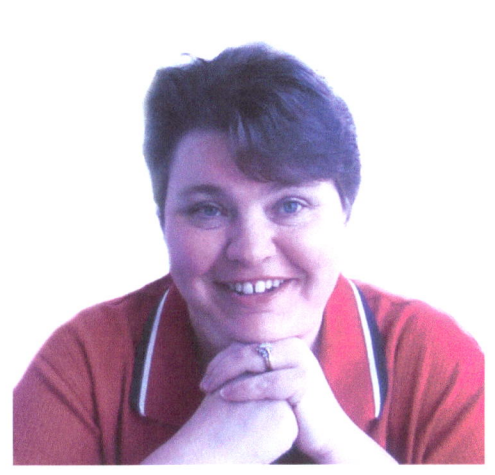

Laurie Sanders, CEO of Black Velvet Seductions, my editor and friend. It would be fair to say that without Laurie there would not have been a book. She has helped and guided me, proofread and suggested areas where I could look for contributors. She believes in the multifaceted nature of beauty as passionately as I do.

Laurie and I usually work together on BVS projects, book covers and any graphic work she needs. She also edits my fictional work but her hand can be seen in this book and I thank her for the long hours she has put into this publication.

Marian Savill is a friend and colleague, who helps me run the studio and generally keeps me organised. She is a contributor to the book but she has also been a tremendous help both proofreading and generally casting a creative eye over the whole book.

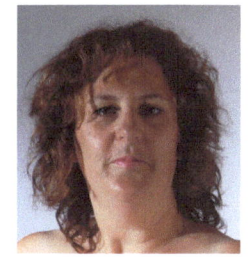

Photograph by Rob Morris

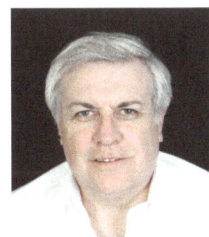

Rob Morris is a friend and colleague. We have worked together on numerous projects. I am a great admirer of his work. His work appears throughout this book as well as in his own section.

Lin Reed is a professional life and portrait model from Cambridge with whom I have been working for the past few years. A popular model, she works regularly with my Monday evening life group.

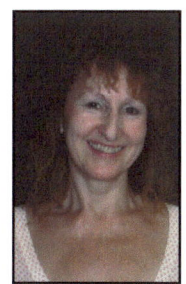

When considering this book I asked Lin to share some thoughts on life modeling and the issues of body shape and beauty. I had thought of a contributors page, as I have done with most of the other contributors, but it seemed more appropriate to have her words near some of my drawings of her.

Beauty And Life Drawing

Like all my comments in this book, these are just my personal thoughts on art. If you put a dozen artists in a room you will doubtless get more than 20 different views on any one subject. Art is very personal to us. One person's masterpiece is another's cow pat.

When you look back through the annals of time, beauty seemed to be a much broader concept than it is today. Classical artists seemed to be more concerned with the natural beauty of their subjects. Artists such as Peter Paul Rubens paid homage to the fuller figure model in their life-sized depictions of biblical scenes. Rubenesque, I believe to be a glorious term for the larger female form.

Even into the 20th century glamour models and actresses such as Marilyn Monroe, a size 16, were considerably more curvy than would be acceptable for models today. It made me wonder, why the obsession with the slender? I have nothing against the slender, but it set me to wondering why others seem to condemn those that are not slender. What message does it send to the youth of today? I am not advocating obesity either but it saddens me to see our TVs filled with documentaries about teenage girls suffering from bulimia and anorexia and lines of teens wanting plastic surgery to help them conform.

I am not for or against any body shape or size, just very against the negative feelings aimed at those who do not conform to what, to me, seems a narrow view of beauty. In my opinion life in every form is beautiful.

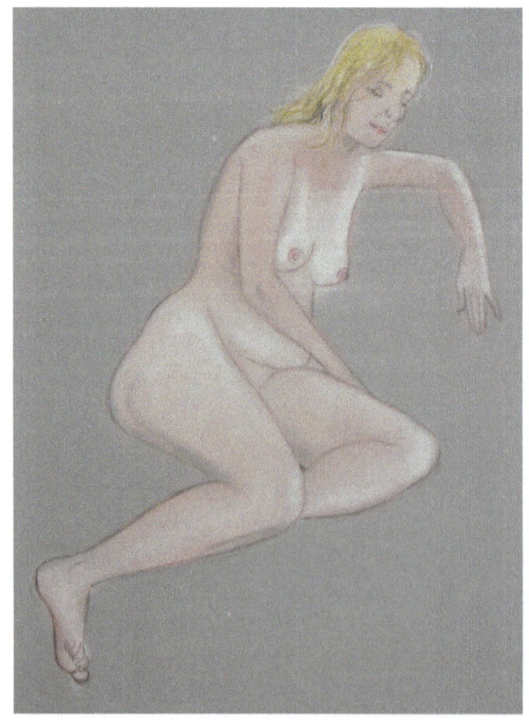

Life study Richard Savage © 2009

There are a number of things that attract me to the human form in life drawing. I think it's the natural elegance of the lines, the roundness of the limbs and the subtle shades of the skin tones. I'm drawn to the way skin reacts under different light. I also find the natural look of tan lines rather appealing.

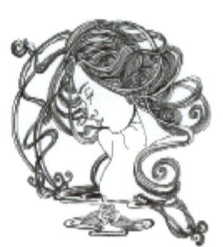

The picture right is a study of Lin in soft pastel and watercolor pencil.

Most of the pictures I do in a life class scenario are very quick studies usually under fifteen minutes. I favor the combination of soft pastel and watercolor pencil because it gives a nice soft image relatively quickly. I do like to spend longer on images as a general rule, but in the life class I think the quick study captures something of the essence of the model. This quick approach has a down side; the drawings look a bit rough around the edges and generally unfinished, but I like that. In the context of this book the pictures have an honesty about them.

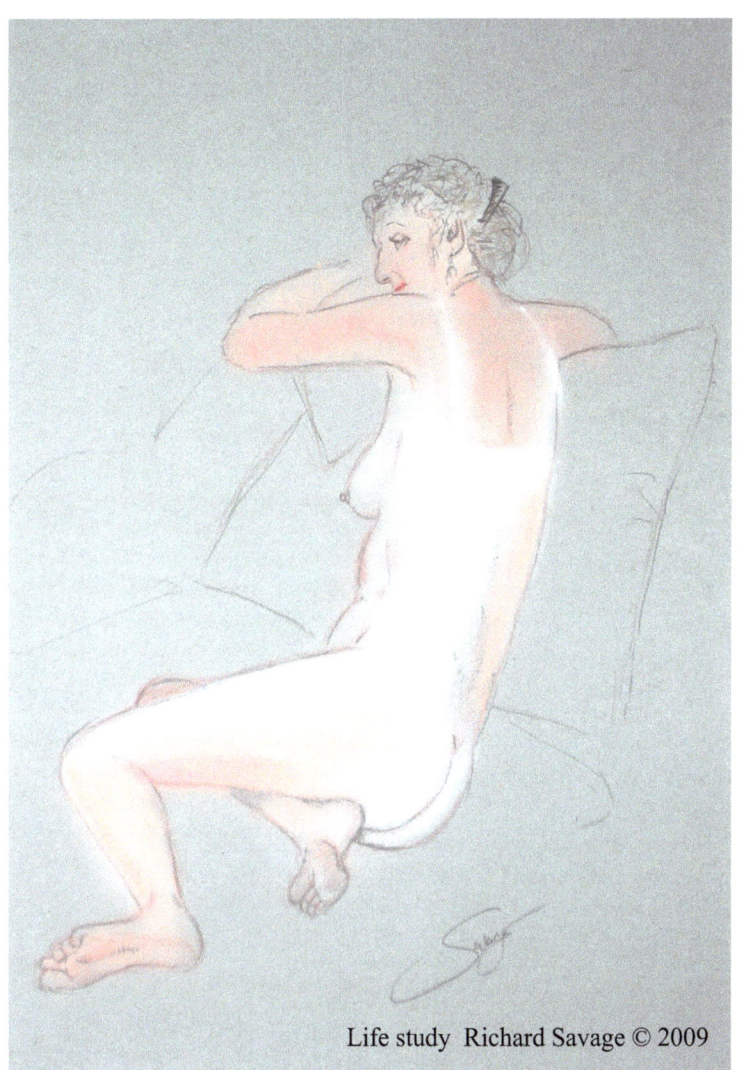

Life study Richard Savage © 2009

Lin

These are just my observations or things I've been told from artists in and around East Anglia. Some artists like a variety to draw and are not so bothered about how good, interesting or inventive the model is. The majority of artists appreciate a model who can hold a pose or get back into it accurately after a break. Poses with a twist, a head tilt or an interesting prop are always appreciated.

Beauty in Every Form

Alana Yvonne Wallace
Founder And Artistic Director Of Dance>Detour

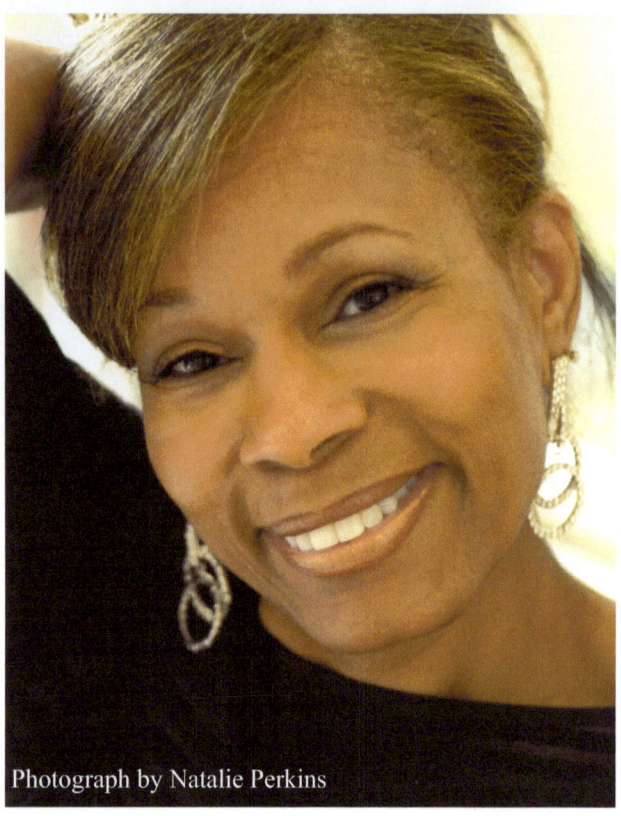
Photograph by Natalie Perkins

At the age of five, I contracted polio. As a child I walked with crutches and leg braces. My earliest memories include times when I would receive *look away* messages from others -- for instance, mothers who would tell their children not to look at me or maybe even swat their hands if they tried to engage with me. These messages were the catalyst for me to choose career paths in the arts that allowed me to be visible. I wanted to prove that it was OK for me (and others like me with a disability) to be seen -- front and center.

I have been in the performing arts, both acting and singing, since I was a child but I never thought the world of dance could include me in a legitimate or professional way.

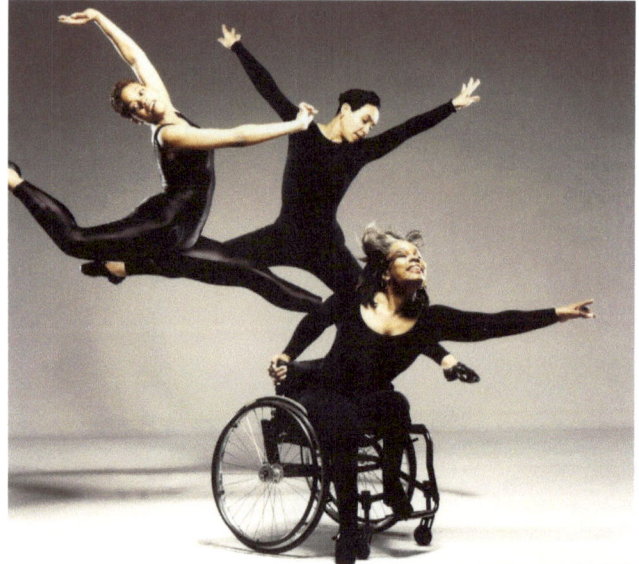
Photographer: William Frederking

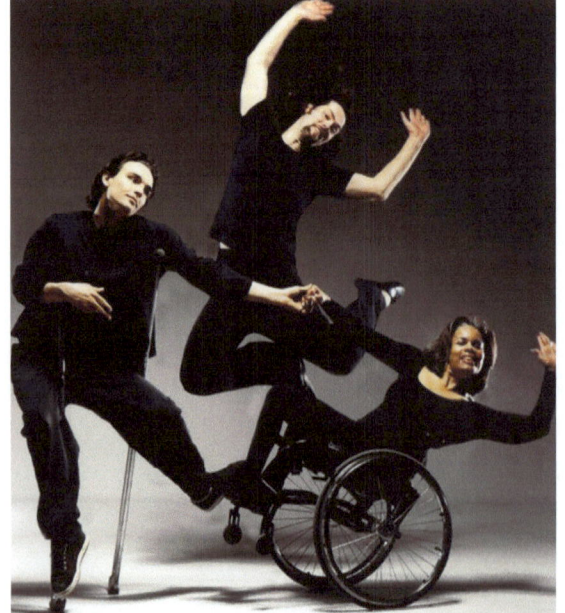
Bill, Dennis & Alana
Photographer: William Frederking

I was introduced to mixed-abilities dance in 1994. I saw a company called the Cleveland Ballet Dancing Wheels perform at the performing arts schools I was attending. I was amazed! I witnessed dancers in wheelchairs gliding beautifully across the floor in perfect harmony with their non-disabled partners. I saw dancers in wheelchairs being lifted out of their chairs and spun around doing moves I never thought possible. But what I was most enthused about was that the dancers who used wheelchairs were equal participants.

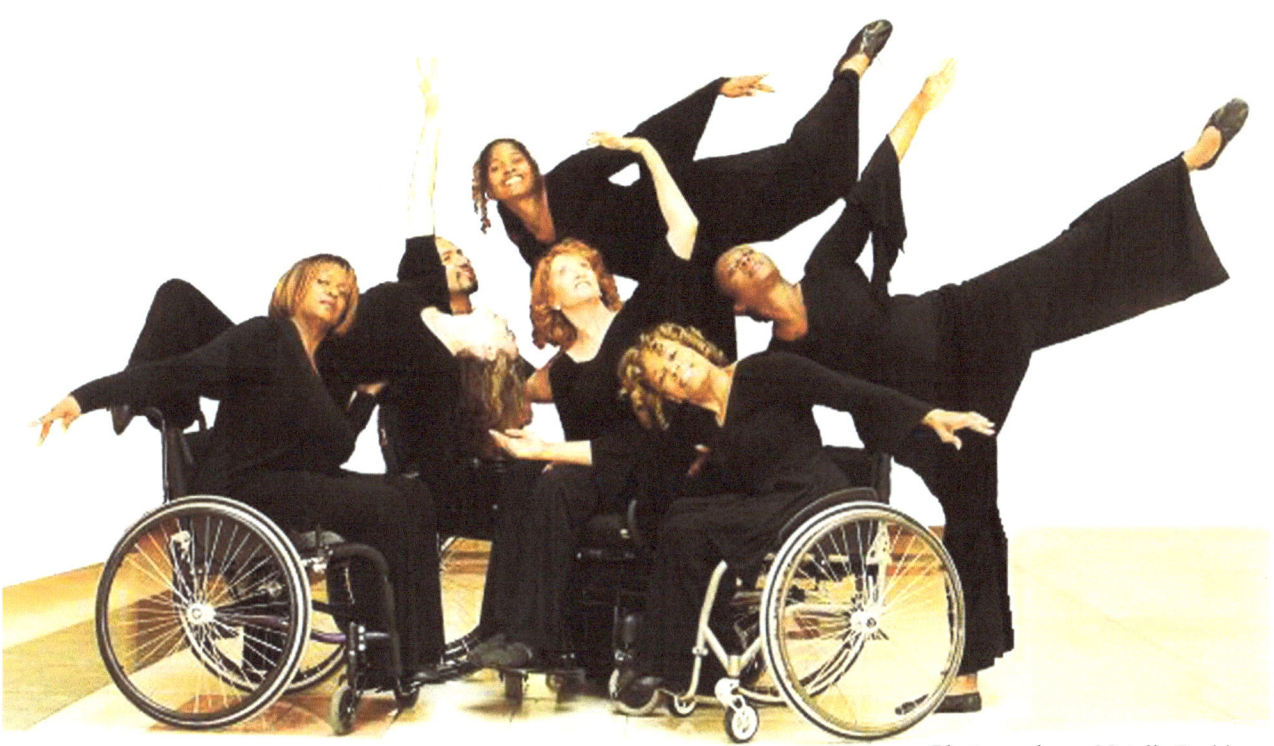

Photographer: Natalie Perkins

This troupe of dancers inspired me to form my own company. Thus, currently I am the founder and artistic director of Dance>Detour -- Chicago's first professional physically integrated dance company. Our troupe is comprised of dancers with and without disabilities who collaborate as **equals**. Our motto is Everyone Can Dance because dance, like beauty, is an expression of your soul.

I have always had my own unique view about beauty. As an African American woman with a disability, who doesn't fit the standard mold, I have fought to dispel the stereotypes and views others hand down to us regarding beauty. Beauty radiates from within. Beauty is a welcoming smile. Beauty is a kind word or deed and beauty is confidence. Sure, I also take pride in my appearance by finding fashion and healthy habits that work well for me at the age of 58. I'm proud to say that I was selected by Dove as one of their Proage Winners who exemplifies the beauty of women over 50.

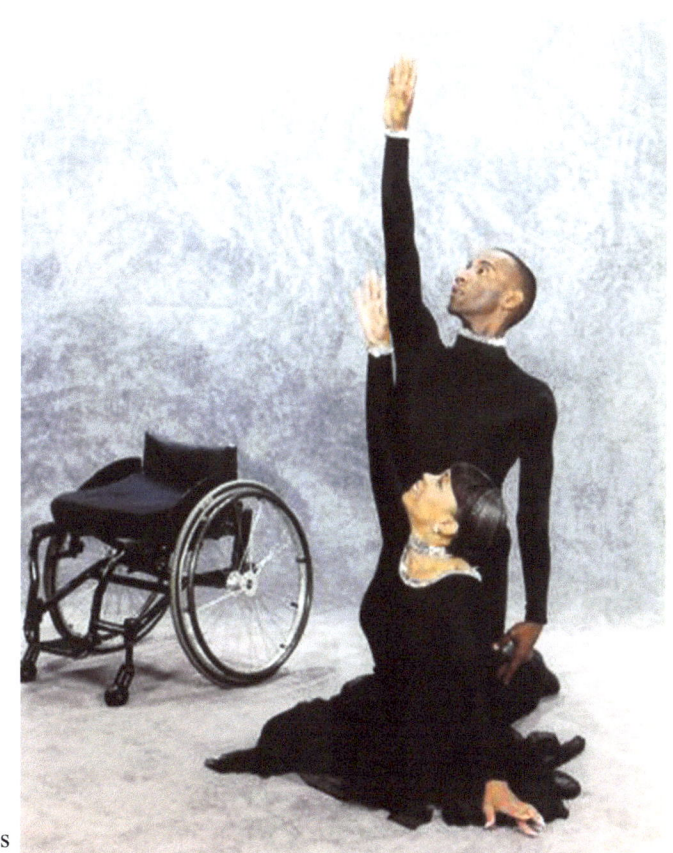

Photographer: Better Image Studios

Beauty in Every Form

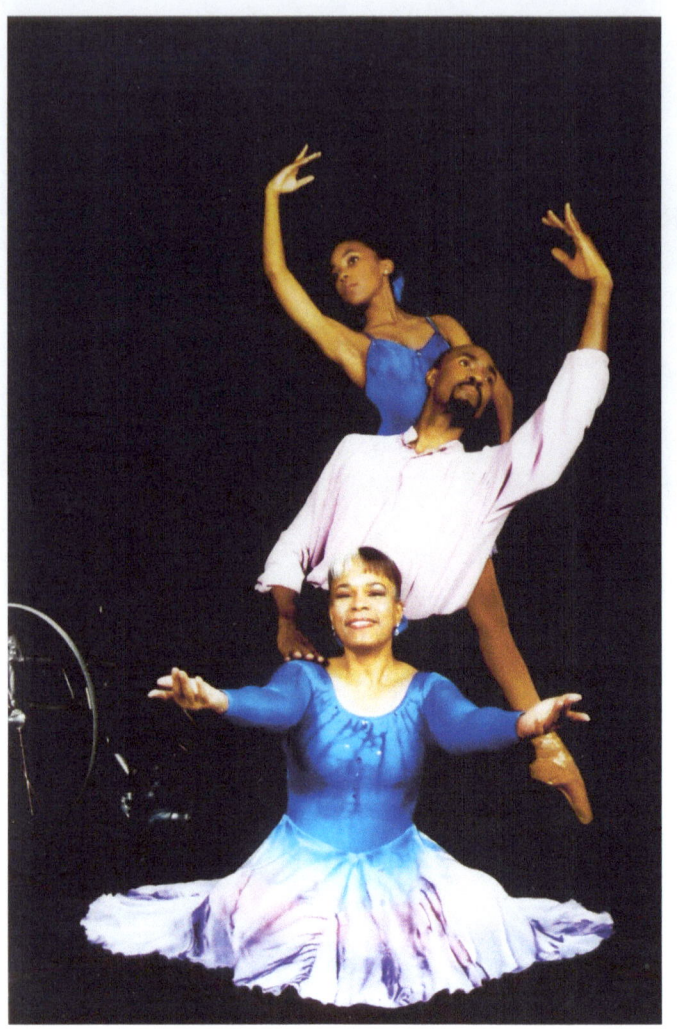

Homer's Photography

In 2007, I came across a small blurb in a newspaper announcing an Illinois pageant for women who used wheelchairs. On a lark - I applied and won the title of *Ms. Wheelchair Illinois 2007*. I went on to compete in the national pageant and I was selected as *Ms. Wheelchair America 2008* -- the first African American woman to hold title in the 35 year history of the pageant.

I definitely don't approach dance from a therapeutic perspective. I view it rather from a professional artistic standpoint. But, I must admit the healing benefits of dance are very apparent. Dance is a great way to exercise, alleviate stress, promote flexibility, burn calories, cultivate social and cultural interactions – and I could go on and on.

All these reasons, individually and collectively, promote wellness and well being. As a post-polio survivor for more than 50 years, I feel dance has helped me to ward off secondary health problems because when I am doing something that I love I feel healthy and happy. Try it—you too may find it to be beneficial!

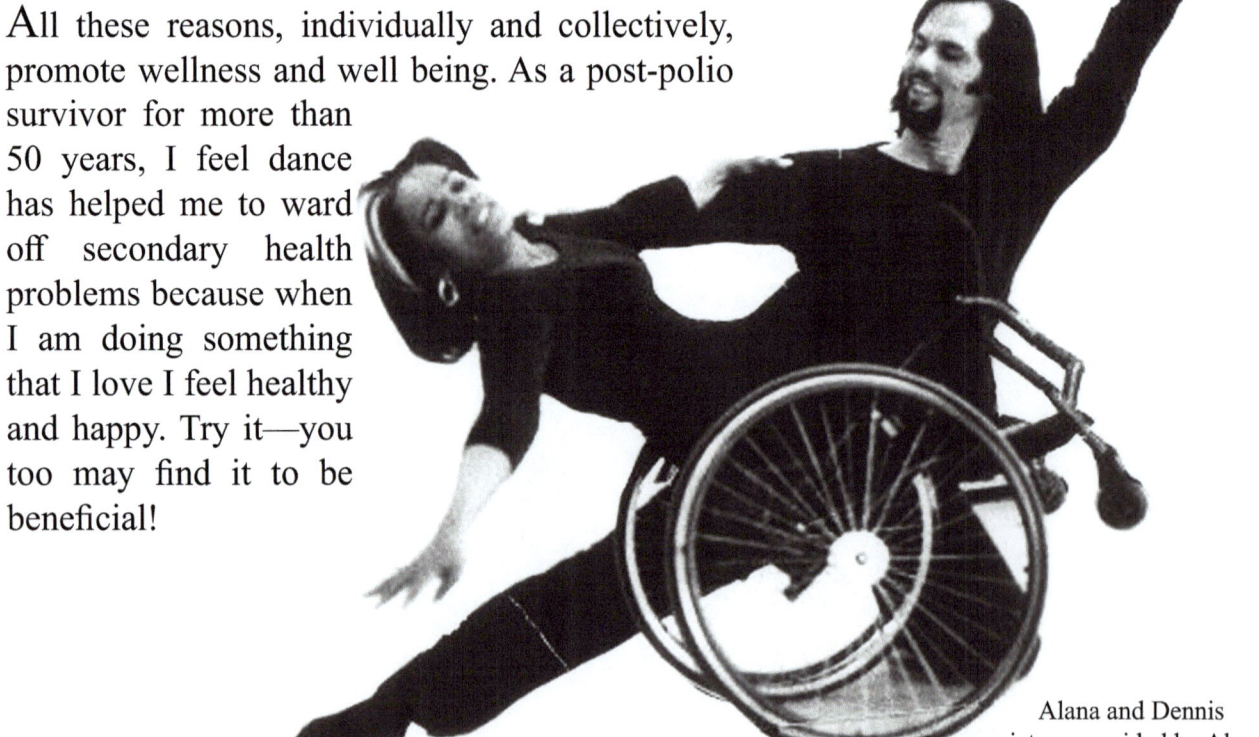

Alana and Dennis
picture provided by Alana

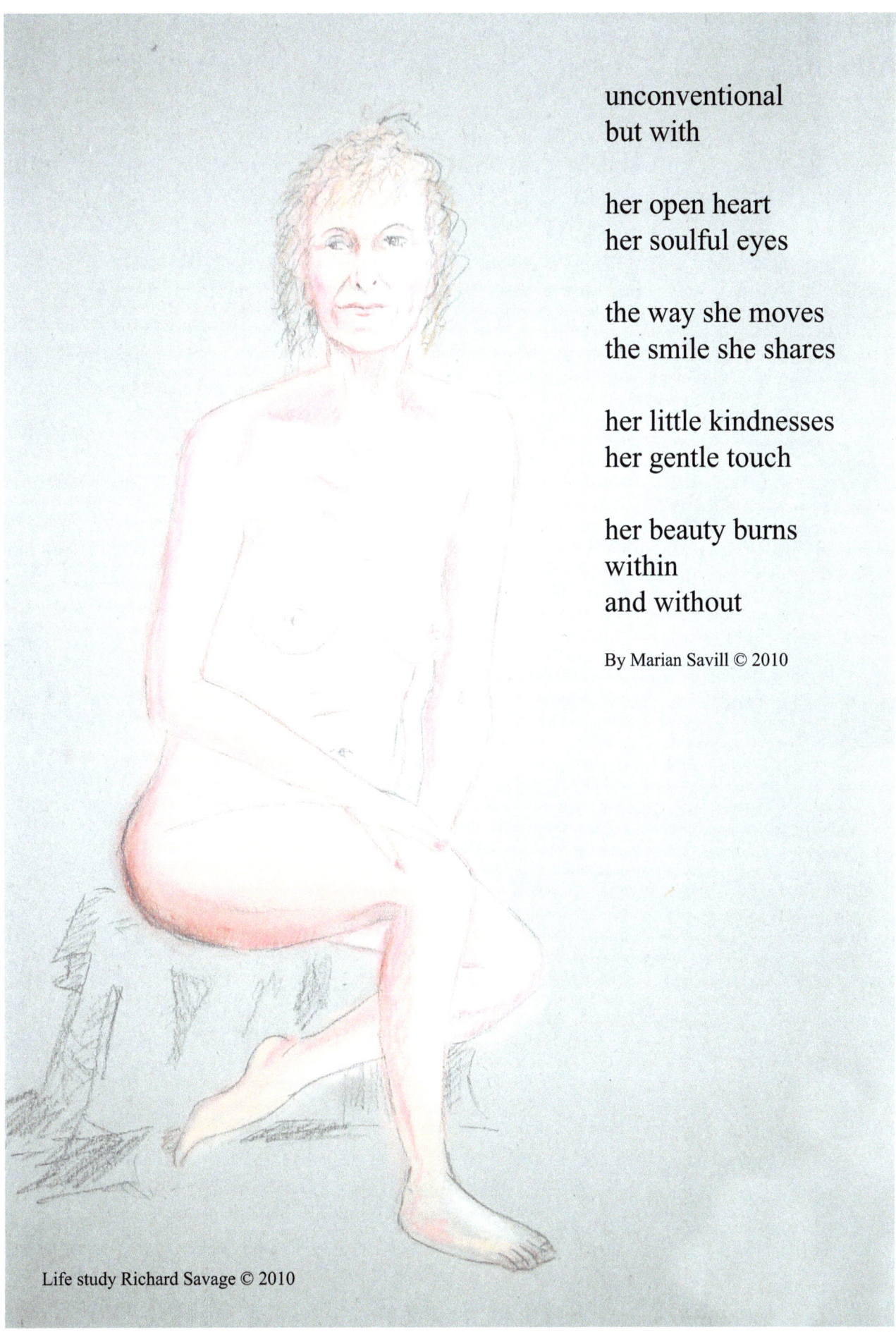

unconventional
but with

her open heart
her soulful eyes

the way she moves
the smile she shares

her little kindnesses
her gentle touch

her beauty burns
within
and without

By Marian Savill © 2010

Life study Richard Savage © 2010

Janice
Author With Black Velvet Seductions

When I'm writing and developing a character I consider body shape only if it will pertain to the story. My work in progress is called **Sumo Sammie**. Even the title gives the reader a first-hand look at my main character's body image.

How do I feel about the stereotypical dark, handsome hero and thin, blond, long- legged heroine? Again it will relate to the story. I have, on occasion, written about characters with these stereotypical looks but they were just their thin icing. I think one line I used in **Killer Caregiver** when my heroine met my male character, Kurt, for the first time sums up what I feel about thin icing: "Looks like a smile has not been welcomed on this face for a very long time."

I believe beauty can be seen if we look deeper than the skin. My character, Abby, is scarred all over her body and her face and I feel these scars should not be hidden from the reader. Abby wears her scars with dignity and this is the way I'd like to see her presented. She is a survivor.

Something I'd like to share with readers is: Never give up on your gifts. They've been given to you personally and for success. Go the whole nine yards to make them a reality and don't quit until success is yours. There's a star out there with your name on it. Find it, claim it!

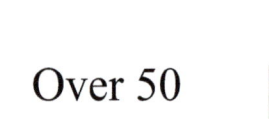

Secretchick
UK Model

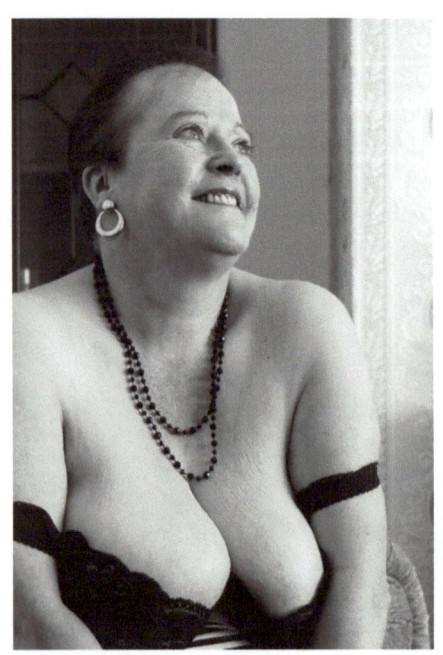

Over 50 BBW and still as beautiful as ever

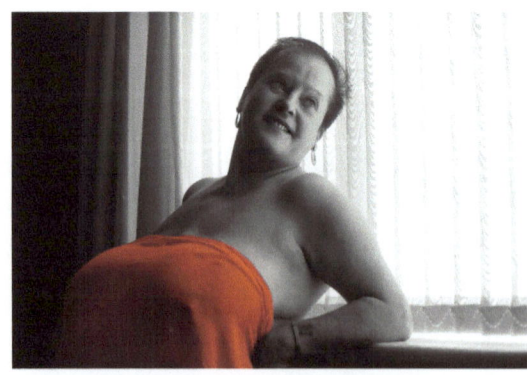

I have enjoyed being a model in the United Kingdom for some years. My message is simple - being over 50 years old and being a large breasted woman is no handicap to looking beautiful. I believe I can still look good and I am definitely not over the hill by any means. It's all about living life to the full.

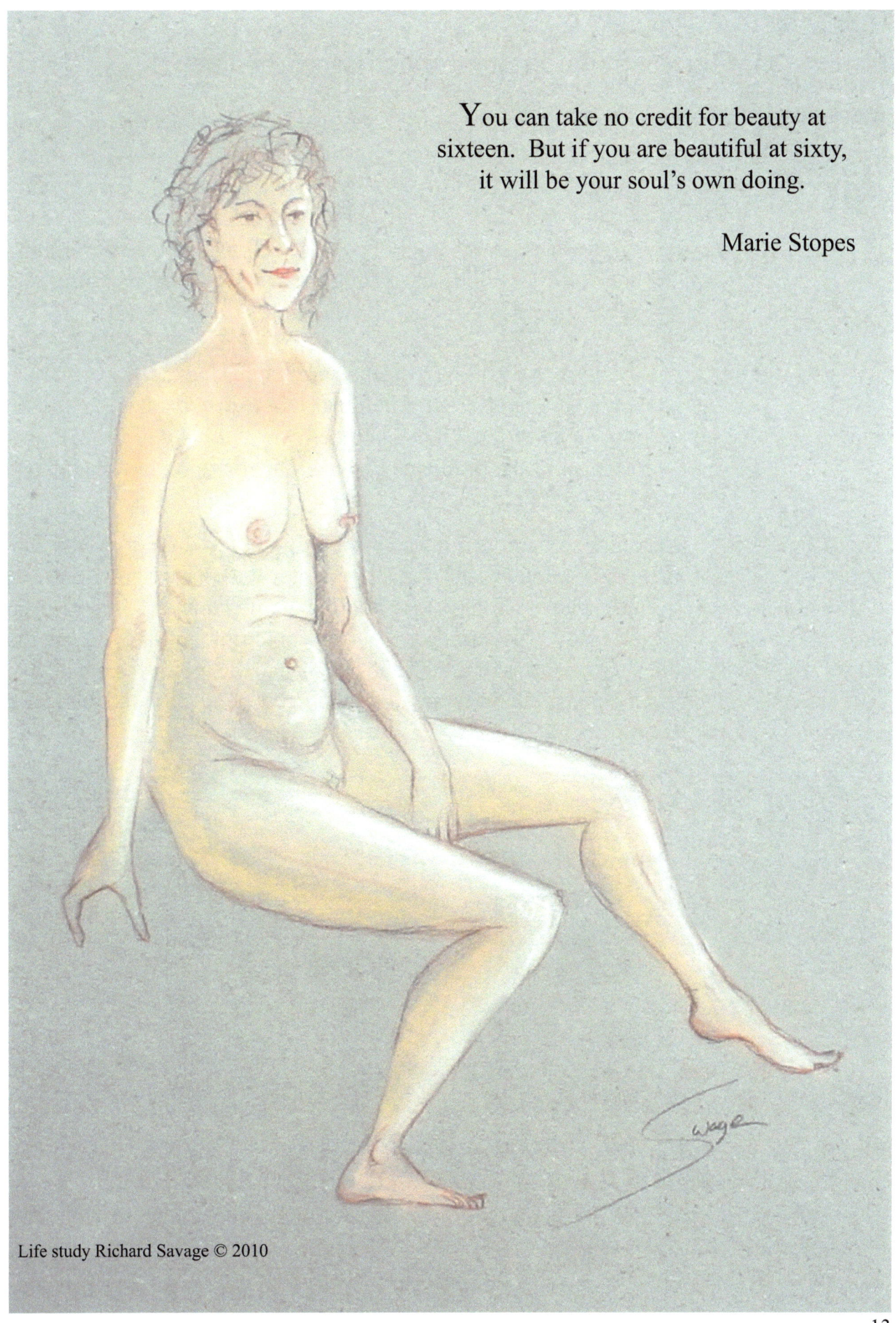

You can take no credit for beauty at sixteen. But if you are beautiful at sixty, it will be your soul's own doing.

Marie Stopes

Life study Richard Savage © 2010

Rob Morris
Professional International Photographer Based In The UK

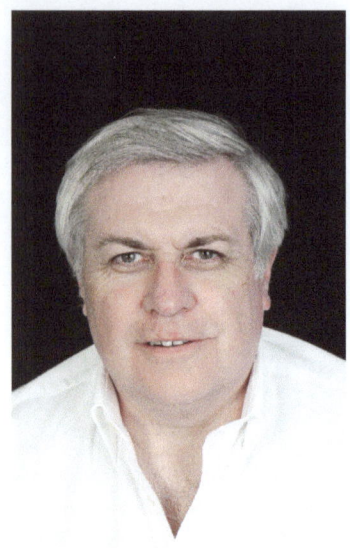

I have been fortunate to have taken photographs for more years than I care to remember, first as an amateur, then as a semi-pro, and now as a full-time professional. My general work and my involvement in local and international charities has allowed me to spend many of my holidays travelling to countries around the world both photographing the work of those charities and also helping to set up projects.

Most of my trips have been to areas like Uganda, South Africa, Lithuania and Egypt helping those disadvantaged by the decisions of mankind. Even that word *mankind* is a misnoma as most of the problems I have seen would not have happened if we were more kind to our fellow human beings.

The people I have seen and photographed have shown a dignity and inner beauty that would shame most of our government leaders. The warmth they have shown me has at times been overwhelming when they have had nothing and in some cases have been close to death. Having said that, I was also able to spend some time in Sri Lanka in the weeks after the tsunami, a natural disaster which had devastated the region. Many people died, others lost their homes and all their possessions and many people around the world helped in whatever way they could.

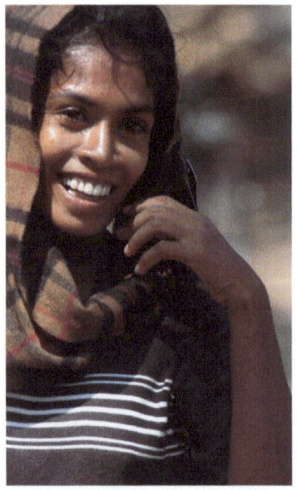 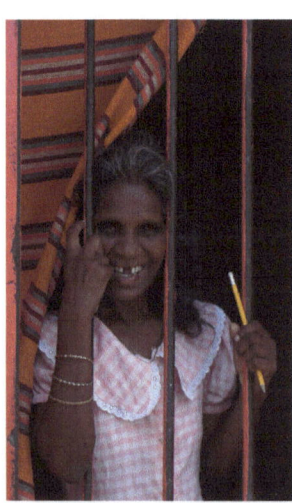 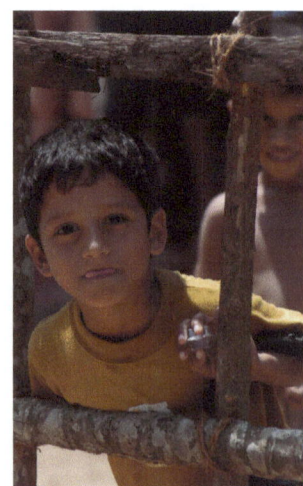 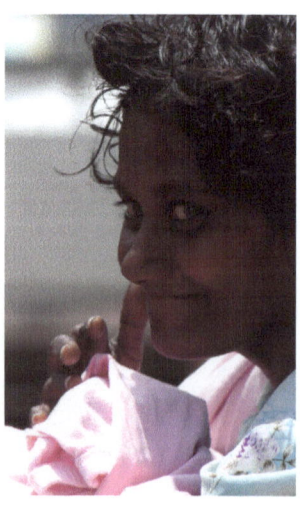

On arriving at Colombo Airport I was expecting to find desperation, weeping and begging but I found a wonderful friendly people putting, or trying to put, their lives back together. Their positive attitude shone through their eyes causing me to decide that my role as a photographer was to show this in any way I could. As I spent some weeks there chatting to so many of the people this became more and more a part of my "mission."

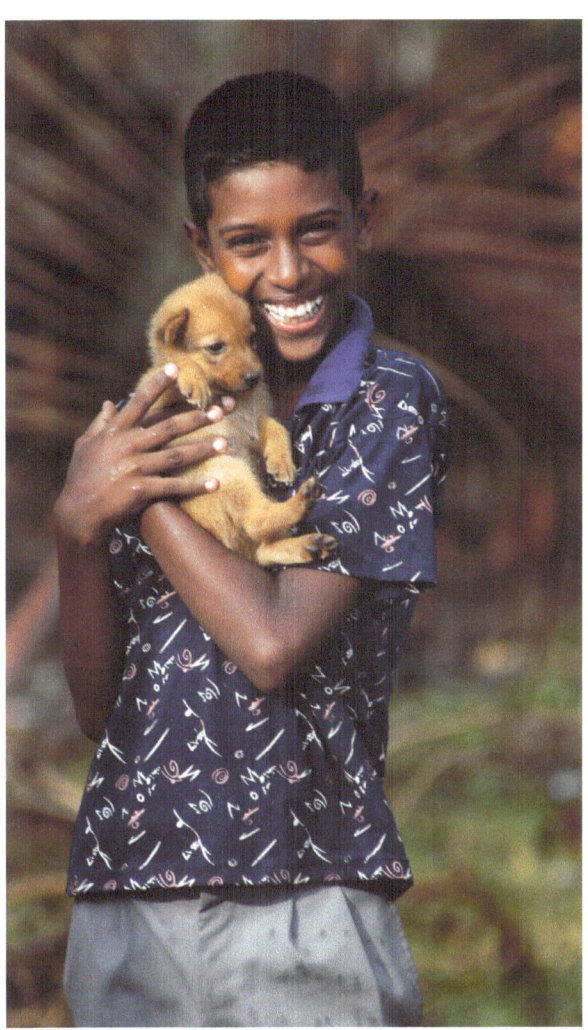

I decided that I would produce a touring exhibition on my return to the UK and that it would be entitled **Portrait of Hope**. This has been used in talks to groups and as a touring exhibition throughout the years and will continue to be for some time to come.

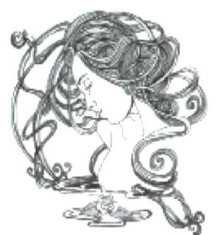

I hope that by using my skills as a photographer I can always bring the true sense of a person to the images whether it is a wedding, portrait, or those I photograph that live what some people call an alternative lifestyle. To me it doesn't matter what a person wears or what they do for a living. I see beauty in all people, and it's my job to bring that to the images I take.

It is also my belief that the *eyes* have it!

Having photographed people for many years I have to agree with the saying "The eyes are the mirror of the soul."

I have been given the opportunity over the years to meet and photograph people all over the world, from every ethnic, cultural and age group.

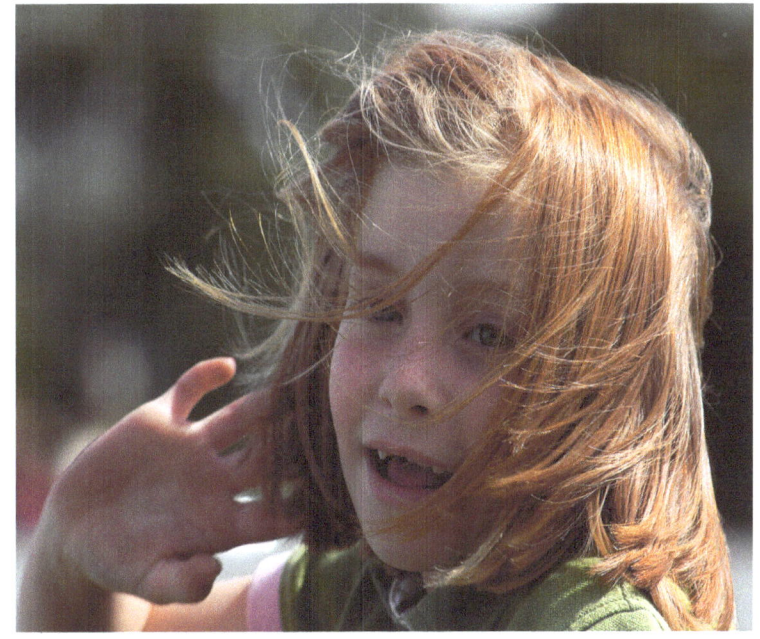

I have photographed babies at birth and, heartbreakingly, also those that are dying. I have photographed the young and elderly and all the ages in between, in times of happiness and in the aftermath of disasters, both natural and man-made.

In all this time my best pictures have had nothing to do with color of skin, what age or size the subjects of them are or if they are wearing rags or the most up to date fashions. My best photos have all, and I do mean all, been those images where I have captured the real person by what emotions they are giving me through their eyes.

Is body image important to me?

Well, I would be lying if I said no, but it is my own body image that I inwardly criticize not anyone else's. I know deep down that it doesn't matter if I am overweight or that I have any of the other *faults* that make my body less than perfect. I know that I am essentially a good person so is that enough?

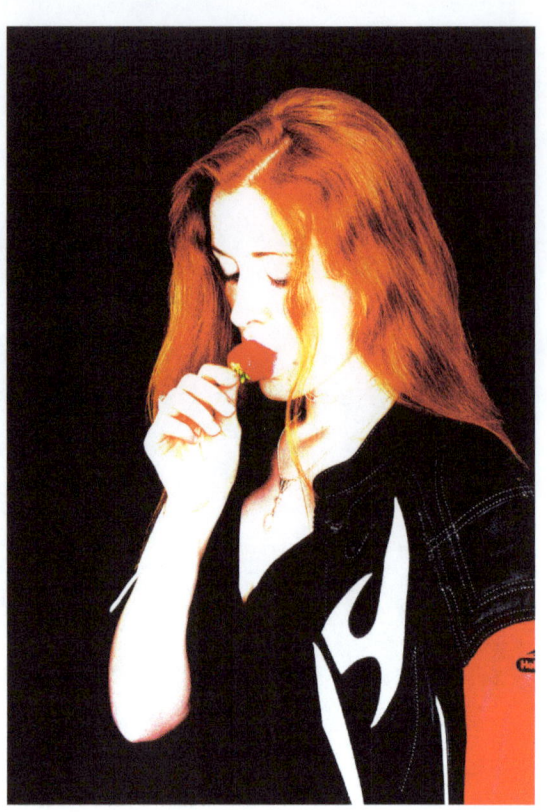

Well, honestly I don't know! So, am I a hypocrite as far as body image is concerned? Again I do not know, I do hope not though.

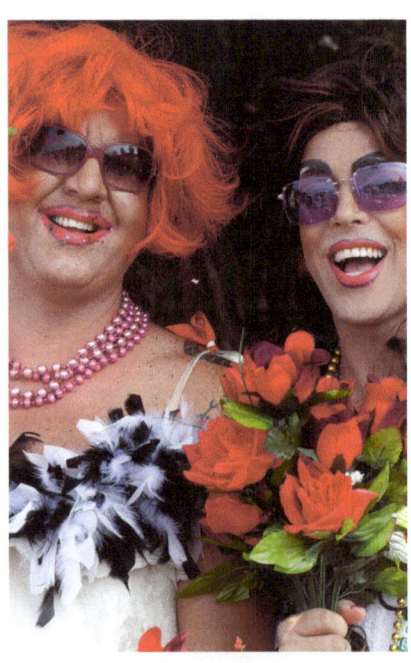
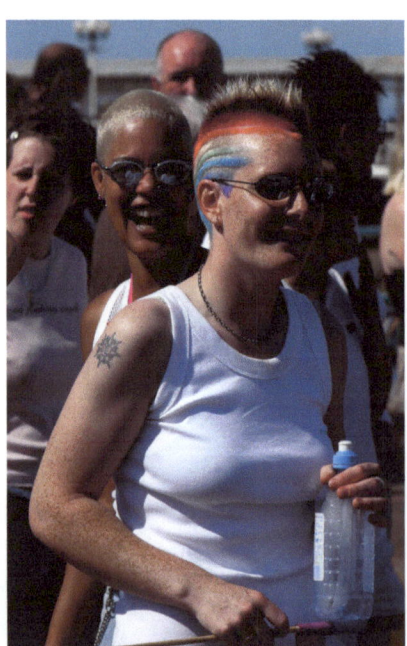
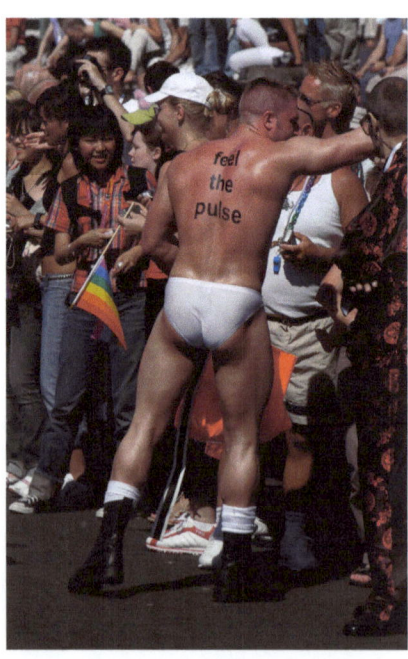

The camera never lies they say, but of course it does. Even without the effects that computer programs can achieve, just by selecting certain lenses or shooting from certain angles I can alter the way a person looks. So, there is the problem when taking portraits of people. Do I flatter them in my images or do I take them how they really are? And is how I see them really how they are? I guess it depends on the viewer and in life we are all viewers.

I've never seen a smiling
face that was not beautiful.

    Author Unknown

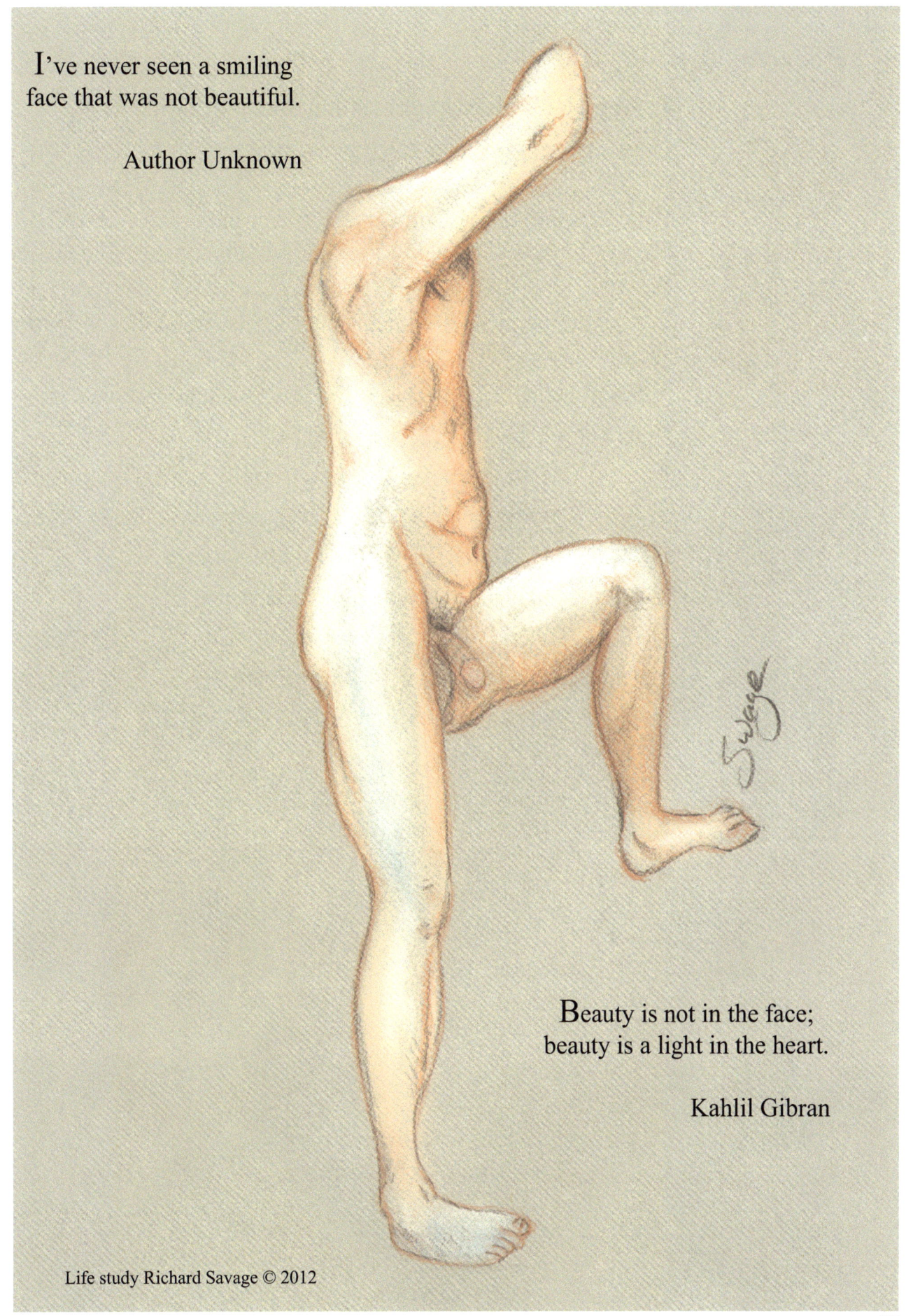

Beauty is not in the face;
beauty is a light in the heart.

    Kahlil Gibran

Life study Richard Savage © 2012

Tabby
A Fetish Model From The UK

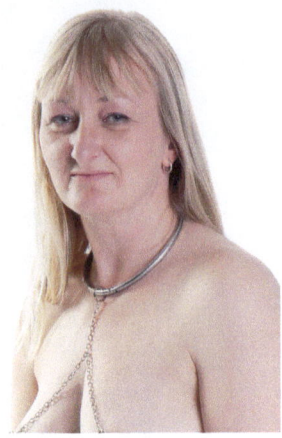

A young girl with NHS glasses and hand me downs

Quiet and shy, the inner voice never loud enough for anyone else to hear

Braces, spots, long hair cut short, appendix scar, Caesarian, blonde, blue eyes, 5ft 4", yeah right, said thoughts that could not be seen

The last to be picked in games but the first to be picked by the abuser

Years of hating the mirror, never friends with the camera

Figure never shown, smile never smiled

Then he was there

The doors to my soul were opened, the light could finally shine

He came, and showed me the beauty in the mirror

He came, and made the camera my friend

He came, and truly listened to my inner voice

He came, and released the joy of my figure

He came, and taught me to love...me

He came, and said, I am beautiful

He came, and now I believe.

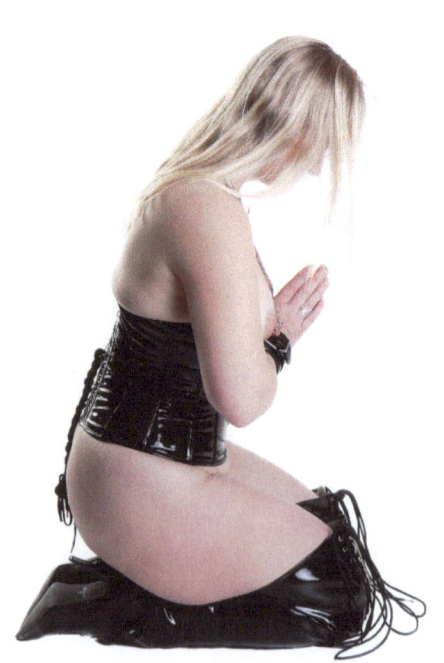
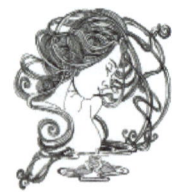
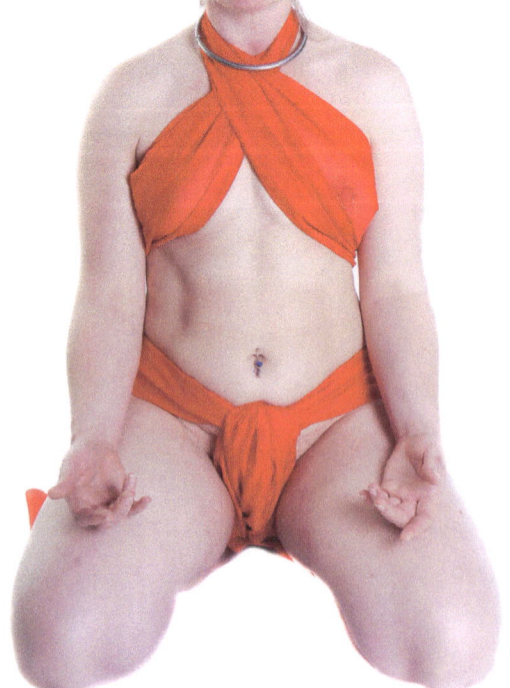

Photographs by Rob Morris © 2009

Drew Turney

Freelance Journalist, Graphic Designer, Author With Black Velvet Seductions, Resides In Australia

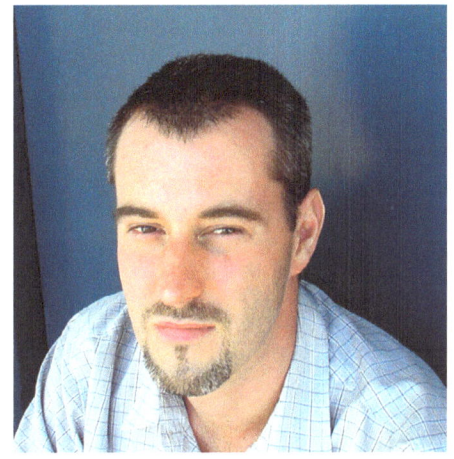

It sounds corny but the drive to bring another world to life is the same as the one that drives us all to eat and breathe.

When I am writing or developing a character I always visualise how they look, considering height and body shape.

The tall, dark, handsome hero is fine because in romance that's the fantasy women are after, but I prefer heroines to be a bit shorter, have a bit more meat on their bones and feel the nagging doubts that they're not beautiful enough after years of media conditioning. Female readers will empathize with this type of character.

It's the same, but the other way around, in pornography which is targeted at men. The woman should be tall, blond, tanned and pneumatic because that's the fantasy being presented to the viewer. What the man looks like is immaterial.

Beauty and body image are elemental forces in our emotions because evolution puts us in competition with everyone else of our gender for mating rights. The modern world of commerce has been very successful in playing on those anxieties. If people knew more about the biological basis for beauty and body image we'd be much more forgiving of ourselves and forewarned about the tricks the advertising industry is prepared to play on us.

You only need beauty to attract a mate but you need a lot more than that to keep him/her.

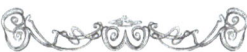

Do you love me because I'm beautiful,
or am I beautiful because you love me?

Pierre Auguste Renoir

Christopher John Ball
Co-founder Of The Association Of Erotic Artists

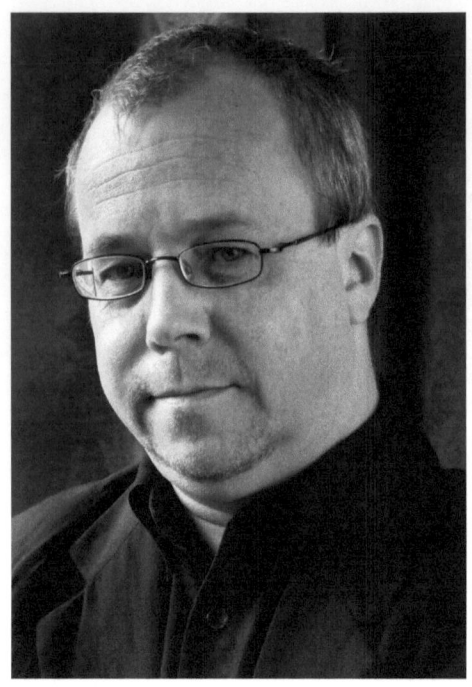

Chris has a BA (Hons) MA, is a widely exhibited and published, award winning, London based, fine arts photographer, playwright and lecturer. With over 30 years experience as a photographer, his work is in public and private collections worldwide. He is the co-founder of the *Association of Erotic Artists* which can be found at www.associationoferoticartists.co.uk

He was selected as a juror for both the 2008/09 *Erotic Signature* annual international arts competition and the *Erotic Review Photographer of the Year 2009*. He recently had work on show at the *Erotic Heritage Museum* in Las Vegas, USA, the *ArtBay Gallery* in Stoke on Trent, UK, the *She Said* Gallery, Brighton, UK and the *Enlightenment* exhibition in Milton Keynes, UK.

Chris also acts as a fine art/photography advisor, international photographic competition juror, portfolio consultant and exhibition curator. He has experience in facilitating and advising on art based/lifestyle TV programming - in particular fine art photography and erotic arts. In addition to his fine art work Chris has also produced several photographic projects of a socio-documentary nature that have attracted Arts Council funding.

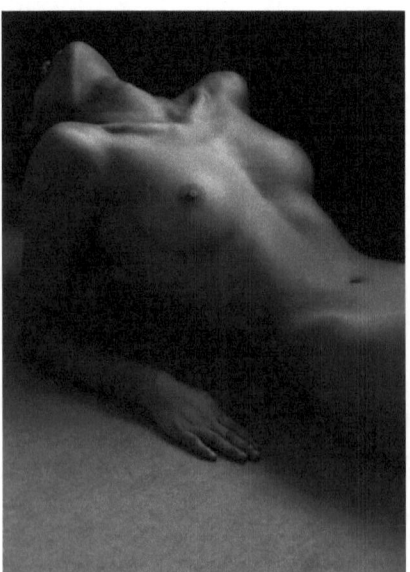

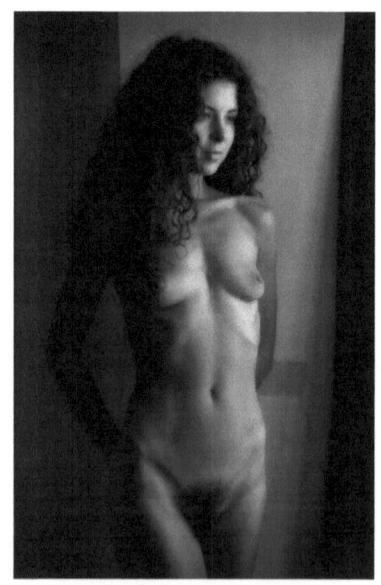

Christopher John Ball
www.classicnudes.co.uk

He contributes articles on photography for various publications and acts as an external moderator for several photographic courses in London. His images have been showcased in Italian, German, Spanish, Hong Kong SAR, British and mainland Chinese publications and also displayed within the pages of several respected online galleries. He has also been interviewed, and filmed at work, for television programs that have been transmitted in Europe, the USA and Great Britain.

Photographs by Christopher John Ball

Photography And The Other

Once you label me, you negate me.

Much has been written by philosophers, such as Aristotle and Immanuel Kant, about the nature of beauty, aesthetics and the values that we place upon what we see and observe; but what does it mean to be 'seen' by another and how does that impact upon us as individuals and how we perceive our own beauty?

To further this examination I have drawn upon Jean Paul Sartre's philosophy of existentialism as defined in his work *Being and Nothingness*. A key concept within Sartre's philosophy is that of the Other - an individual/ Existent other than oneself who is singled out as different. An Existent's definition of the Other is part of what defines or even constitutes the self and cultural identity. It is also used by societies and groups to exclude Others whom they want to subordinate/oppress/control.

The starting point of Sartre's philosophy of the Other is that the Existent does not derive the existence of the Other, by the Existent's own cogito/thought, as something that it must prove. The Other is an undisputed fact whose existence is given simultaneously with its own and therefore can never be an object of knowledge. It is another I who is not I and never merely a probable object.

Though the Existent encounters the Other within the depths of its own being; here it encounters not reasons for believing in the Other's existence but the Other itself. The Other is not revealed as an object of knowledge but as a personal presence - although this Other must ultimately be understood as a subject. It usually makes its first appearance as an object which has come into the Existent's field of vision or attention - though it soon becomes clear to the Existent that this object differs alarmingly from the other objects that surround it.

This alarm and unease is generated due to the sudden eruption into the Existent's world of the Other as an object that threatens its stability. Stability is threatened because the Existent becomes aware that its world is one that can also be seen by the Other - resulting in the inescapable conclusion that the Existent cannot avoid being seen by this new Other. Further unease is caused in the mind of the Existent due to the unavoidable conclusion that this new Other, upon seeing the Existent, cannot help but objectify it and make it part of its world.

In Sartre's Existentialism the world can only exist for a subject, and therefore the Existent knows that the Other is confronting it as a 'subject' who is 'objectified' even in the Existent's own eyes.

At the initial sighting the Existent perceives the Other in terms of the spatiotemporal categories governing its attitude towards other objects, i.e. the Other's distance from the Existent can be measured in feet and inches and details such as height and build can be assessed. At this stage if the Other was to disappear the Existent's universe would not be radically altered. From the point at which the Other notices the Existent's presence the Existent's awareness of the Other, as being more than another object, becomes more acute.

Therefore the Existent can no longer view the Other's relationship with its surroundings as merely the juxtaposition of similar things. What arises now is that, while the perception of the Existent towards the Other can still be described in terms of distance etc, there is a sudden change in the Existent's own connections with the surrounding objects; i.e. they no longer belong to a spatiality that is purely the Existent's, they are now part of a spatiality that is shared with the Other; the Existent's whole universe is in danger of being thrown into confusion.

This Other is not only something that 'sees' what the Existent 'sees' and, in so doing, helps to pull the Existent's world out of 'shape'; the Other is also a being who 'sees' the Existent. Therefore, the Existent's fundamental relationship to the Other must be defined in terms of being-seen and this becomes an irreducible relationship belonging to a world of everyday experience.

Not only has the 'look' of the Other disturbed the Existent's universe, by being forced to accept that it is no longer its own, the Other has created the feeling within the Existent that it too has been absorbed into that universe as one of its objects.

Therefore, in looking at the Existent, the Other has transformed it into an object thus depriving the Existent of its 'transcendence' and 'subjectivity.' The Existent is robbed of its freedom and the possibilities which lie at the root of its existence are petrified and alienated by the Other's look.

The ultimate effect this has on the Existent is that it becomes, as stated, an object in its own eyes and not just merely in the eyes of the Other. The Existent realizes that it is no longer a free subject but an object; this is brought about not through knowledge but through the fact of the Other's presence as a freedom other than the Existent's own. This is what Sartre called 'Being-for-Others' and it is for the Existent to recognize its Being-for-Others and transcend it so as to give meaning. For Sartre, the important aspect is not what the Other makes of the Existent but rather what the Existent makes of the Other. It could be argued that the above discussion could hold great relevance when applied to photography; specifically the genre of portrait photography.

Throughout history the artist has chosen to depict other human beings as subjects within their art. This has extended from the earliest cave paintings to the images displayed within the windows of most high-street photographers today. Of course there are many social reasons for this but, due to the thesis topic, any discussion should be from an existential standing.

What would happen to the Existent if the Other, instead of just looking at the Existent, proceeds to photograph said Existent? For the sake of this argument let the camera be one of the instant image variety such as digital. Let us go back to the previously mentioned first sighting of the Other by the Existent. The Existent would still be able to judge the Other as an object in spatiotemporal terms. If the Other were to disappear at this point the Existent's world would not be radically altered. The Existent's reaction to being noticed by the Other would remain the same as previously discussed i.e. an inability to treat the Other as a mere juxtaposition of things, the feeling of the Existent's world being stolen and the confusion associated remaining.

The Other, instead of just looking, now begins to photograph the Existent. The Existent is aware of the camera as an object that can be used to record images that can be used to represent what the Other sees i.e. the Other's world. As has been described, the Existent is also aware that its world is a world that can be seen by the Other and therefore it can be photographed by the Other, thus intensifying the Existent's own sense of objectification.

This can be made more intense by the Other allowing the Existent to see the resulting images. The sense of unease experienced by many people, when either being photographed, or viewing the resulting images, draws testimony to this. Another factor arises out of this situation; the Other has made a decision as to when to make the image.

The creation of a work of art entails an individual Existent wanting something to exist that has certain properties through the said Existent; therefore a work of art is an appropriation because it expresses a synthesis of a 'self' and 'not-self' and becomes the creative embodiment of 'my' idea in a concrete Existent. This is now independent of its creator though it will always remain, in some sense, 'mine.'

What happens when the subject of this art is another Existent? If it is an appropriation i.e. a form of exclusive possession of something set aside for future use, how does this affect the Existent? It cannot be said that the Existent photographed has become the property of the Other but photographs have been used, ever since the medium was invented, to say just this. One example would be during the time of slavery in America prior to the Civil War. Photographs were made of individuals who were thought of as 'owned' i.e. the Negro slaves. Prisoners are also photographed; have they not been 'appropriated' by the state? Photographs are used in contemporary society as means of identification, but what are they identifying?

They cannot, existentially, be thought of as identification of an Existent due to the aforementioned changing qualities of the said Existent.

Photographs are, at best, what the Existent was not, what it is or is capable of being. Yet, when the Existent confronts its own image a sense of apprehension is often felt, nobody reacts neutrally to an image of themselves.

If the Other can show the photograph to the Existent, the Existent is aware that this photograph can then be shown to other Others. What happens to this photographic object when it is shown to other Others? By situating objects in context the Existent gives them meaning; therefore as the photograph is an object meaning is given to it by the viewing Existent.

Does this have any really adverse effect on the Existent depicted within the image? If one makes, what would be described as, a pornographic image of a female Existent, how could it be viewed in existentialist terms?

If the viewing Existent is a heterosexual male, he will be aware of her as a sexual object; an object upon which to focus and direct his sexual desire. This of course comes as no surprise to the Existent who acquired the image, or to the producer of the image, but the object that is being held and viewed is a photograph and not a woman. The male Existent viewing the image is capable of making this into a sex object by appropriating sexual desire upon the image. In doing this, it could be argued that, the male Existent objectifies sexually, not only the woman depicted in the image, but women in general. This is because he is Other than the subject; for him it constitutes no problem, he sees himself as 'different.'

For a female Existent viewing the image this 'difference' as to gender does not exist, so how is the female Existent affected when viewing the image? She will be aware of the bodily similarities that she shares with the subject depicted, but she will also be aware that she is not the subject and is in fact Other to the subject.

She will be aware that what she is holding is a photograph, an object that 'holds' an image of something that is similar to her, yet different. Therefore, unlike the male, who it could be argued has the distance he can place from the image on the grounds of gender i.e. sexual difference, if the subject is regarded as an object within a patriarchal society i.e. a sex object, is it any wonder that the female Existent feels that she too is an object?

If the photograph is regarded by the male viewer as depicting a sexually available object, then the female Existent, due to the special empathy arising from sexual similarities, sees herself as an available sexual object in the eyes of the Other.

In turn she will also see herself as a sexual object even in her own eyes for the same reasons as previously described in the section dealing with the Existent being seen by the Other.

An argument often put forward is that pornographic images degrade women because they are seen, not as depicting a woman, but women in general. The effect this has is adverse existentially because it anchors women in the object world by denying them individuality. This makes the task of transcending that which women are seen to be that much harder for the female Existent.

This also has an effect on the male; if the Existent feels unease due to the Existent's world being thrown into confusion when viewed by the Other. Is this unease not then compounded by the Existent being attracted to the Other, when this Other is female?

This makes the sense of objectification more intense because the male Existent is attracted to the objectifier; the desire to escape the Other's world makes the sense of entrapment more acutely felt. Of course this is not to imply that woman is the seducer/temptress as depicted in many fictions: the 'Adam and Eve' story being one example.

Women are also attracted to the opposite sex and must feel what has been described above. There is, of course, one major difference; woman through no fault of her own, lives in, what has been described as, a patriarchal society. This creates an unfair advantage for the male Existent, and increases the sense of objectification of woman. The male Existent has attempted to overcome his sense of unease at being attracted to the female Other by objectifying her, even in her own eyes, before she looks upon him. He is objectifying her before she can objectify him; it is almost as if she is an object before she enters his world. Therefore to the male Existent the female Other has been rendered as less of a threat, or even no threat, to his world due to her being, at best, only slightly removed from the object world. She is not simply an object but another Other who is not male, and is therefore set apart from objects but equally set apart from male Others. She could be described as being in a state of limbo.

It could be argued that the denial, by the male Existent, of the individuality of the female Other, and therefore her opportunity to transcend that which she is 'seen' to be, is equally denying his own individuality and is thus condemning himself to an 'inauthentic existence'.

We have discussed how this relates to the opposite gender but what about Others that are seen as abject/absent such as the disabled?

Artists have often used disability as metaphor or analogy to convey ideas about evil, suffering, vulnerability, human frailty, punishment and sin; it has long been part of their vocabulary. Such themes were especially popular among European artists producing works based upon religious subject matter. The individuals with disabilities featured within these works have, more often than not, acted as passive cultural objects or signifiers. Rather than being seen as other Others the disabled are seen as physically different or 'other to'; apart or abject from Others.

People with, or to use the oft used alternative and more weighted term 'suffer from,' a disability are rarely asked about how they should be portrayed; even within the creation of promotional material in support of a charity set up to alleviate their physical 'problem.' The 'disabled' are hardly ever seen as, or encouraged to be, active creators and consumers of culture, art and media.

As has been discussed, feminists can argue that art, especially erotic art, objectifies women as sexual objects, passive and available. The disabled are also objectified but with the fundamental difference in that they are seen as not having sexuality, sexual identity or gender; they are 'seen' but in a manner that excludes them. It could be said that the very thought of the disabled having sex or having a sexual identity is, at best, uncomfortable to many and even repugnant to some; this is an uncomfortable truth.

Yet, in reality, the number of disabled people is far higher than many would like to admit – especially as it would include many who would not consider themselves disabled. The fact is if you are wearing glasses then you are disabled. Spectacles are of course a socially acceptable disability that has its own multi million pound industry supporting designers and high end labels to support it.

Whilst not realizing that they are doing so, many couples introduce disability into their sex play. A partner may blindfold another in an attempt to heighten the senses. This blindness, though temporary, is thought of as an enhancement to pleasure. Yet we never say to a blind person, 'Hey, you must have great sex'. Another example maybe the binding of a partner by ropes to restrict movement; an enforced paralysis again created to enhance sexual play. There are those who fetishize particular disabilities and have used new technologies to create arenas where images of said disability, or appliance associated with a disability, can be admired and shared; though the role of the disabled individual being viewed is still passive and often without their knowledge or permission.

If it is a hard enough task for women to transcend that which they are 'seen' to be, their 'being for others,' then it must be that much harder for the disabled. The disabled Existent, viewing the Other, cannot help but see reflected back that which society/culture labels as a non-aesthetic or an absence; something that society, through popular culture, encourages and enforces. For as Soren Kierkegaard, the father of Existentialism, famously stated *Once you label me, you negate me.*

Charlotte Hough
Writer From Fort Worth, Texas

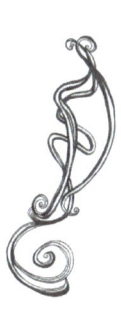
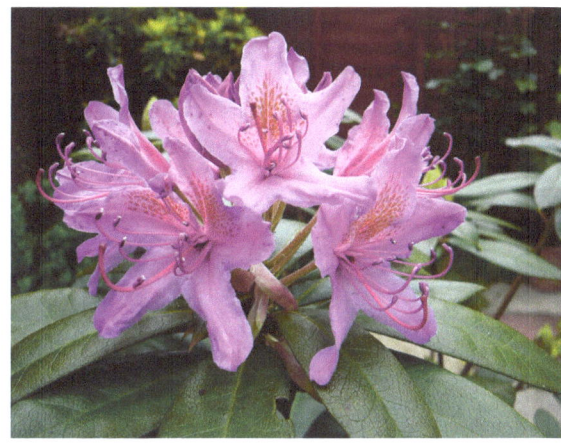
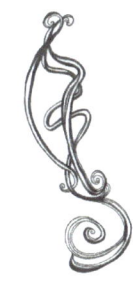

Alabaster Jar

Touching the soul, restless sea; igniting the mystery of your hidden eyes. Give us the dance of the morning and of the night, as our voices cry out to golden embers that light the sky.

Between the pages of a book and the soft caresses of a baby's sigh, passion cannot recreate your beauty. Neither the cold winds of winter nor the barren deserts of summer can hide your face, your hands, your heart. Grafted upon invisible wings, you soar into our time of waking and rest.

I hear your gentle voice echoing through the landscapes of my mind. What I searched for and what I found, all the same you are to me. Hands that speak of vision, nothing can destroy. Time and love make new, make alive. Dreamers and lovers experience music no one else but you can hear.

To hold you is to love you. In pieces or in shards, even dried bones are swept inside your powerful hands. What is picked up, what is laid down; all passes through. Hide my heart, or break it as you wish. Whatever you do, take me with you. Take me with you.

Truth, and goodness, and beauty
are but different faces of the same all.
A thing of beauty is a joy forever;
Its loveliness increases; it will never
Pass into nothingness.

John Keats

Beauty in Every Form

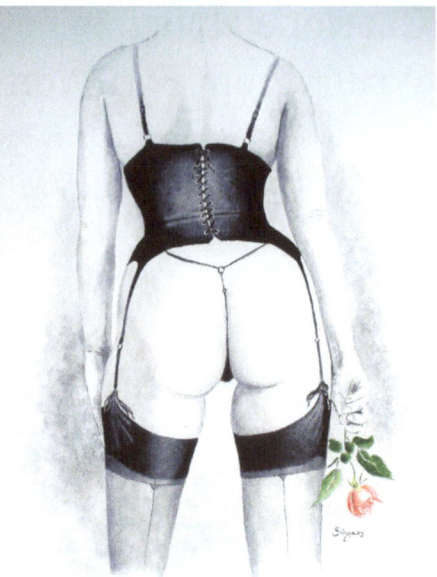

A Rose for My Rose, acrylic on paper
Richard Savage © 2003

In my opinion there is a big difference between life drawing and erotic art. With erotic art there is a naughtiness in the clothing and a joy in that naughty feeling. There is a salacious quality in seeing a glimpse of something that should be hidden that I don't find in life drawing.

I do find life drawing sensual, yet there is a contrast between the two pictures on this page and the life study opposite.

For me, there is a directness in the life work, something immediate. An economy of drawing; in such a short time you have to get to the essence of the picture in just a few lines.

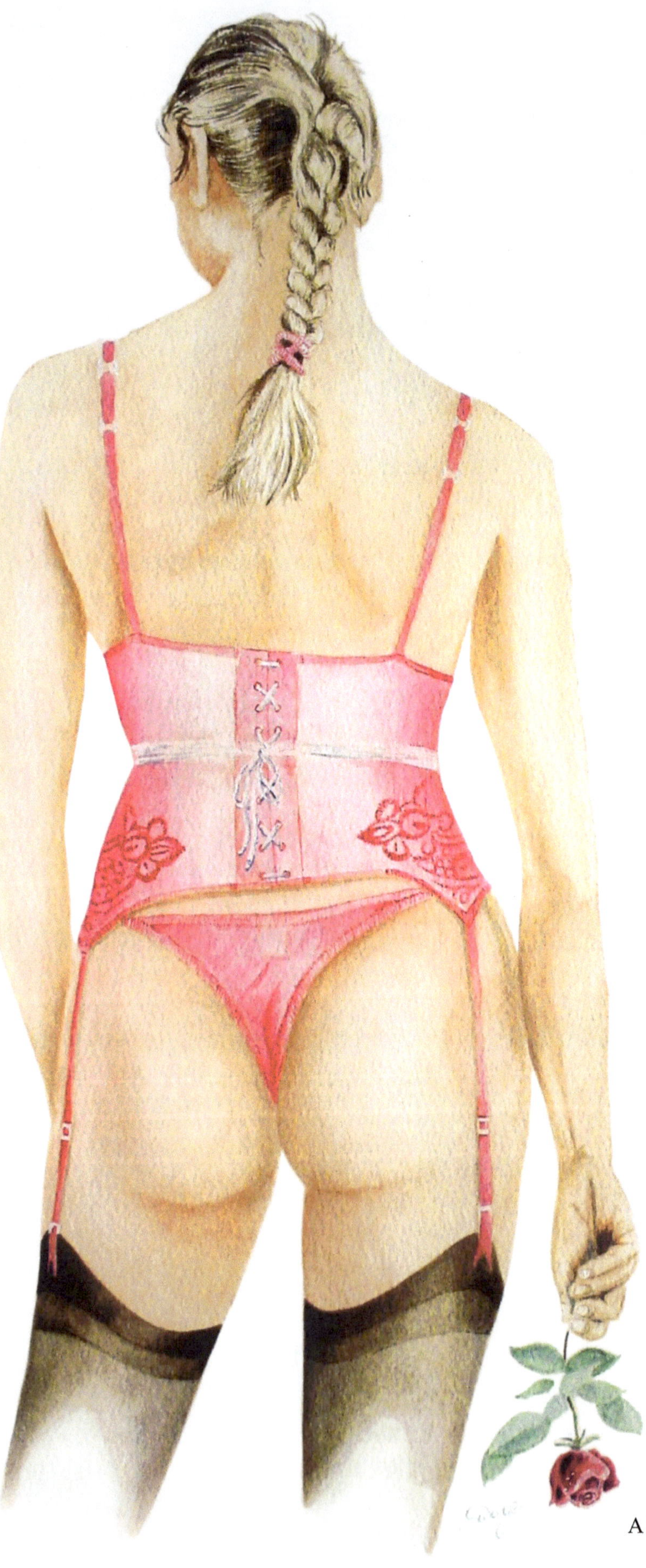

A Rose by Any Other Name, acrylic on paper
Richard Savage © 2003

Typically I would spend ten to fifteen hours working on a painting of this nature. In contrast the life studies take fifteen to twenty minutes. I enjoy both the time constraint with the life drawing and the abundance of time with more polished work for very different reasons. There is a rawness to life drawing, an immediacy and an honesty. In a painting where time is less of a factor you can spend that extra time polishing the image. The painting blends the lines of fabrics and there is more time to smooth out the skin tones. There is the temptation to remove blemishes and enhance the image, where with life drawing the approach is more warts and all. Having said I enjoy both time factors, I must confess, given a free choice, there is something in my personality that compels me to take my own sweet time about things.

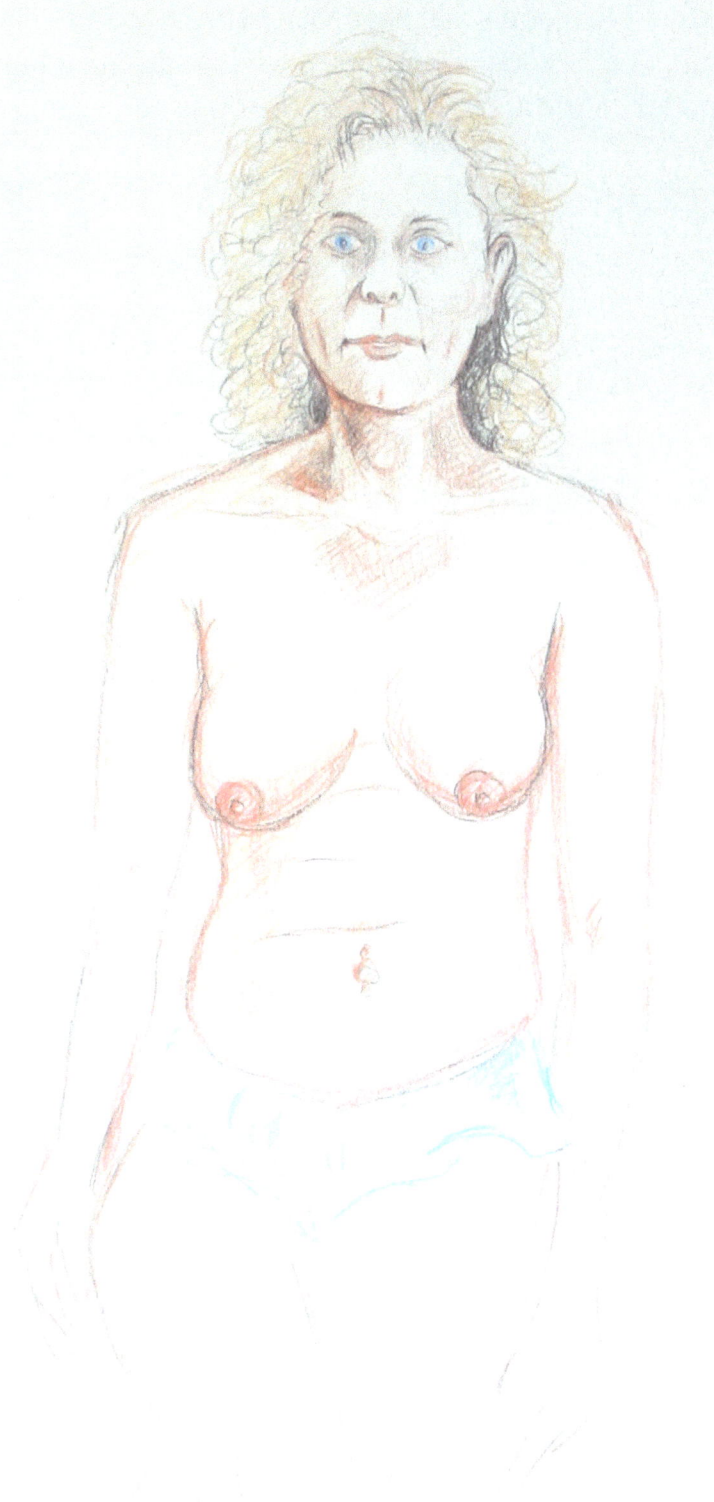

Study of Veronese Richard Savage © 2005

Most life models that have visited our life drawing group, have been happy to pose nude, but not everyone is comfortable with that, so at our group my emphasis is on making the model comfortable and using the opportunity to draw folds in fabric.

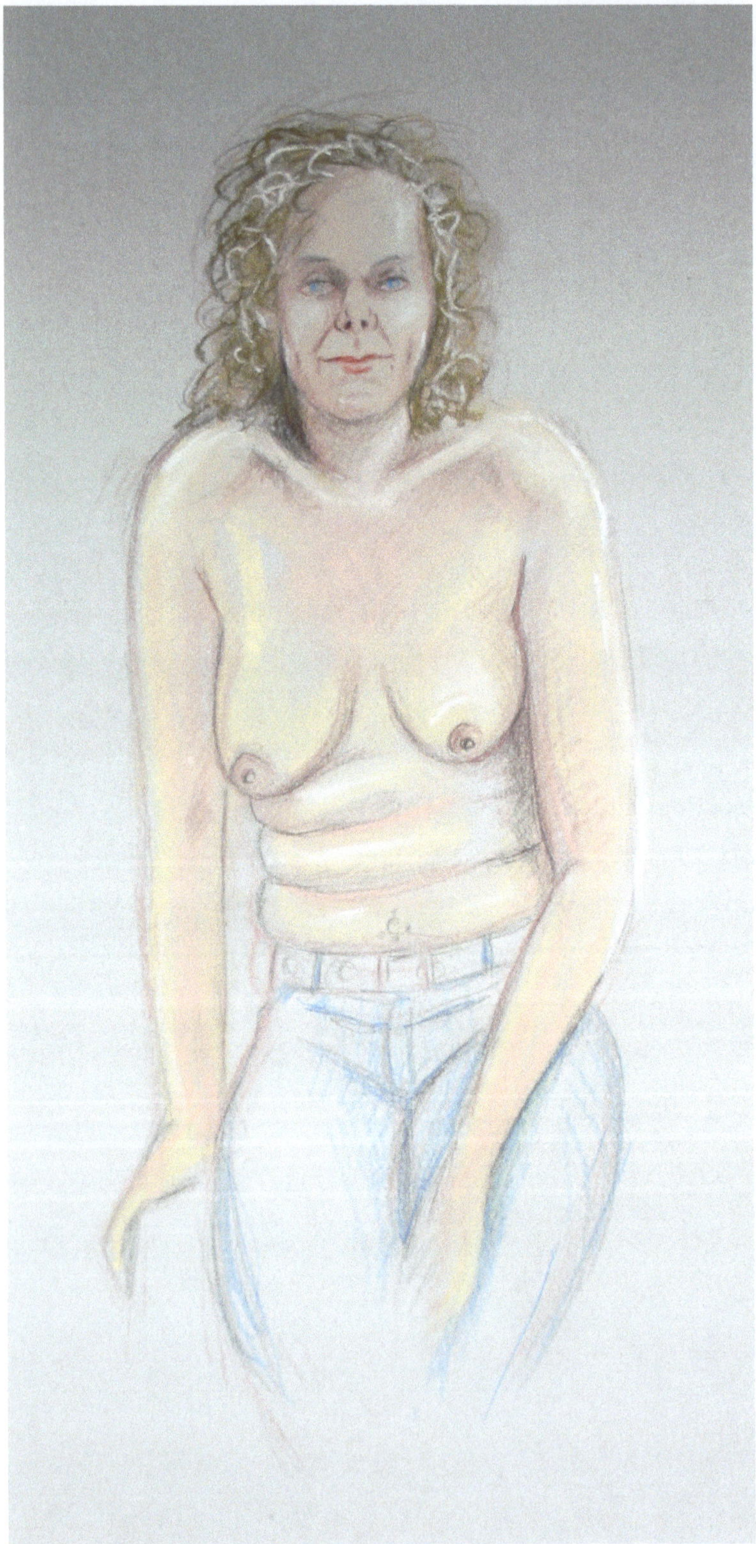

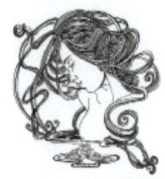

Another interesting feature for me is that the introduction of clothes seems to make the image more erotic. I feel there is a kind of naughtiness in seeing someone half-dressed. There is the lure of what you can't actually see. For me, erotic is much less about what you can see and more about what an image makes you think.

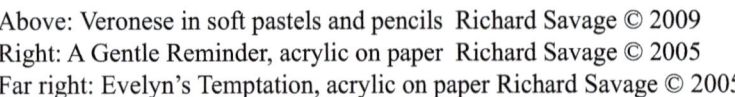

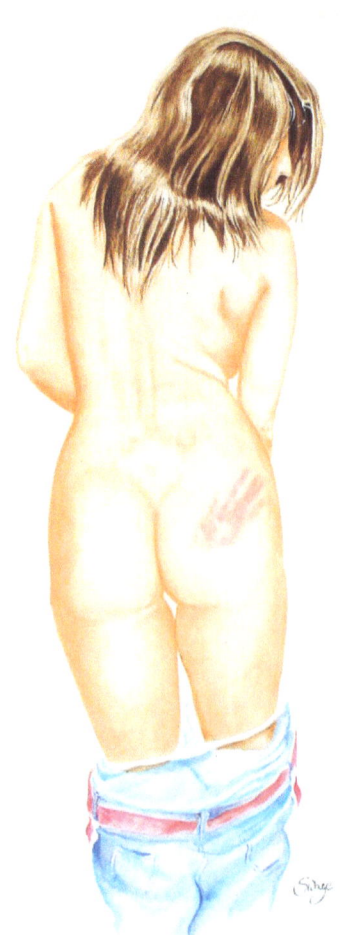

Above: Veronese in soft pastels and pencils Richard Savage © 2009
Right: A Gentle Reminder, acrylic on paper Richard Savage © 2005
Far right: Evelyn's Temptation, acrylic on paper Richard Savage © 2005

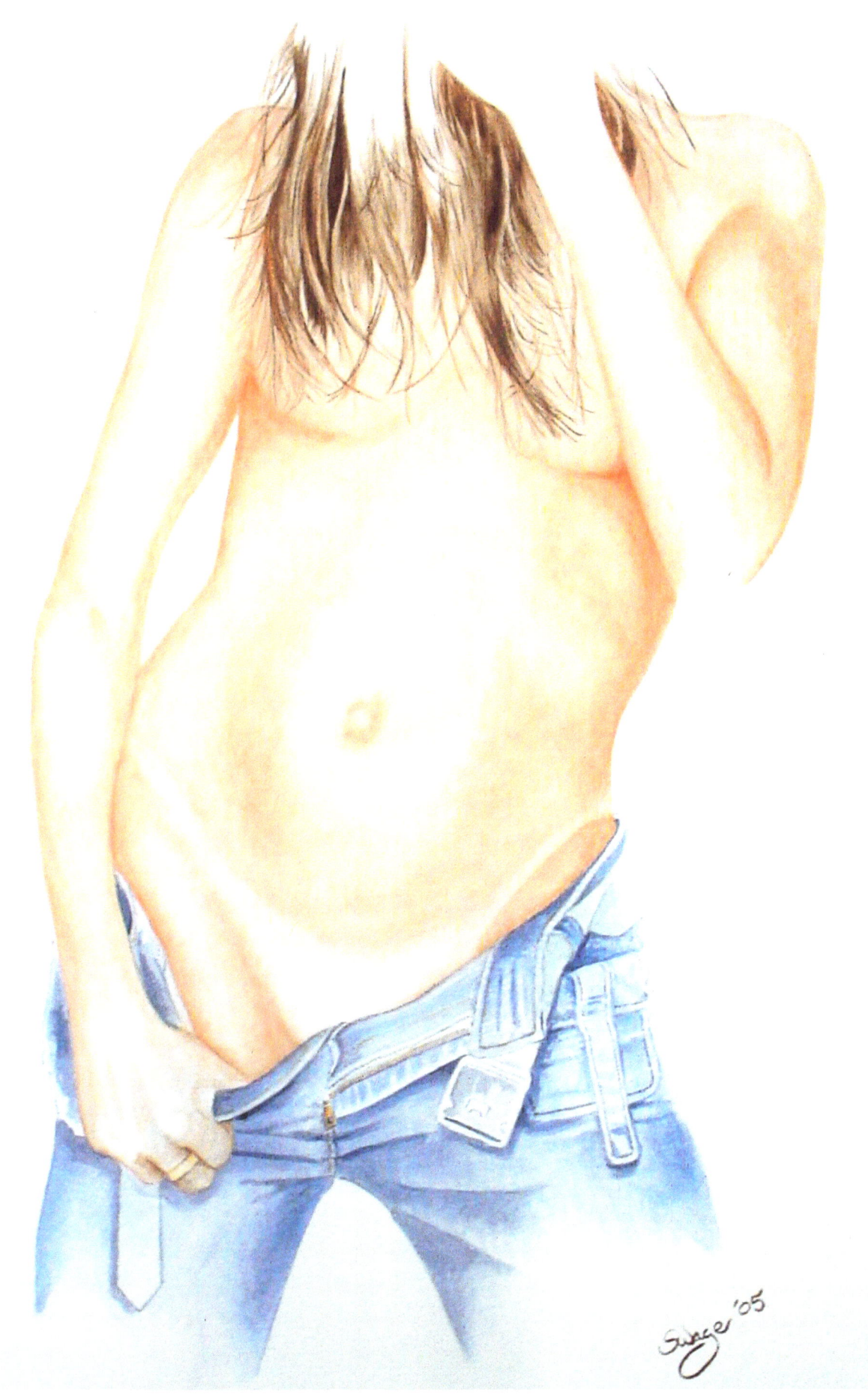

Tim Rosier
Fetish Photographer From The UK

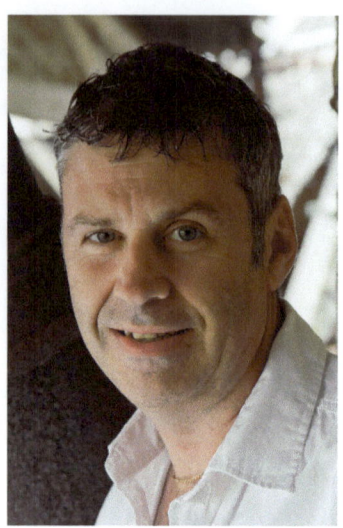

Tim Rosier was born in 1958 and resides in the UK. He came to photography only recently, in 2006. It started as a part time hobby and has since grown into a hobby that uses up all his spare time. Tim is currently just about to start his last year with Anglia Ruskin University where he is pursuing a degree in photography.

Tim's photography is mainly based on the female form. He has always been attracted to fuller figure models as he has been an admirer of the work of artists such as Peter Paul Rubens and Gustave Courbet ever since a visit to the Louvre in Paris. He always looks for curves in his models especially around the hips and tries to utilize these curves in his images.

He believes ladies of the fuller figure get a rough time in this age of magazine covers constantly showing size zero models. He tries to show the inner beauty of fuller figured ladies in his images.

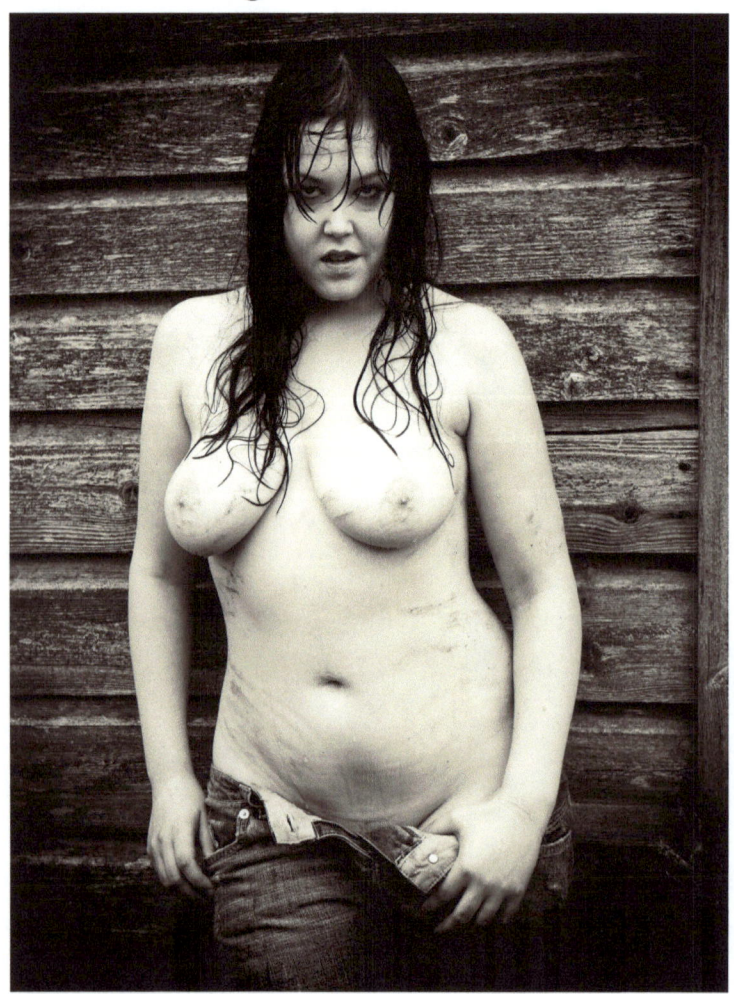

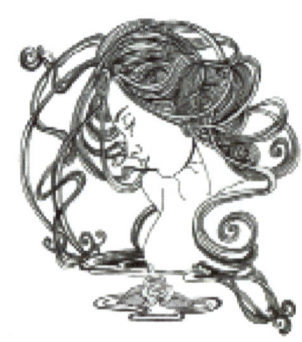

The eyes are the central focus in the picture (left). Tim believes it is the eyes that reveal the inner beauty in everyone.

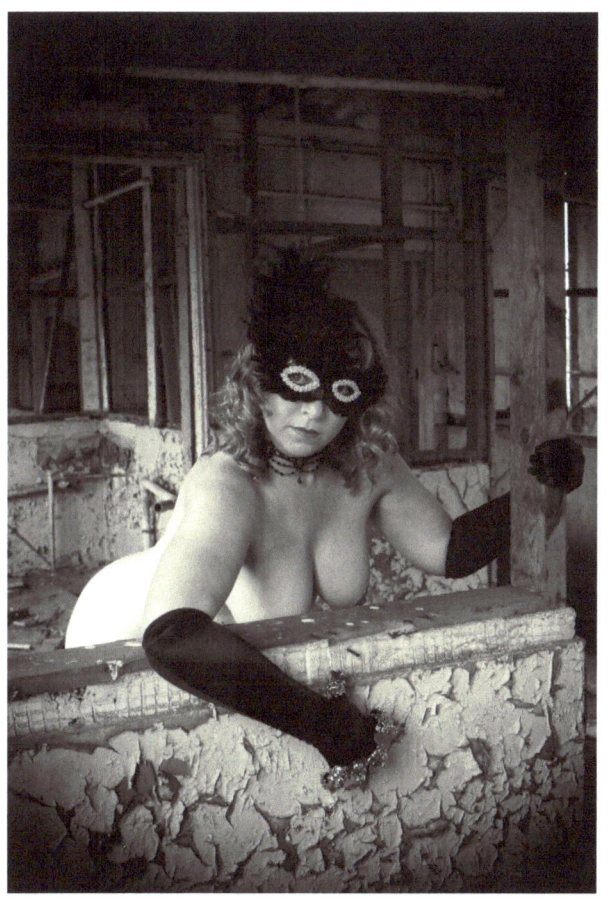

Tim does utilize a home studio, but prefers to be out in the environment, working with natural light and occasionally off camera flashguns. He likes the challenge of finding old falling down structures to pose his models in. The structures create the contrast of beauty in a decaying environment. They also add to the atmosphere and aid in the story telling of the final image.

Tim was asked what his favorite shoot was. After thinking long and hard he answered, "The last one. Every shoot brings a new challenge, new images, as well as further opportunities to learn something new and continue to improve my skill set."

Since starting photography this has developed into a family hobby where his wife photographs men and he photographs women. More of their work can been seen at www.venusadonis.co.uk

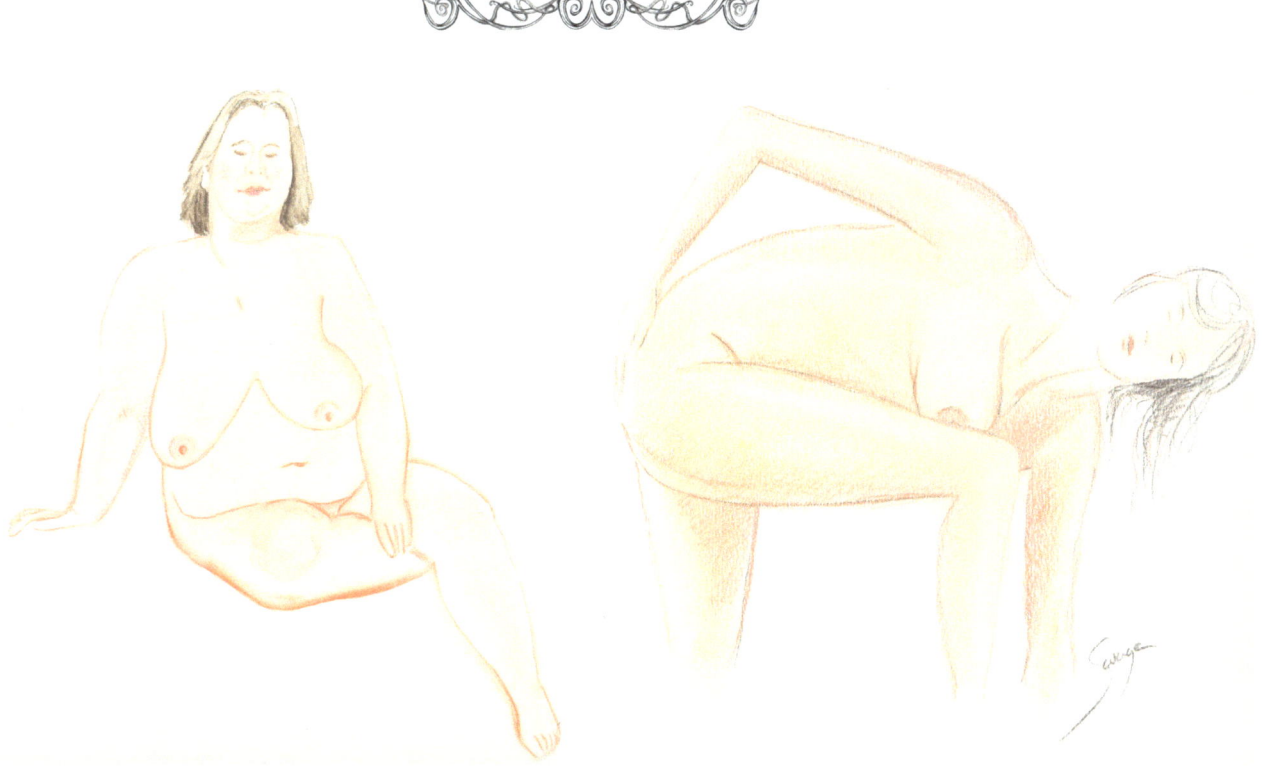

Studies of Carol (left) and Lucy (right) in watercolor pencils and soft pastel. Richard Savage © 2012

Beauty in Every Form

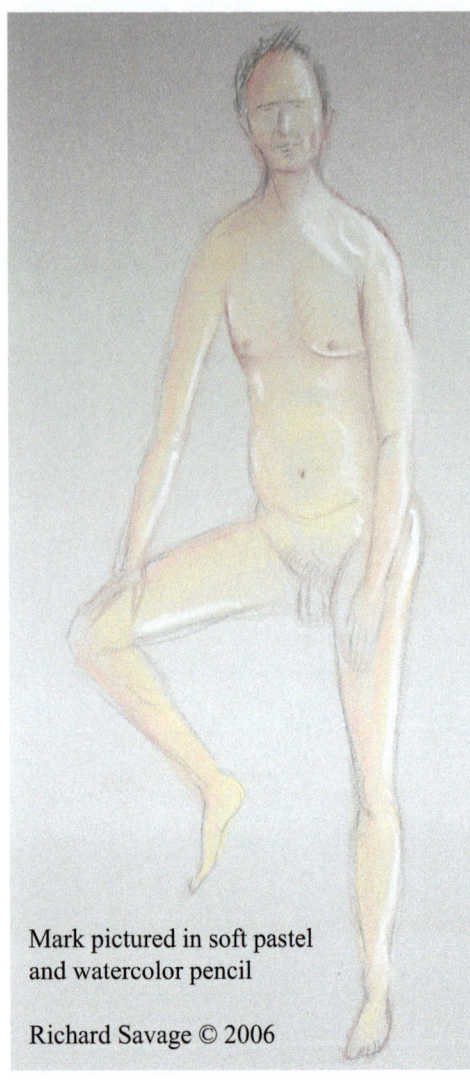

Mark pictured in soft pastel and watercolor pencil

Richard Savage © 2006

Chris pictured in watercolor pencil
Richard Savage © 2012

Male Models

It is truly not a lack of interest, on my part, that I don't paint or draw the male form that often. In life drawing terms I am happy drawing and painting either the male or female form. I would say until recently the problem has been a lack of available male models.

I have never really found a high demand for fine art projects that involve images of the male form. It is a shame that a lack of demand and male models has led to only a small number of pictures of men in my portfolio.

My studio life group now has a number of male models. Mark, seen on the left, a very patient model was our first. There have been a number since including Clifford, Kevin, Gary and Chris.

Below Back to Basics, acrylic on paper
Appeared in the Washington Museum of Contemporary Art
in 2005   Richard Savage © 2005

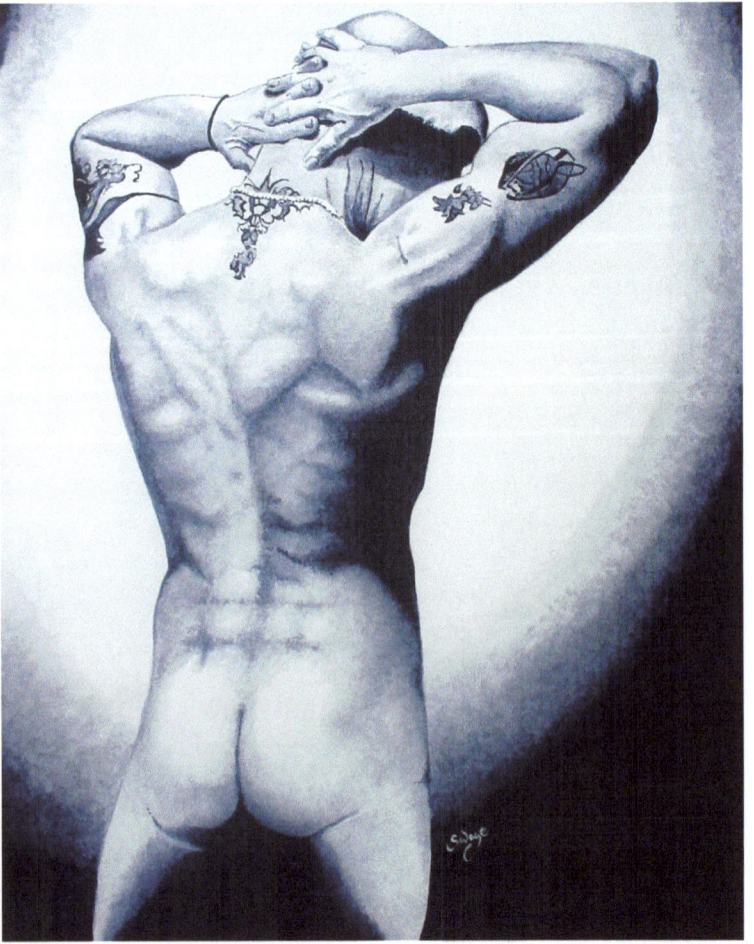

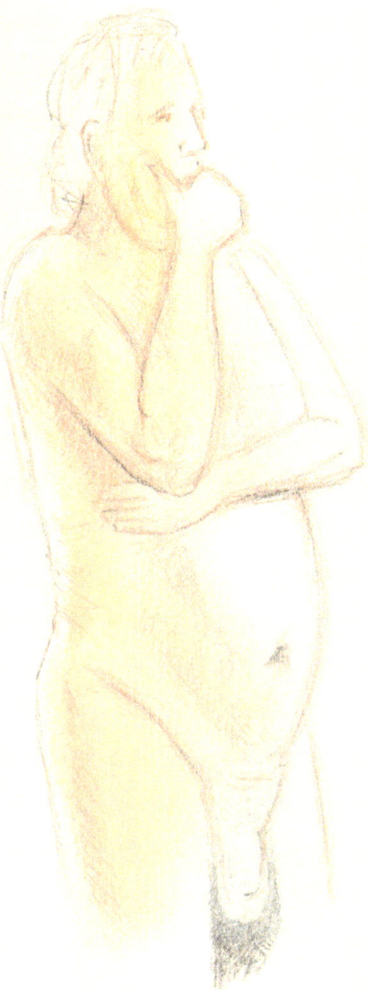

Richard Savage © 2011 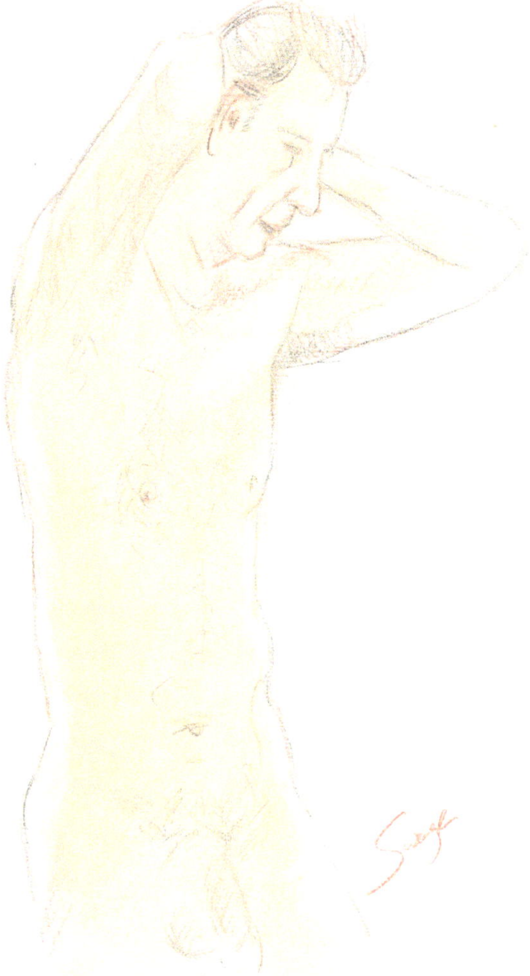   Richard Savage © 2011

The pictures on this page are rendered in soft pastel and watercolor pencil. The models are top left Clifford, top right Kevin, below left Clifford, centre Chris and bottom right Clifford.

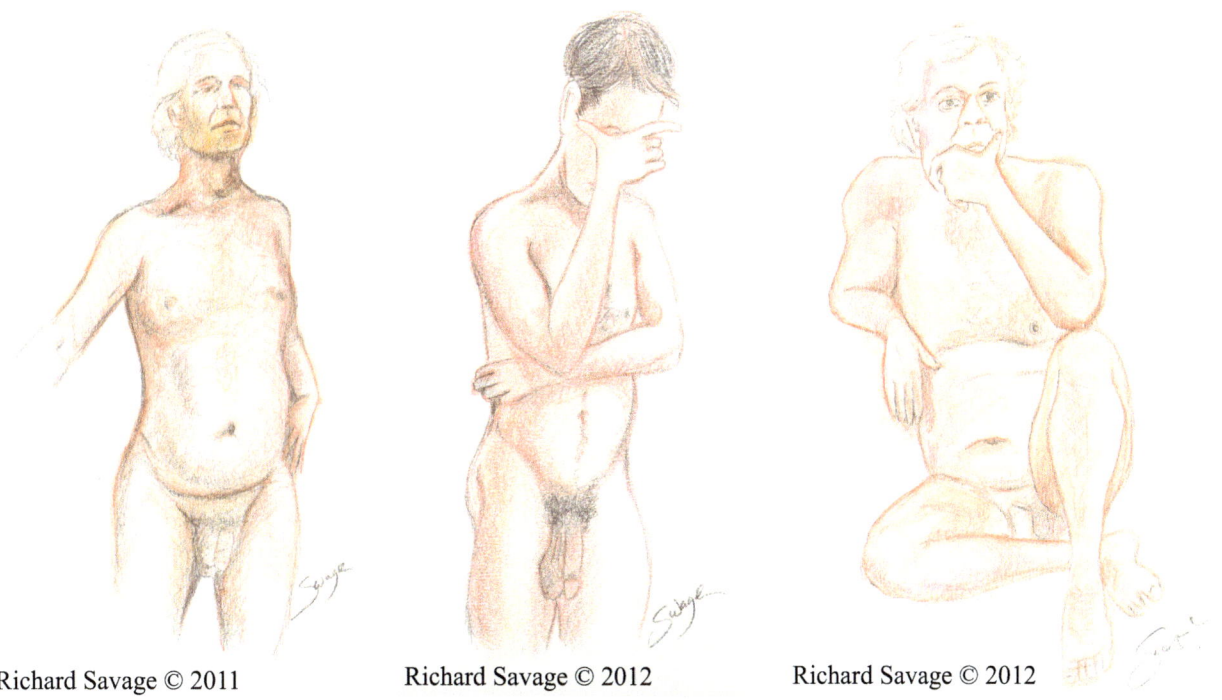

Richard Savage © 2011   Richard Savage © 2012   Richard Savage © 2012

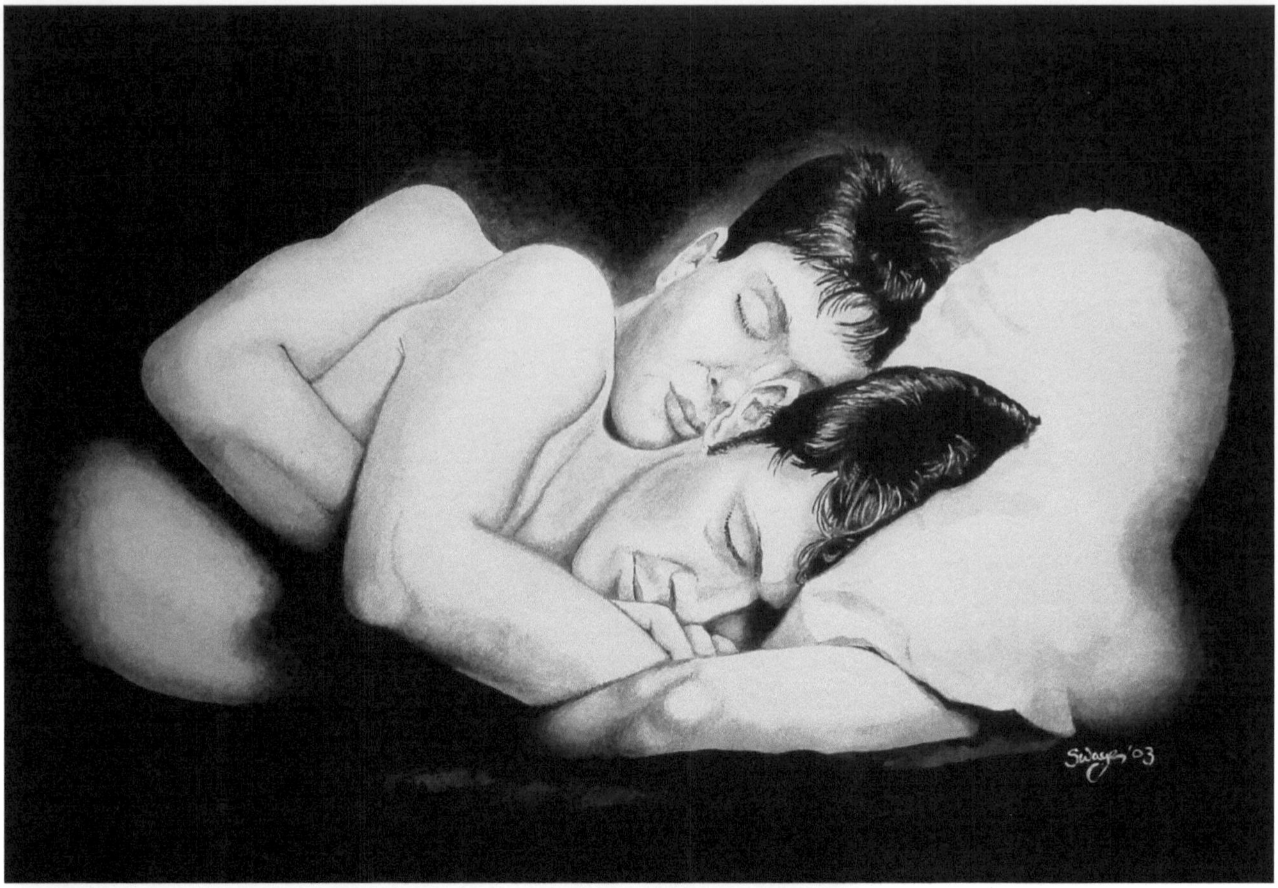

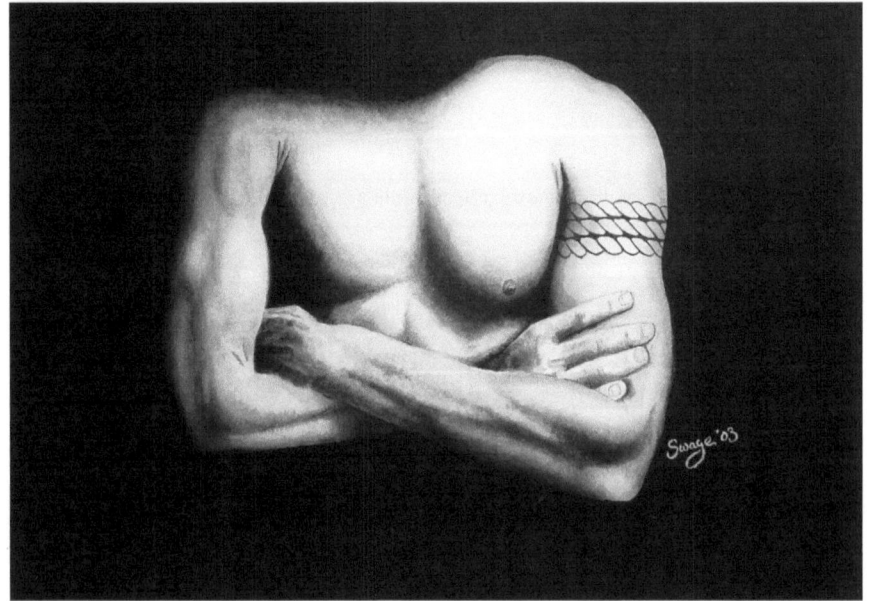

Pictured above is
Sweet Dreams,
acrylic on paper
Richard Savage © 2003

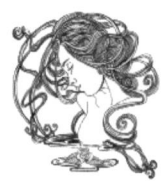

Pictured left is
In Safe Arms,
acrylic on paper
Richard Savage © 2003

Lin

Male models don't seem to be as popular as female models, some groups actually never have male models.

Popular male models are those who have muscular bodies and who take up poses with ropes or bars which accentuate their muscles.

Andy
Fetish Photographer From The UK

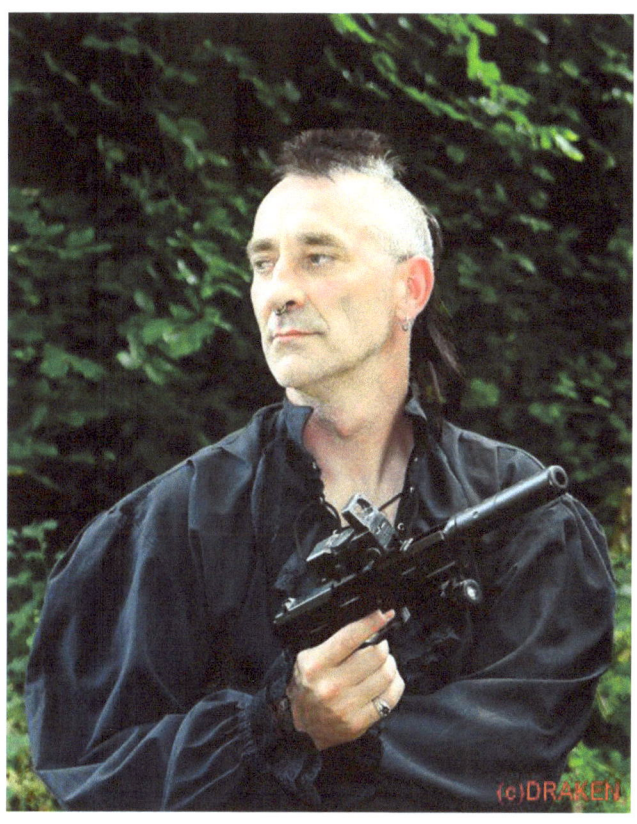

I have spent most of my adult life around people who practice alternative lifestyles. This is mainly due to alt people's acceptance of others for themselves not based on looks, social standing or fashion statement. Through this I met my wife, model Belladonna, who at that time wore tattoos with pride, something the normal people found ugly on a woman.

Since being together we have developed together within the alt/Goth/fetish community, where we have found all walks of life and personal looks to be accepted.

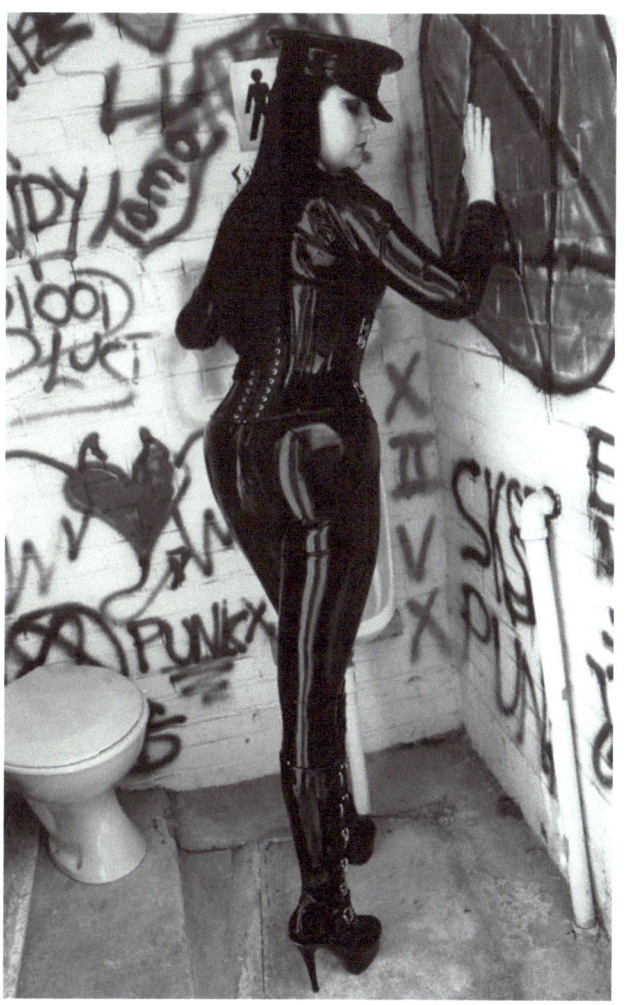

As a photographer, I have always felt more comfortable and satisfied with the alternative genre imagery. So much more can be achieved and others look at the end work as a whole rather than concentrating on the *stunning* model.

I have found that the world of glamour photography is quite a bore. When you have photographed one *pretty* blonde/brunette etc. in a set of poses, you have covered all the *pretty* models have to offer, as these are images of appearance with no input of personality or character.

© Andybelladonna

To work with the models I photograph is a pleasure as there are no hang-ups over dress size, leg length, etc. as there are with glamour models. I find that each person has a feature that is attractive to me and I use this to produce images that both the model and myself are pleased with. None of the models are unattractive, each is individual and the results we produce are governed by our personal tastes.

On the personal side, I am attracted to people who show a great personality/character through the way they present themselves and how they treat others. Their style is an extension of themselves and the appearance they have is a product of the person. I find that these individuals have a depth that is of interest and they are able to express themselves in a personal style.

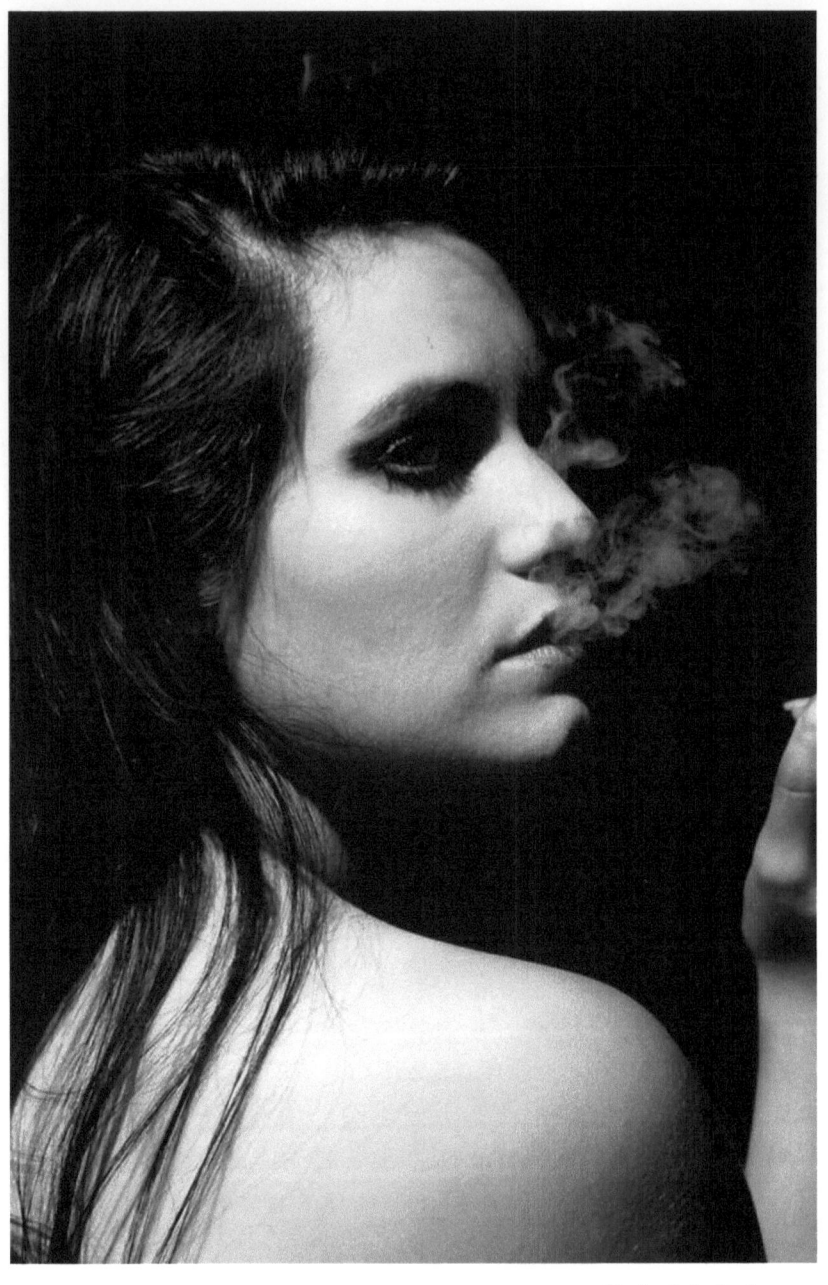

© Andybelladonna

The people I am attracted to do not rely on socially accepted standards of beauty.

I feel that the world of advertising tells us what we need not only in consumer products but in a person's looks. Society has now reached the point of being told what is attractive in a person and that only certain looks are beautiful. This creates a problem of prejudice based on acceptable beauty.

We should all accept a person for who they are and how they treat others. There can be something beautiful found in everyone.

myspace.com/belladonna666 and myspace.com/andybelladonna

Belladonna
Fetish Model From The UK

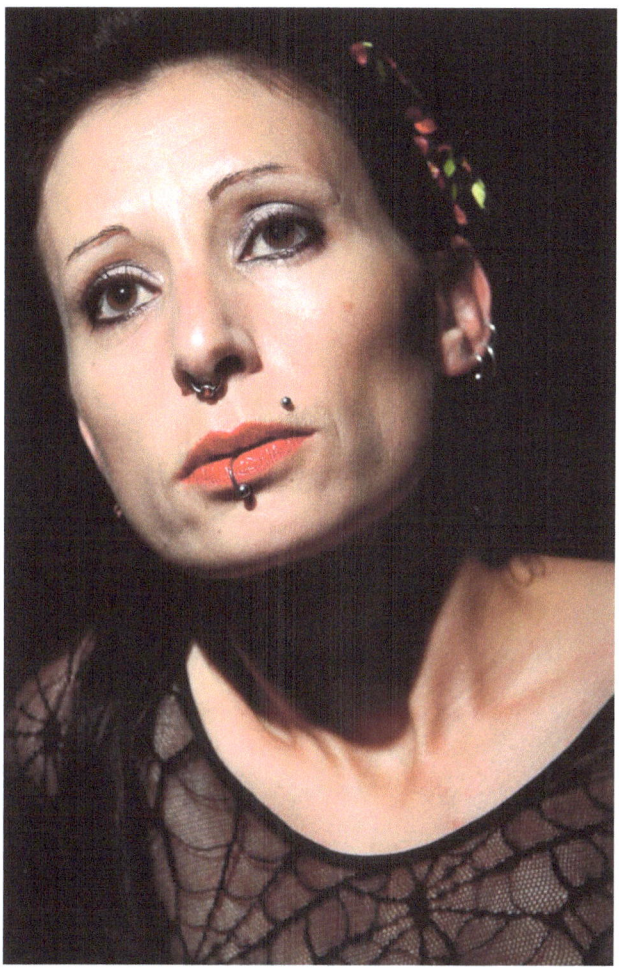

© Andybelladonna

For the past 5 years I have been an 'alternative' model. I have worked with lots of different women, many of whom you would be unlikely to see in mainstream publications.

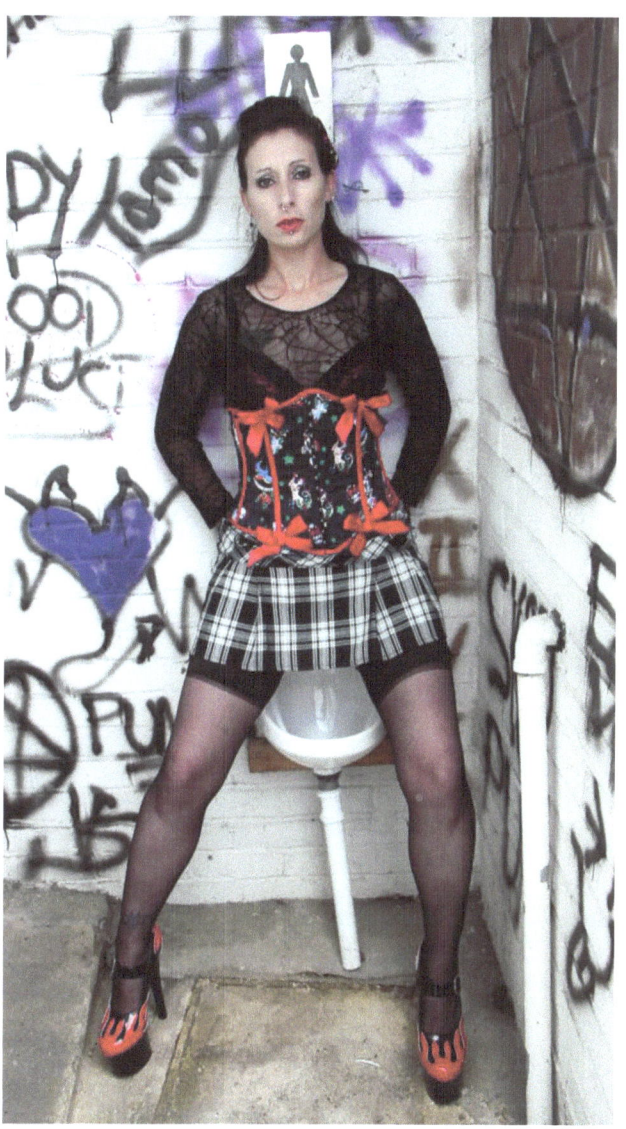

© Andybelladonna

It seems that beauty, as portrayed by the media, falls into set guidelines; a woman must have a certain body shape, facial structure, height, etc. We are given the impression that this is how we should look and it is presumed that we want to look this way. But when I look at pictures of these 'beautiful people' they appear to have no personality or character.

In contrast when I see a picture of an alternative model, to me, their character seems to be shouting out loud above their exterior. Perhaps I am biased but I think that women with body modifications and a unique sense of style are far more beautiful than those without. Part of this is because to me it portrays that the woman is emotionally strong, independent and doesn't conform to anybody's rules or ideals. This inner beauty makes them even more beautiful on the outside.

Beauty in Every Form

Nori Zay
Model From Washington DC, USA

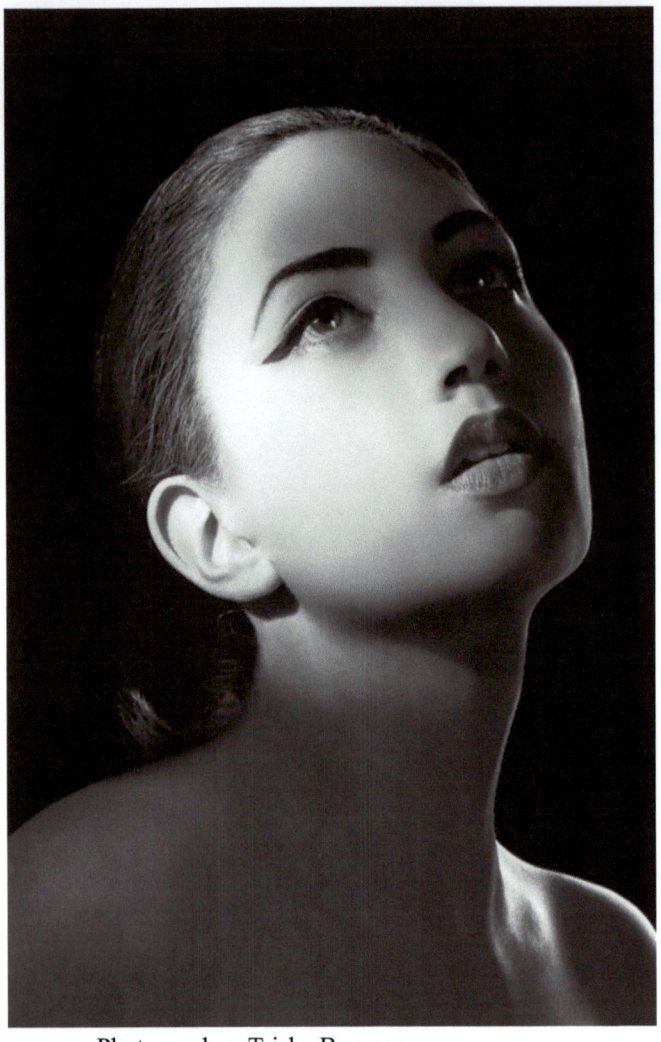

Photographer: Trisha Bowyer.
Makeup & Hair: Viva La Kayleigh

Beauty is what people see, and different people see different things. Growing up in America, unfortunately, means that the disgustingly tall and bizarrely skinny people are the ones that have the cards in their hands.

The guy on the street is told that it's the girl with the swollen t-shirt and the puffed-up blonde hair that is beautiful.

Compare that to someone like me, average-sized with blue hair and multiple surgical scars, and I might as well have been wrapped in police tape and faded into the background.

I spent the early part of my life trying to conform. I bought brand-name jeans and wore my hair straight, tried to lose weight and even bought bottles of self-tanner and push up bras, in a vain attempt to be like everyone else. I wore carefully considered necklines to conceal one large scar and only wore one-pieces to hide the majority of other scars.

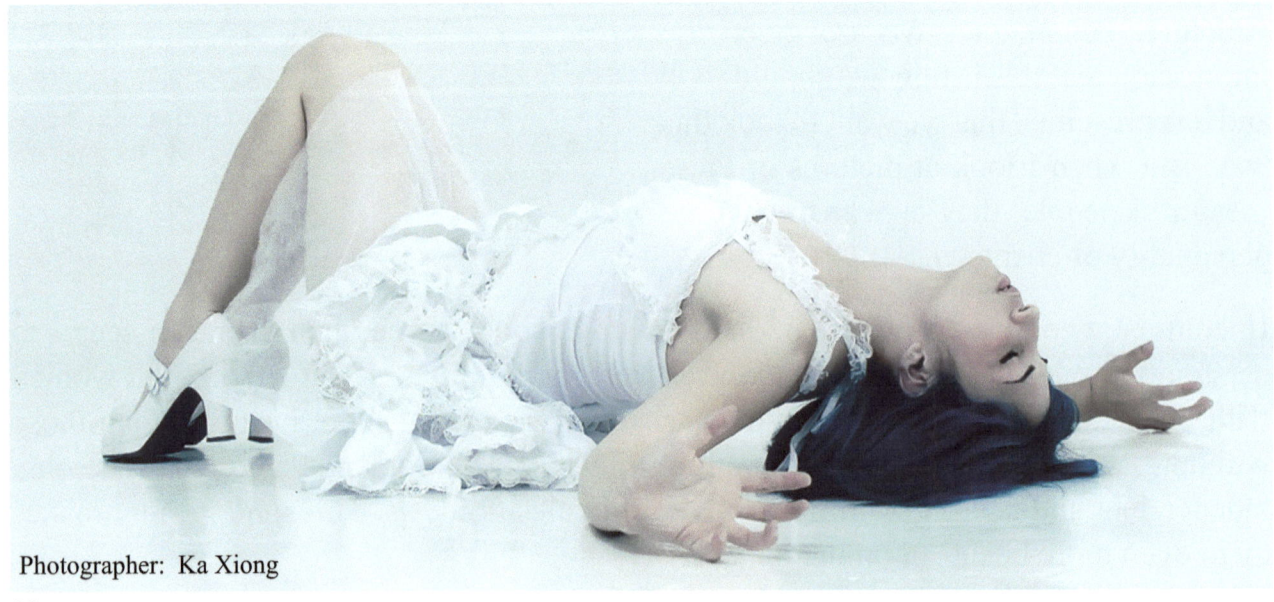

Photographer: Ka Xiong

It wasn't until about a year ago that I accepted myself as beautiful, or any form of attractive, to be honest. I'm not sure why but a spur of the moment decision to dye my hair pink prompted a lot of changes in my life. I started to wear the clothes I wanted, to check myself in the mirror and give a nod of approval. Suddenly I felt like an attractive person. My chest didn't get bigger, fat didn't slide out of my skin and my hair still isn't long, thick and shining but I broke out of the stereotype and tried to be myself instead of what everyone said I should be.

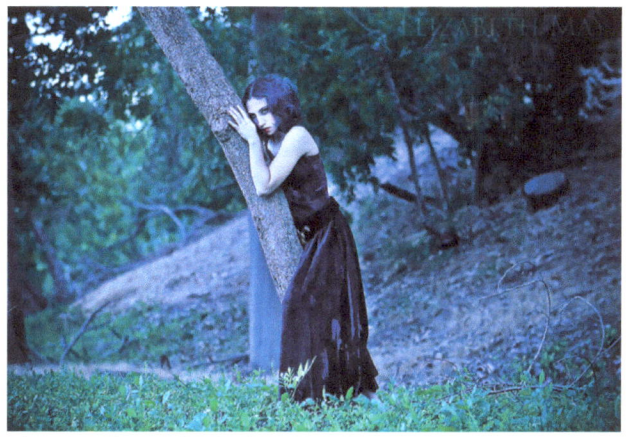

Photographer: Elizabeth May. Makeup: Donna Aguilar. Hair: Kittycut. Wardrobe: The Art Farm

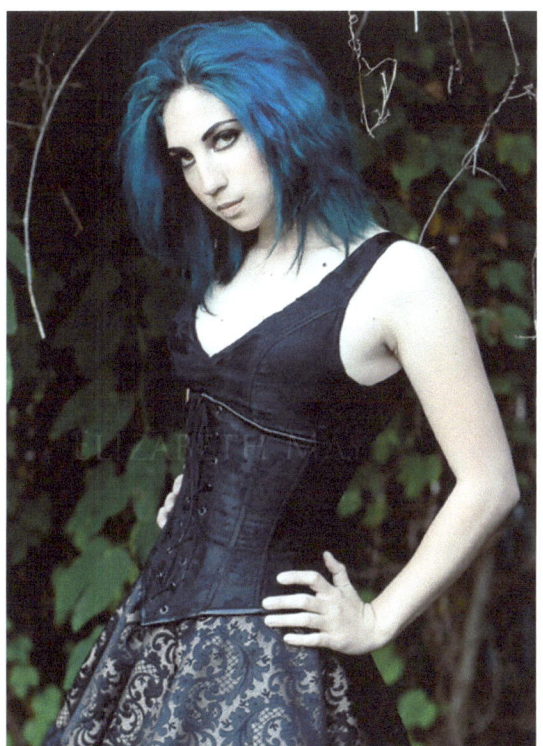

Photographer: Elizabeth May.
Makeup: Donna Aguilar.
Wardrobe: Karen von Oppen

The people who have turned a disinterested eye away from the spewed out junk that says all girls should look alike have an appreciation for those who make an effort to be who they want to be.

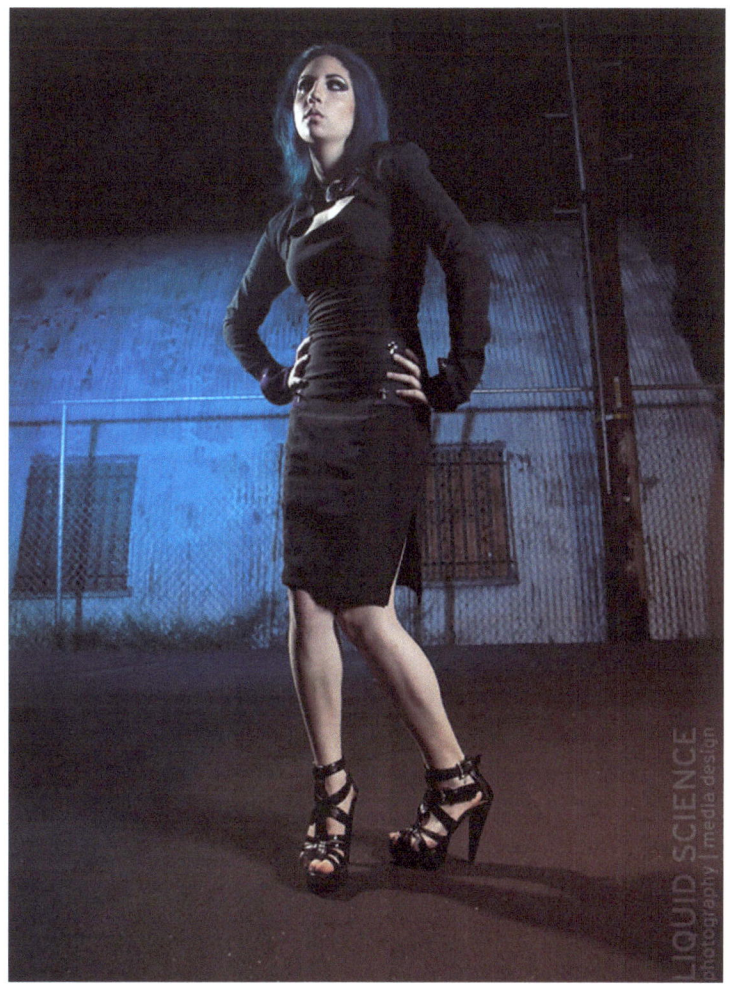

Photographer: Liquid Science.
Makeup & Hair: ToriUnicorn MUA

When the media tells us what beauty should be, some people try to be it. Some people are it. Some people have the confidence to break free from it stand out in the crowd whether they like it or not. And that is beautiful.

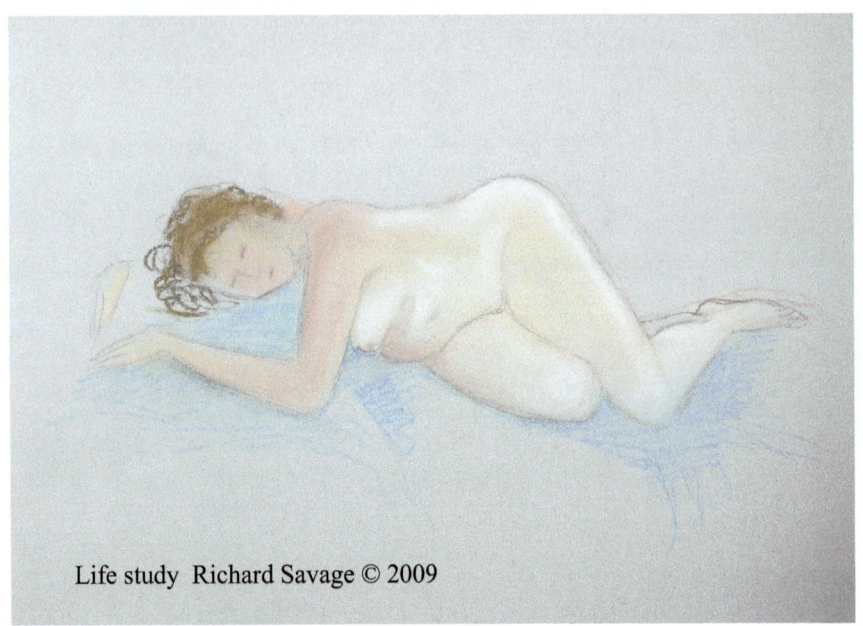
Life study Richard Savage © 2009

My life model, Lin, in three relaxed poses.

When she asks, "What pose would you like?"

I will often say, "Just relax." I love the soft languid poses. I often feel Lin is at her very best when just totally chilled.

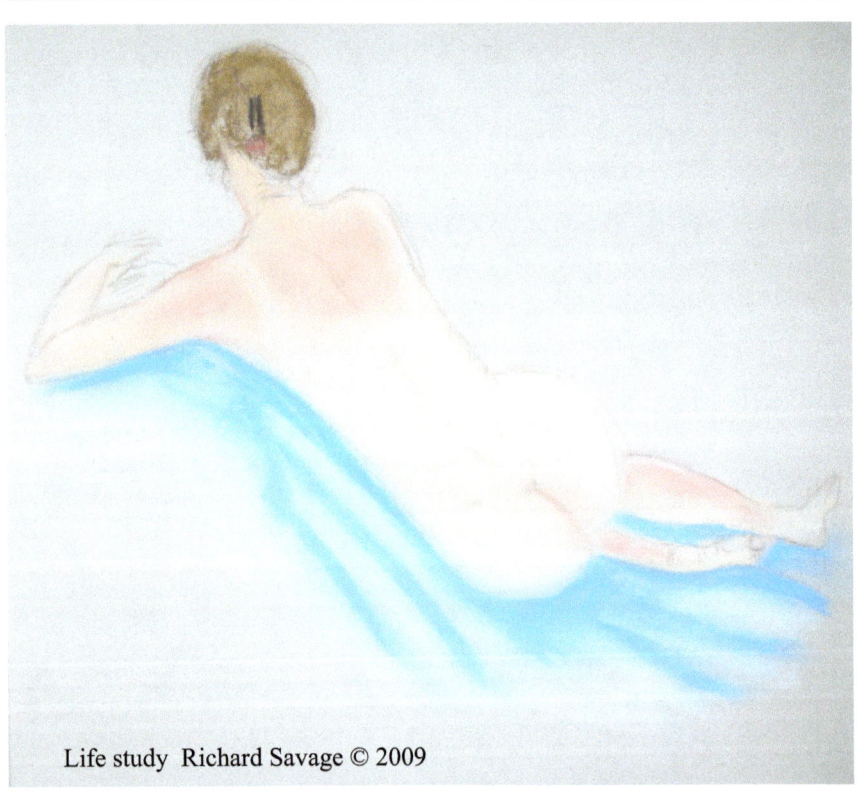
Life study Richard Savage © 2009

Lin

The majority of female models seem to be fairly slim. Slim and curvy seems to be liked but shapeless is not. Thin, straight, shapeless models of either sex do not seem to be popular

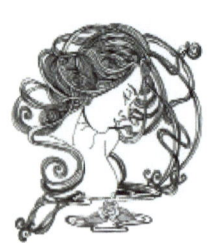

Lin

Back views are popular with the people I pose for. A lot of men particularly like bums and buttocks.

Life study by Richard Savage © 2009

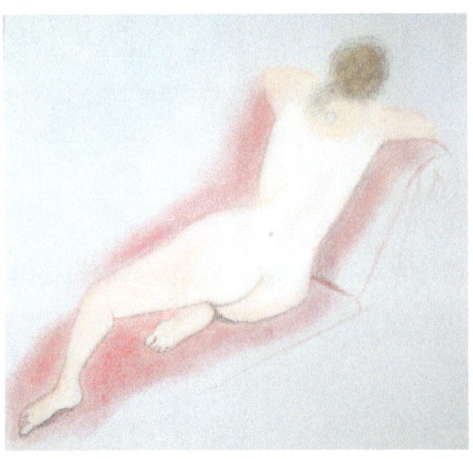

Becky Vigor
Artist From Sheffield, UK

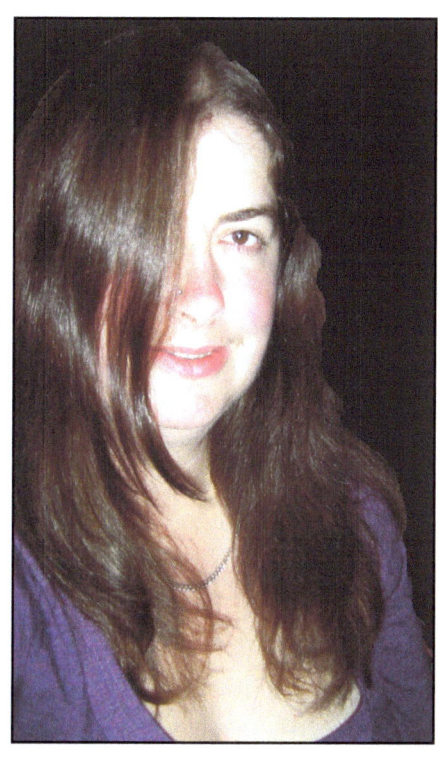

When I think of what makes a person beautiful I guess, like most people, part of what I think about is what they look like. Being visually impaired doesn't alter that, it just means I get a different picture.

With most things in the visual world I am at somewhat of a disadvantage when it comes to details. A lot of this I can flesh out by touch – a beautiful glossy leaf feels smooth and cool to the touch, a beautifully embroidered cushion has many soft and sensuous textures. When it comes to a beautiful woman, though, I don't often get to fill in the details. I can hardly go up to a woman in the street and say to her; "Excuse me, I think you may be beautiful but I am visually impaired so I can't be sure. Would it be ok if I stroke my finger along your cheekbone and cup your breast in my hand? And can I then do the same to your friend for purposes of comparison?" Our culture simply doesn't allow for this aspect of accessibility and I'm not sure I'd want to be subject to it myself.

So instead I move more readily into the non-physical realms of personal beauty – the voice is the obvious provider of clues. I like those with plenty of tone, a good regional accent and a relatively low pitch. And of course what the voice talks about has something to do with it! Once I fell in love with a woman who wrote beautiful emails, whose essence was conveyed so clearly by the written word that it was simply a bonus to discover later that she was also in possession of a beautiful voice. It was only much later that I was able to satisfy my curiosity on the point of cheekbone and breast.

The flip side is how others see me. It's hard to gain a confident self image when I can't make clear comparisons between myself and other women, when I can't really tell how much they can see of me. I just don't know how obvious things like the texture of my skin and the colour of my eyes are at a distance. How far away do I need to move before they won't notice if I scratch my nose? It's so easy to err on the side of either negligence or hyper-vigilance and never know.

I have to hope that beauty, or lack of it, is only part of what we notice, what we want. I have to hope that most people will be happy with a mix of ingredients, and that most people, even those with perfect sight, can recognize a soul that is trying to be beautiful.

Beauty in Every Form

Marian Savill
Mixed Media Artist And Writer Living In The UK

I Am More Than My Dress Size

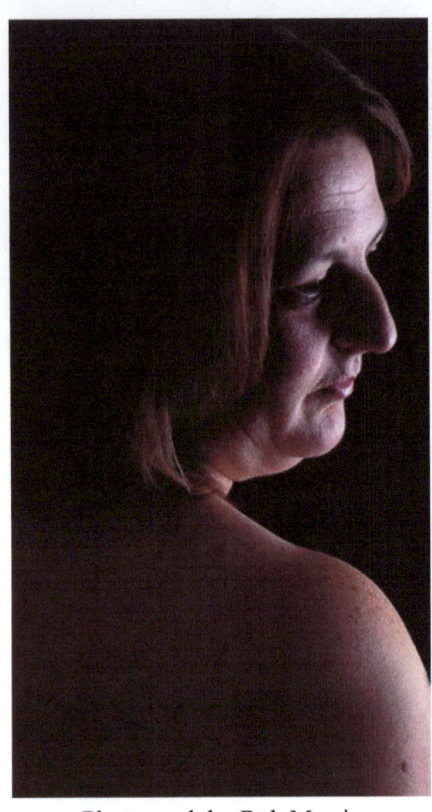

Photograph by Rob Morris

I am a mixed media artist living and working in Cambridgeshire. I took the plunge from being employed (by the local library service) into being a full time artist in 2007. Most of my artwork revolves around the use of recycled or used materials. I create assemblage, jewelry and mixed media pieces using materials which have had a previous life. I love to transform the unloved, the unwanted, the discarded, into distinctive individual artwork.

This year I started to explore body image in some of my artwork. My self portrait, Fragmented Acceptance, brought many deep rooted feelings to the surface as I planned and subsequently created the piece of art work. The art work is a self portrait which I submitted to the Royal Academy of Arts Summer Exhibition. I found the inward reflection as I created the piece both fascinating and absorbing and I certainly plan to continue to explore the subject of body image in my future artwork. I hope by exploring the subject of body image I can use it to promote the positive effects of self acceptance and encourage others to express themselves without bowing to societal and media pressures.

In my early teens, at secondary school, I was tall, I had a deep voice for a girl and I resolutely wouldn't follow the crowd. I was different. I began to be bullied and these unhappy times led me to start to use food as my comfort, my weapon, my everything. During my late teens and into adulthood, my weight increased as my self-esteem decreased. Body image issues began at school where negative thoughts were imprinted and made me more conscious of my differences. It has taken a long time to get to where I am now, and to be in the position where I feel confident enough to be celebrating in a book that is discussing the essence of what beauty is really all about.

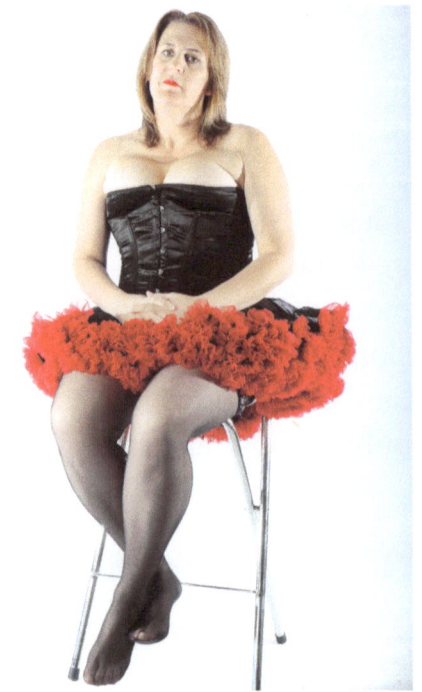

Photograph by Rob Morris

The first naked photo shoot I experienced was a total revelation to me! It was singularly the most empowering thing I've ever done for myself as a woman. Suddenly the scales fell away from my eyes and I saw myself for what I am, not for what I thought I was, for what I had spent years believing I was. Participating in that shoot was like opening a door for which I'd never had a key. I have now had several naked shoots, including one for a charity calendar. They continue to empower me and strengthen my belief in the power of self acceptance.

For many years I have wondered just why it is considered ok to judge me on my size? Why is it that I feel that I am judged to be a lesser person because I am larger than life in body and personality? Why is it ok to celebrate differences unless they relate to size? I am not my dress size. I am not a number on the scale. I am much more than either of those things.

Don't look at me and judge me for not being a size zero, look at me and see, really see, that women of all shapes and sizes should celebrate their bodies for what they are, not for what others dictate they should be. We should revel in all our glorious, beautiful differences. We are all different shapes, we all have different sized bums, boobs, legs and tummies, we have stretch marks, scars and cellulite. We have brown eyes, blue eyes, long hair, short hair, big feet, small feet... the list is endless. These things make us what we are. They make us real. They give us our wonderful individuality. We are all unique, we are all truly beautiful.

I look at my beautiful daughter and know that she is suffering the full force of media driven hype about the *perfect body*.

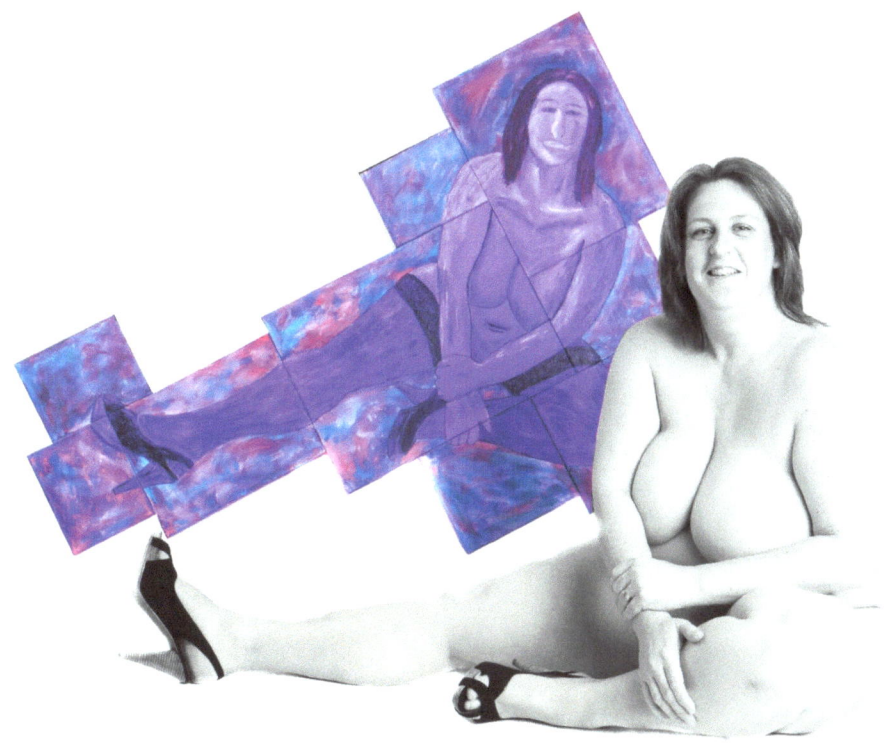

Photograph by Rob Morris

We owe it to our children to be role models for positive body image. Loving ourselves just as we are is the best way to demonstrate to our daughters that it's ok to be real, it's ok to love what we are, it's ok not to try and make ourselves something we're not. What's important is how brightly the flame burns not the size of the container it burns in.

Katie
Student From Cambridgeshire UK

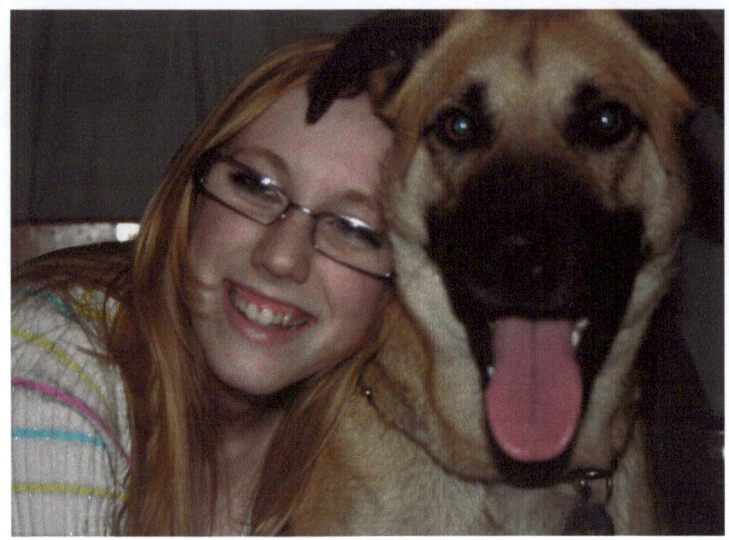

They say that beauty is in the eye of the beholder, if that is so then we all see people differently. Therefore to be happy with yourself is the most anyone can do to feel they are truly beautiful. Someone my age goes through a lot of peer pressure to fit in and be the same as everyone else, but sometimes individuality and personality are the very things that make us who we are. To be comfortable with ourselves is what makes us beautiful. If we go through our lives forever changing because we're not comfortable with who we are then we can never hope to feel beautiful.

Personally, I believe that once someone finds their own style then they can be their own person. Only then will they truly be happy within themselves. Conformity is the impulse to fit in with the people that surround us. While it does make us feel stronger to be part of a group it's much healthier to be your own person and do as you believe will benefit you.

Lin

Women seem to be more open and forthcoming about the type of models they like. Men do not air their preferences very often. Many women have told me they find larger ladies interesting to draw if they get the chance but huge women are not liked if there is just bulk but no shape. I guess that might be the same with men. I don't know why there are not more large models. I don't know whether it is because there is not the demand or whether larger people are not so confident, comfortable or eager to be drawn naked, after all nothing is left to the imagination!

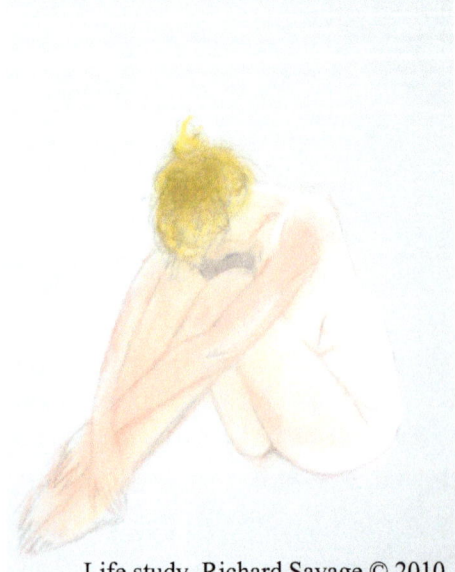

Life study Richard Savage © 2010

Lin

For me, there are all kinds of aspects to beauty. Just a rounded curve of a belly, the roundness of a bottom, a smooth easy line.

Face shape is another whole area. Some people are very self-conscious of having round faces, no cheekbones. Others are self-conscious because they have no chin.

There are all sorts of things that we ascribe beauty to, or not. The thesis is that there is beauty in all shapes, all sizes, all ages, all statures, all face shapes, that there is beauty in all of us, no matter our size, stature, shape, or the shape of our face, or indeed whether our skin is tight or whether it has a wrinkle here and there.

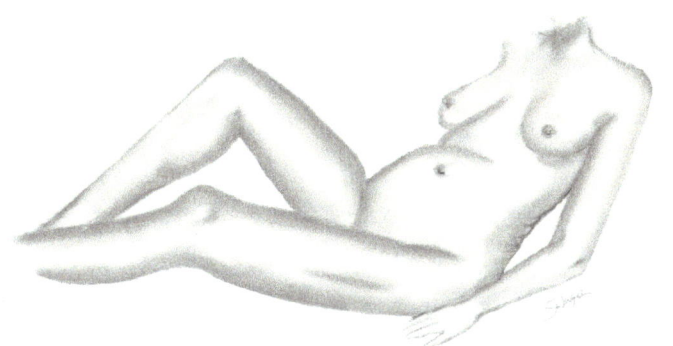 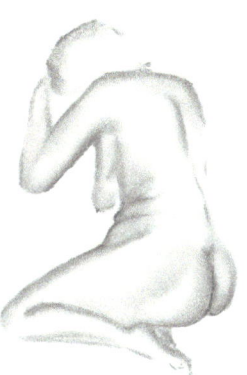

Two studies of Lin in charcoal. Richard Savage © 2012

Kat the Leopardess
Model From California USA

I think it is less about conventional vs unconventional beauty. You cannot limit beauty to any one aspect of your life, nor any one preference in the sea of possibility. Beauty comes in all forms, none to be marginalized or excluded. It's all about size acceptance, inner beauty surpassing societal *guidelines*. Remember that the surface is never as important as the soul that the vessel holds.

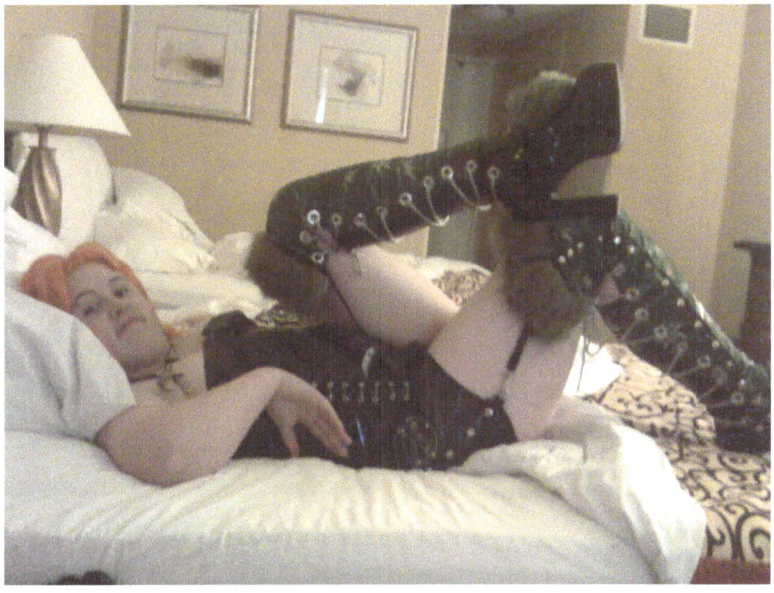

Beauty in Every Form

Tracie
Fetish Model From The UK

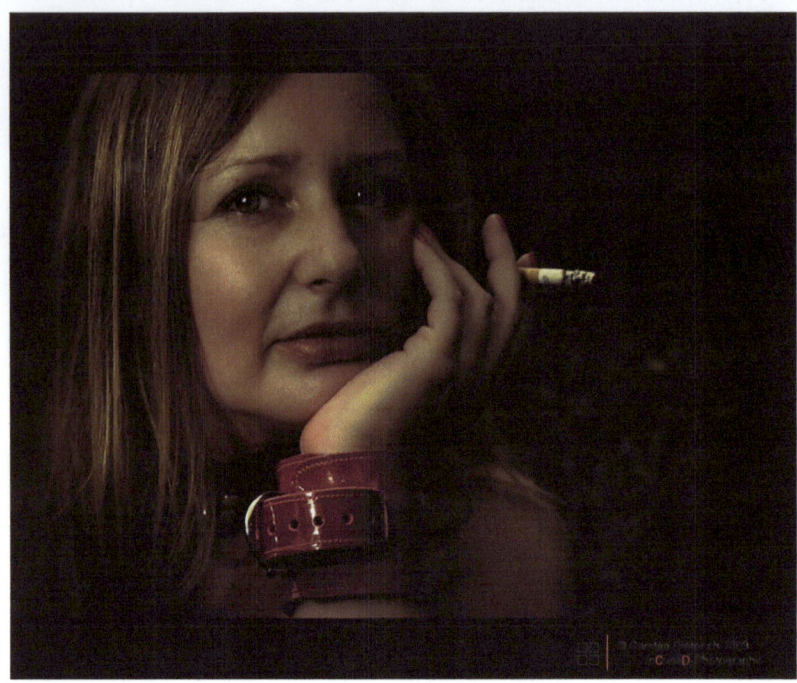

I'm a 44 year old mother of two girls and grandmother of four. I am size 16 and five feet 3 inches tall and 13 stone (though fluctuating downwards at the moment). I can confidently say, I've never looked or felt as good as I do now. Maybe that's maturity, growing into my skin as they say, but it's all good.

Photography by Carsten Dieterich

I came onto the BDSM scene a year ago and I've been on a voyage of discovery since then. I know I'm attractive facially but I've had body image issues since I was a teenager.

I have spent much of my life struggling with my weight. I've got stretch marks from having the children, surgery scars too, though not large ones, the usual stuff. A few months ago I was asked to pose for a fetish photographer.

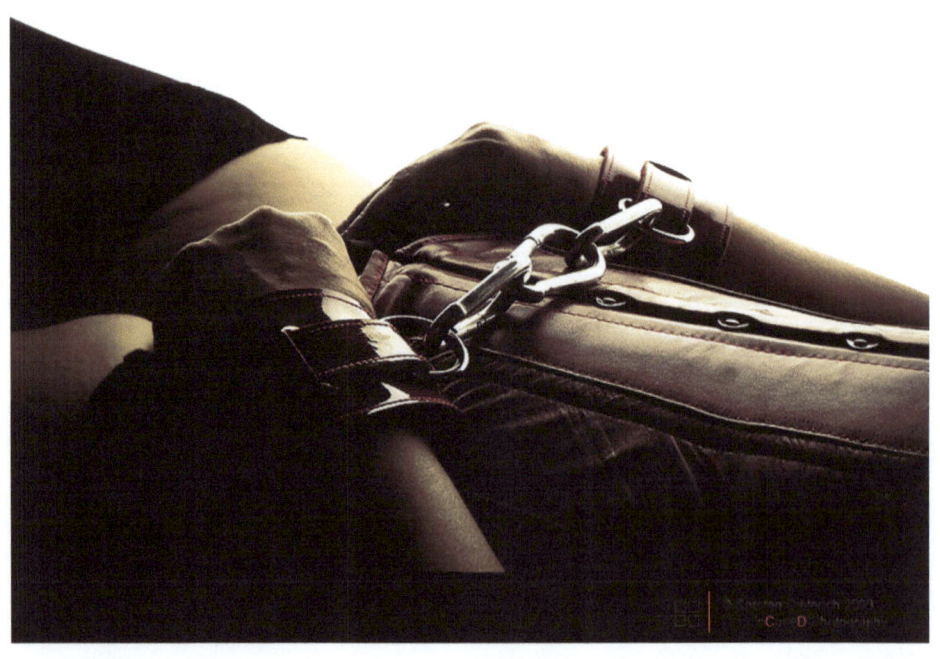

Photography by Carsten Dieterich

For some time I've been growing in confidence and acceptance of me and my body. The boost I got from the two shoots I've done this year was so good I'm going to do a few more. A year ago I wouldn't have said that, no way would I have done this.

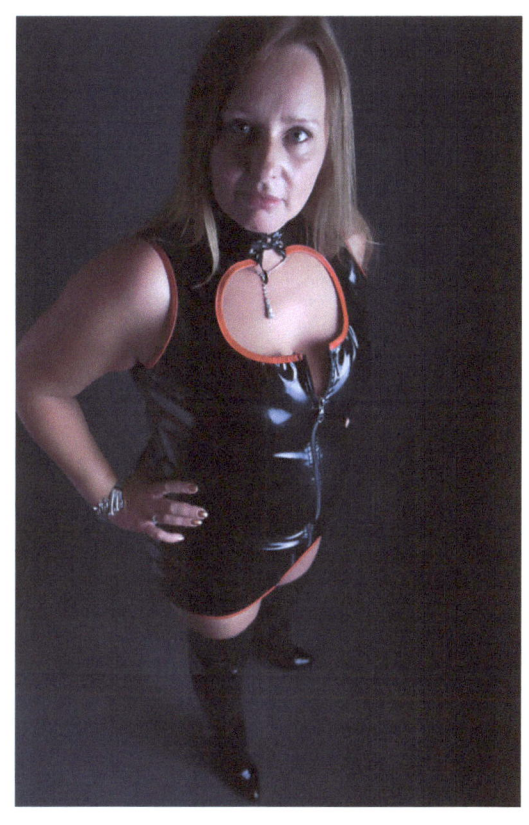

I feel there is too much emphasis on the perfect figure. Most of the people I talk to are happy with 'real' curves, not that there is anything wrong with slender people either. We all make choices about our bodies and what we put into them, but there is also a genetic thing going on. I will never be in a size 10/12 unless I'm really quite ill, so there is no point beating myself up about being something I can't be. Yet we all do.

I agree that there isn't enough positive imagery around about different sizes and shapes and looks. After all isn't it the person inside of us, inside the exterior, the way we think that's more important?

I think that's what is happening to me now. I'm happy with who I am and what I am, so that happiness is transferred and yes, visible just by looking at me. That for me comes from finding myself through BDSM and the like minded people I've met.

Jill Bickford
Founder Of LivingEarthBeauty.com USA

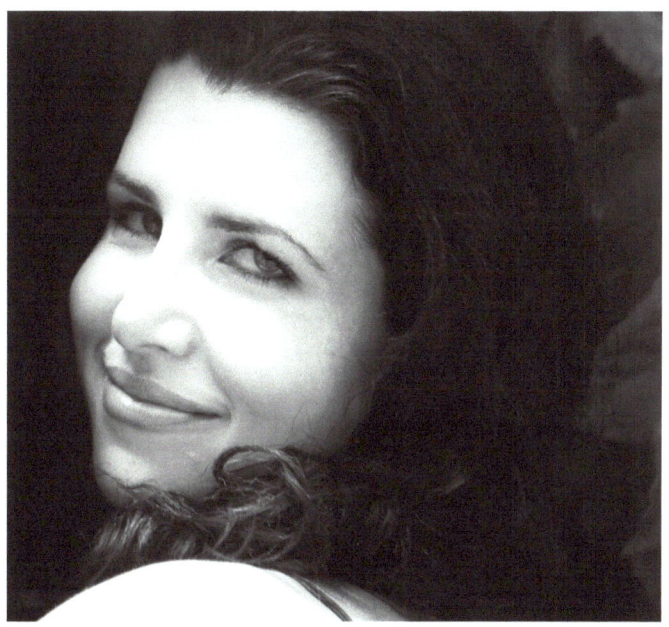

Beauty is the visual expression of love. Beauty is expressed in the fragrance of night blooming jasmine, the love-silk of a rose petal, the devotion in your love-filled eyes, the smooth curve of your hips, the dewy glow of your cheek, the delicious ache of your heart. Beauty is literally the light of the universe. And you are the most beautiful, intricate, and complex expression of love in the universe. Your radiant beauty liberates the hearts of all beings.

When you look at other human beings as what they truly are, infinite divine beings, there is nothing to see but beauty.

Jill Bickford
www.LivingEarthBeauty.com

Beauty in Every Form

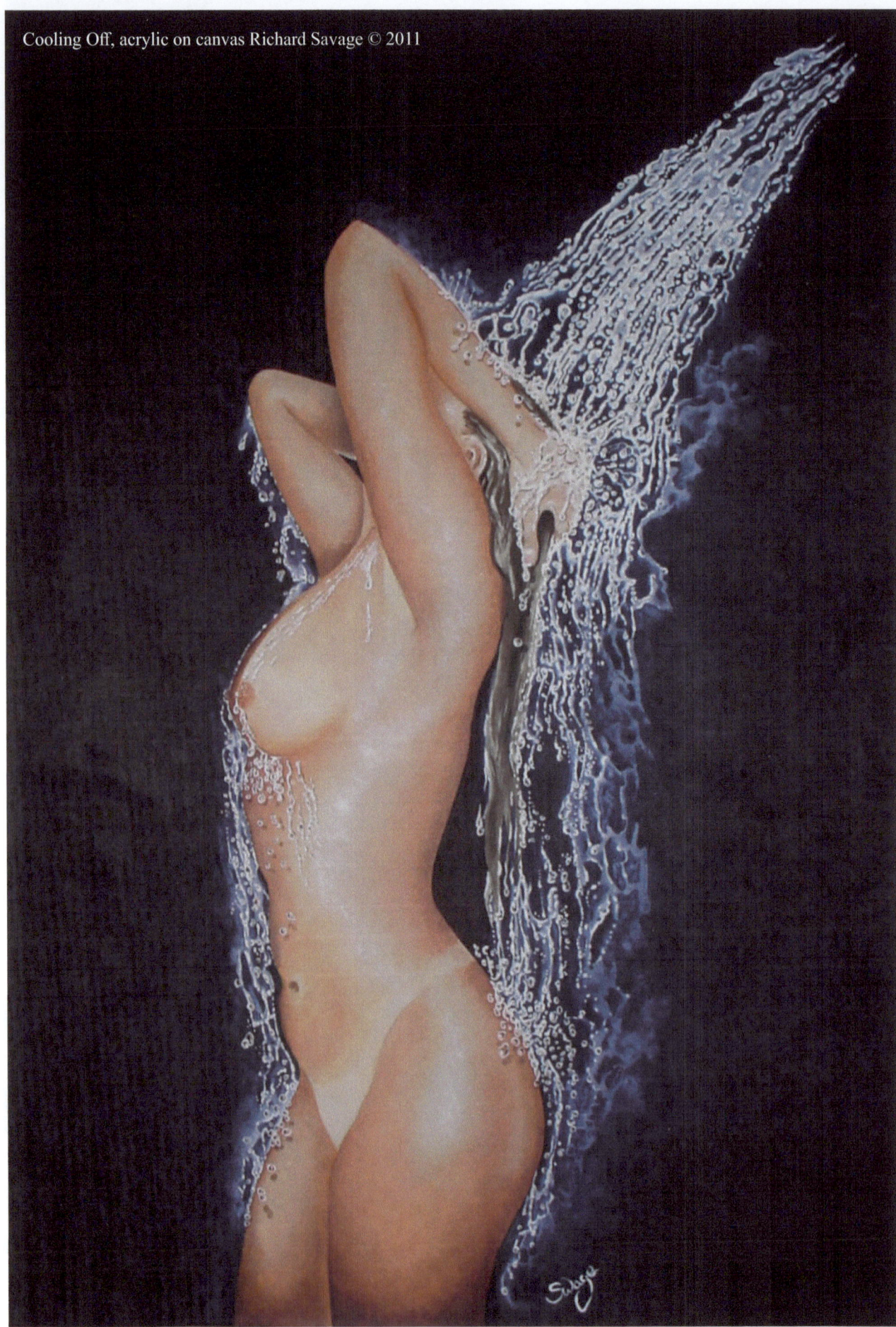

Cooling Off, acrylic on canvas Richard Savage © 2011

50

Beauty comes as much from the
mind as from the eye.

Grey Livingston

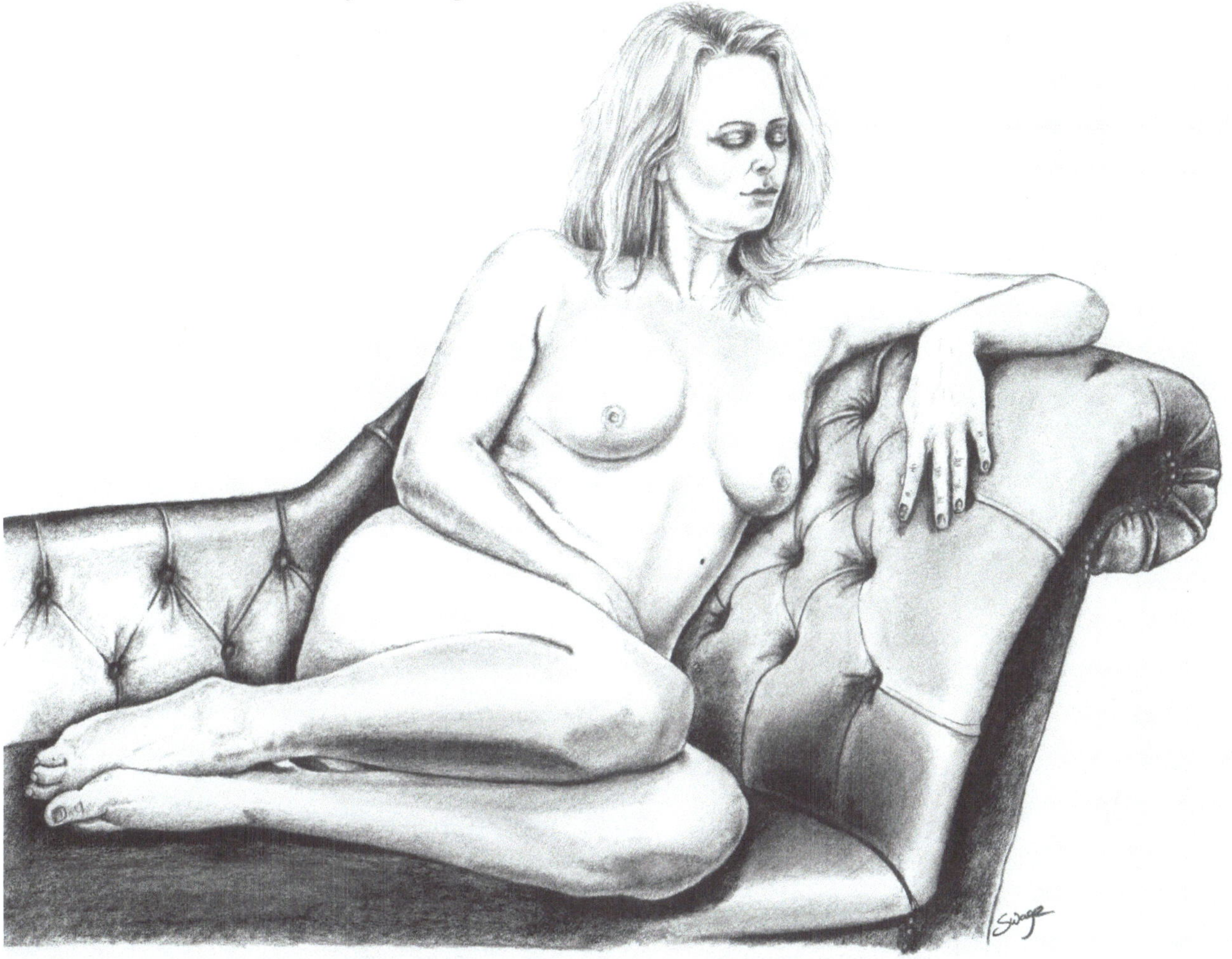

Contemplation, pencil on pastel paper Richard Savage © 2013

I often contemplate the similarities and differences between life drawing and erotic art. At first sight both seem to deal with very similar subject matter, that of the nude model, yet my approach to each seems to be worlds apart. I would like to think there is a little more polish to my erotic work. In recent months there has been an addition to the repertoire, a halfway house; life drawings from photographs. To illustrate the point, the picture above is of one of my newer models, Charli, and right, Veronese, both drawings of life, yet the image of Charli is drawn from a photograph.

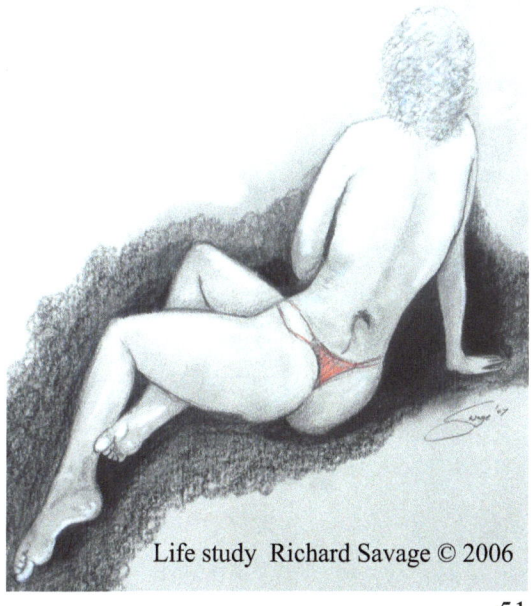

Life study Richard Savage © 2006

Bill Clearlake
Photographer San Jose, California

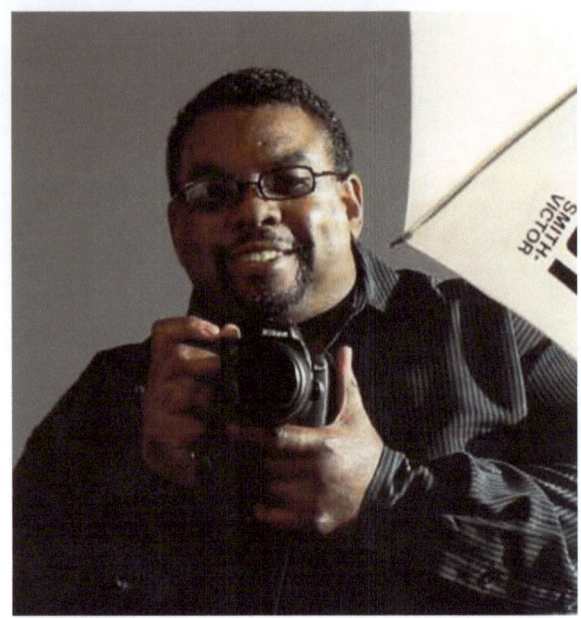

My love for photography began when my father gave me a Kodak Brownie camera for my 8th birthday in 1963. Since then I've used photography as a tool to chronicle my life and also as a means of artistic expression.

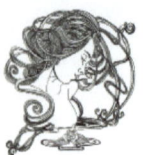

I find beauty everywhere, in the shape of a lamppost, the petals of a flower, the inquisitive face of a child, the gentle landscape of a woman's body.

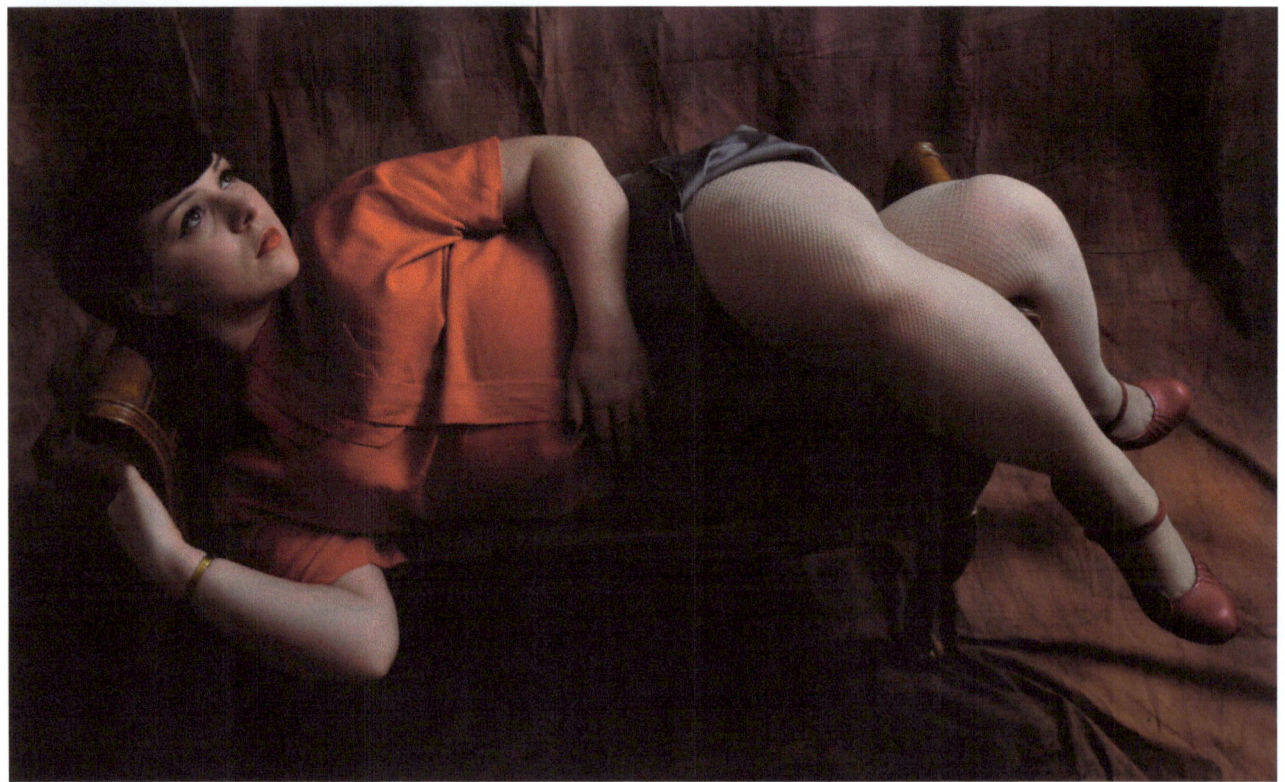

Photography by Bill Clearlake

I've done photojournalism, artistic nudes, street photography, portraiture, travel and commercial photography, and weddings. I've documented street demonstrations, a riot, as well as corporate and social events. So long as it's legal and within my physical abilities, I don't think there is anything I would not attempt to show the beauty or reality of through photography.

Photographing models has given me some of the best experiences I've had and some of the closest and most intense relationships. My favorite models aren't necessarily the prettiest, but they have a knack of expressing themselves with their faces and bodies. They create ever changing vistas of beauty and emotion and all I have to do is not screw up the photography.

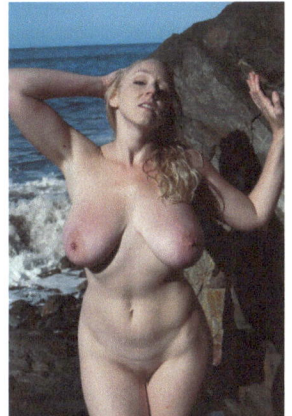

Photography by Bill Clearlake

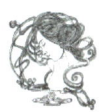

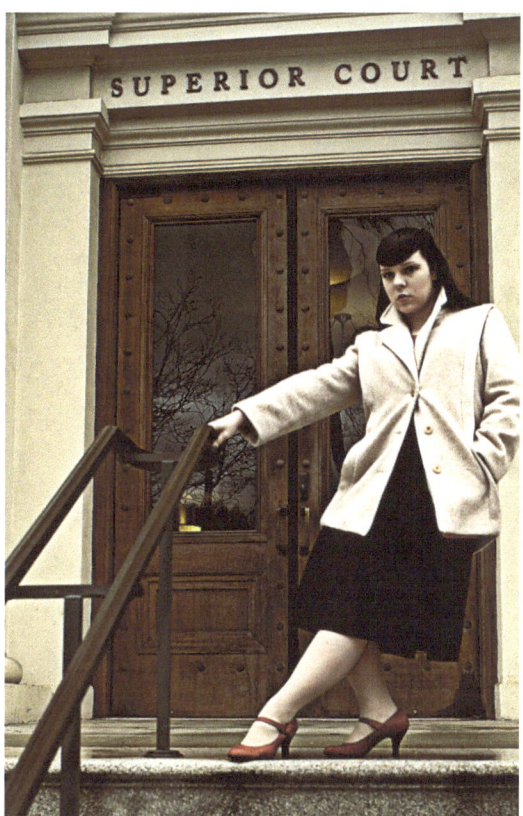

Photography by Bill Clearlake

I truly enjoy doing location fashion photography and finding locations where the colors and textures compliment the garments and models I'm photographing.

Photographers who shoot models are encouraged to seek unrealistic levels of perfection, choosing the tallest, thinnest models - whose looks are already out of reach of the average woman's ability to achieve - and then digitally altering them to inhuman, doll-like perfection. And while this has been considered to be *industry standard* for fashion and glamour it seems that there is a growing desire in the public for a return to realism.

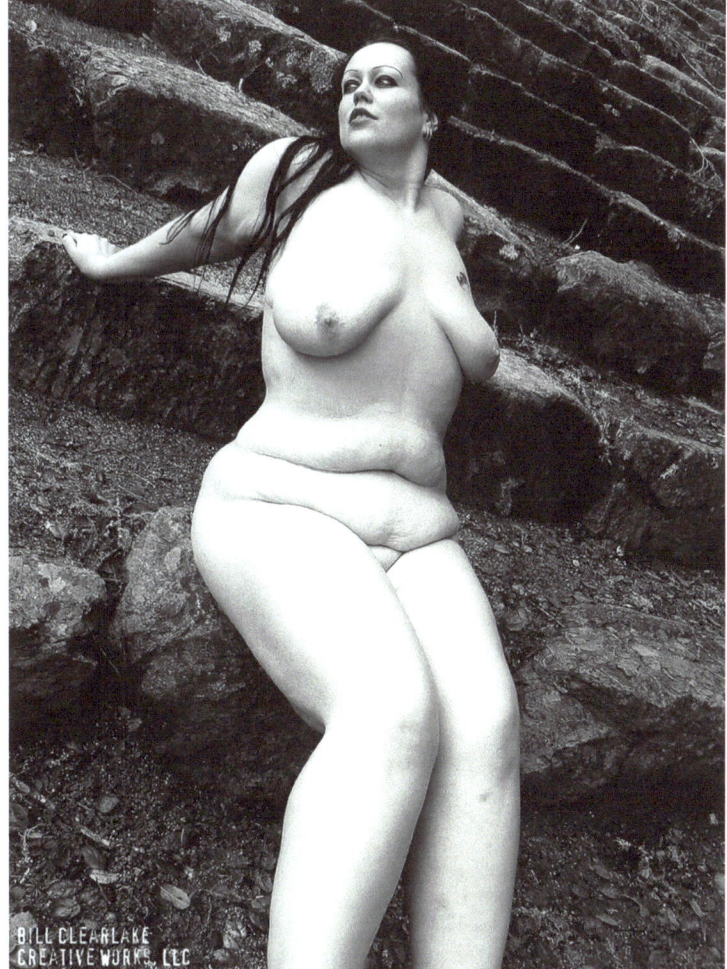

Photography by Bill Clearlake

Photoshopped perfection will probably remain the standard for the near future, but good, basic photography and natural beauty seem to be making a comeback.

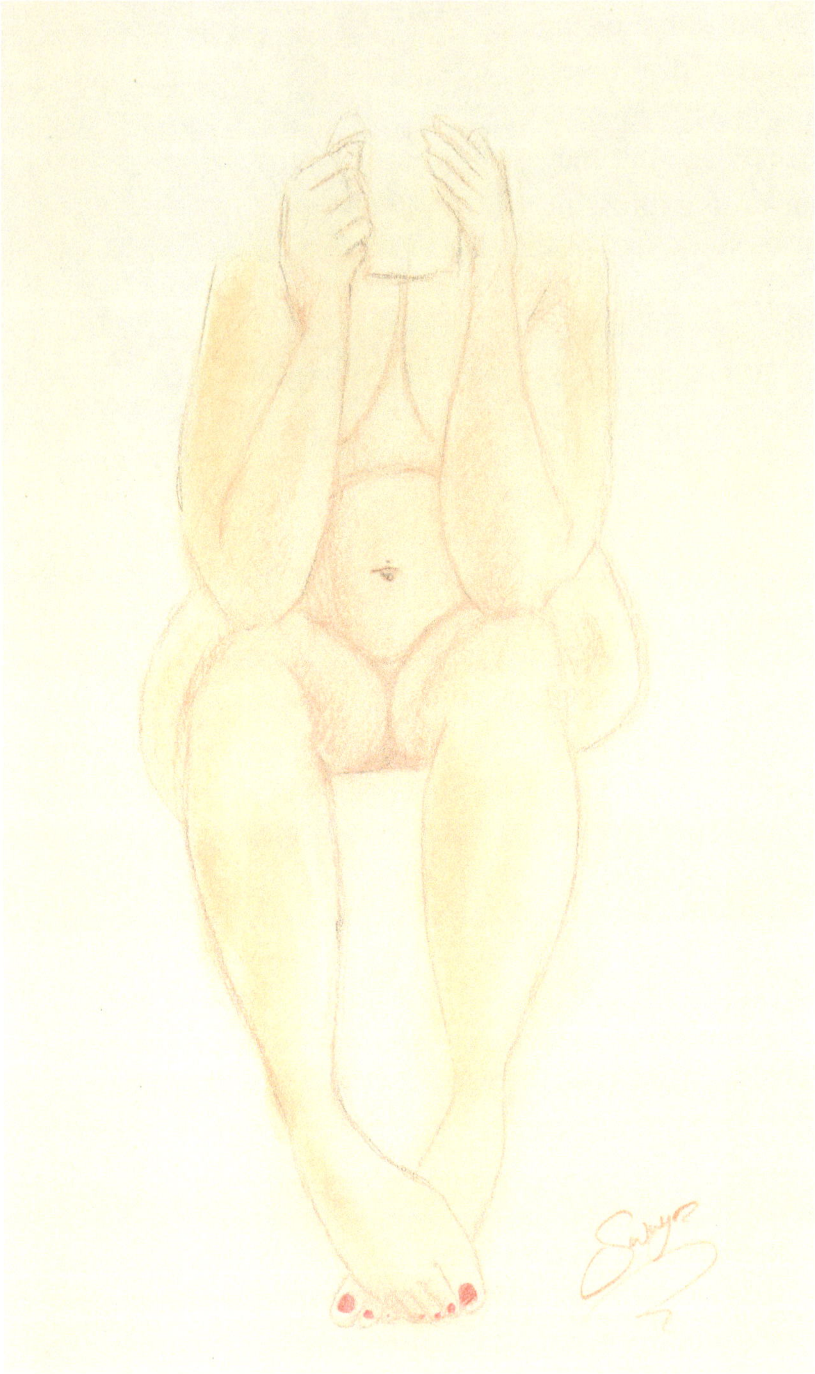

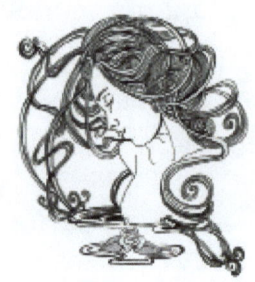

Life study Richard Savage © 2012

Left Tabby, one of my regular life models. The sketch is in soft pastels and watercolor pencils.

Right are two studies of Veronese.

I use a lot of soft pastels in life drawing, mainly because of the nice soft tones you can get, but I also like them for the speed factor. I usually limit the group to spells of no more than 30 minutes, partly for the comfort of the model, but also it concentrates the mind on what the essence of the pose is and the primary shapes.

For every beauty there is an eye somewhere to see it.
For every truth there is an ear somewhere to hear it.
For every love there is a heart somewhere to receive it.

Ivan Panin

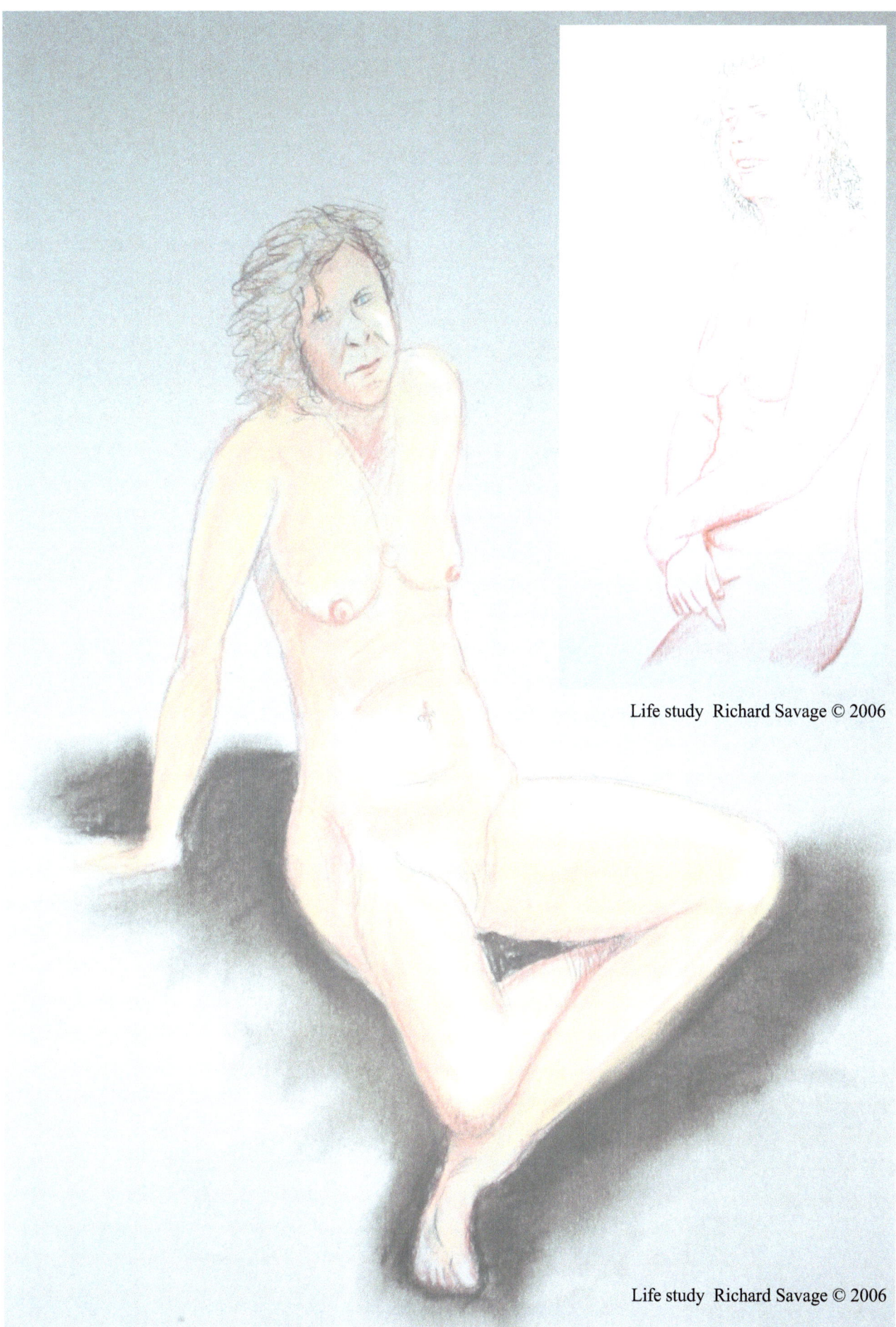

Life study Richard Savage © 2006

Life study Richard Savage © 2006

Beauty in Every Form

Nicola Priest
Arts Student From The UK

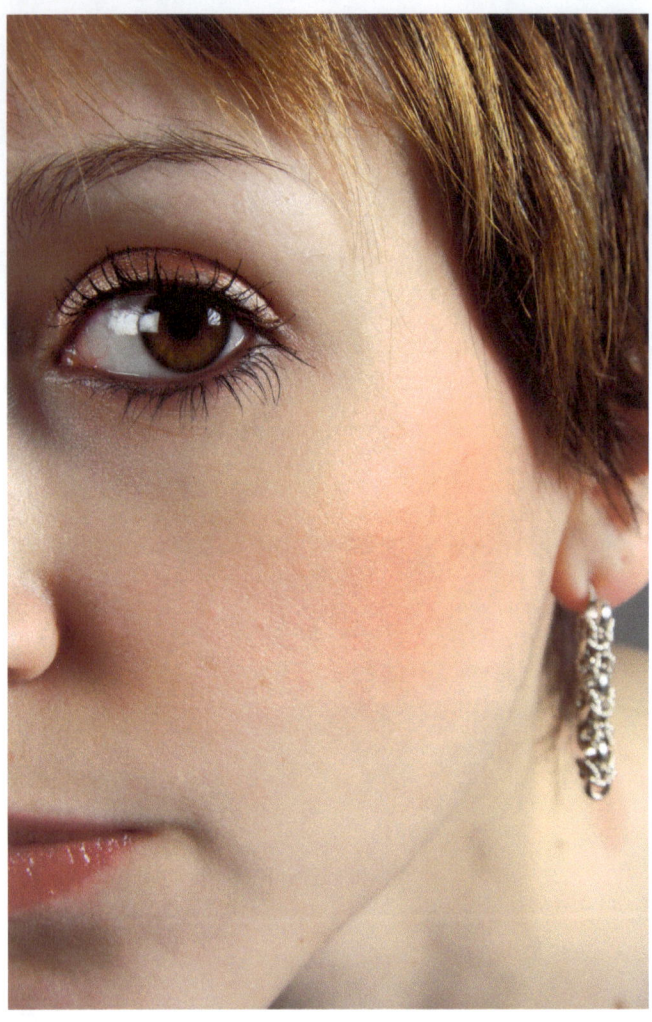

Why is there an obsession with identity and self? Why do we stereotype, and why can we not accept one another as we are? I am convinced popular culture contributes to this obsessive behavior. The media has a vast influence on our society and we have become transfixed and dependent to the extent we rely on it to provide us with enlightenment on how we ought to appear and feel.

Vanessa Beecroft is an artist who highlights the impressionability of media intervention on our opinions of self. Beecroft's relationships with these issues are also personal. She has struggled for numerous decades with her own identity which contributes to feelings of self doubt and uncertainty.

The employment of predefined stereotypes allows us to understand context. These stereotypes influence behavior, interaction, prejudice, and self worth; it is the prelude of an invariable struggle with individual identity and self.

It is imperative that society perceives the effects of stereotyping and the ultimate consequence it has on personal identity and self worth. If we can resolve these issues I am convinced we will be content.

Art work by Nicola Priest

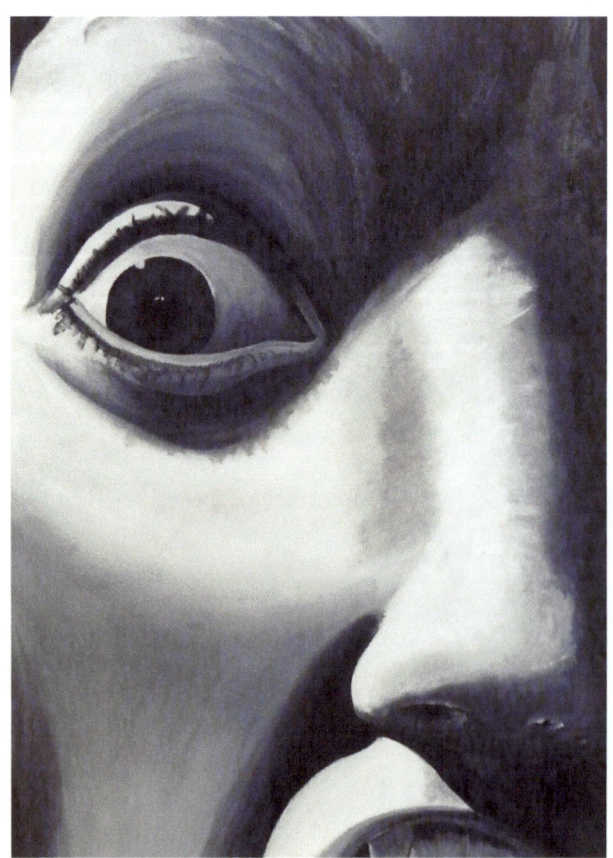

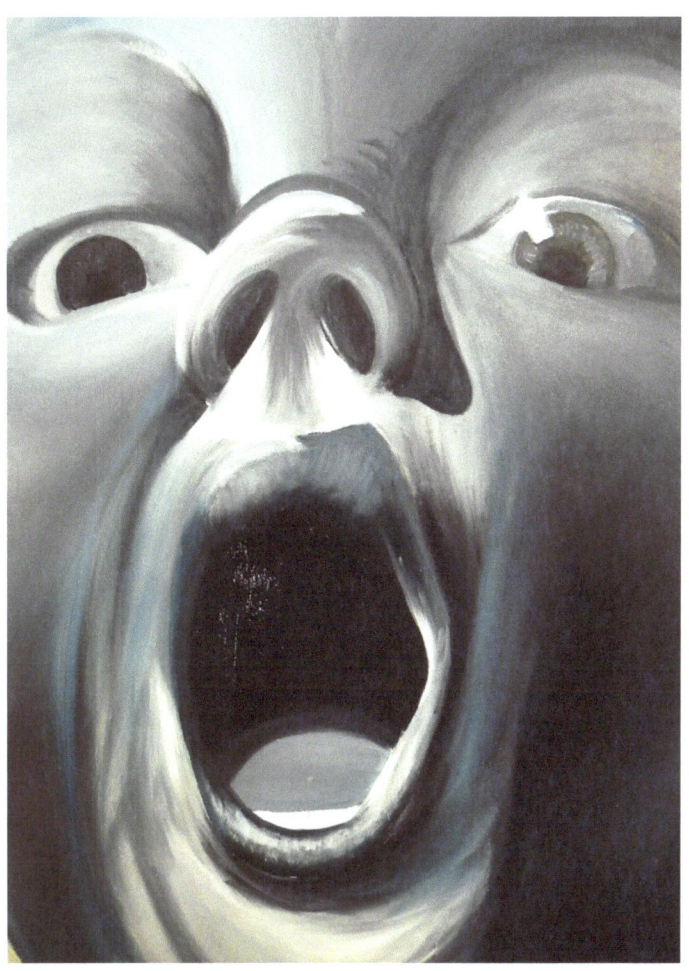

The artist, Gillian Wearing, has addressed these issues in her work, 'Signs that say what you want them to say and not Signs that say what someone else wants you to say.' Wearing exposes people's ability to stereotype and formulate judgements on personal appearance.

"Uncontestable evidence that quick judgements based on observations of facial expressions, posture, clothing style, age, and gender are often woefully inaccurate, people today are programmed to read signs. Signage, however, is typically monopolized by the authorities that control behavior, manipulate action, Drink Coca Cola, alter opinions, or identify landmarks. Wearing replaces stereotypes."
Weintraub 2007

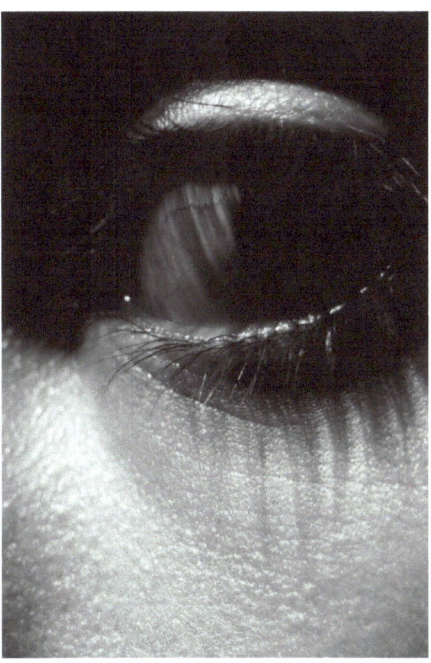 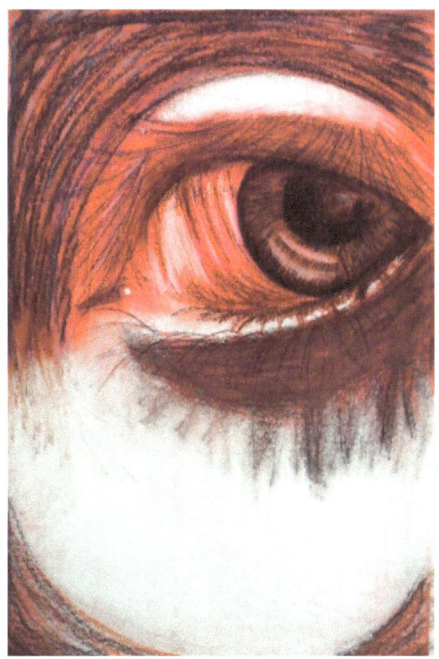 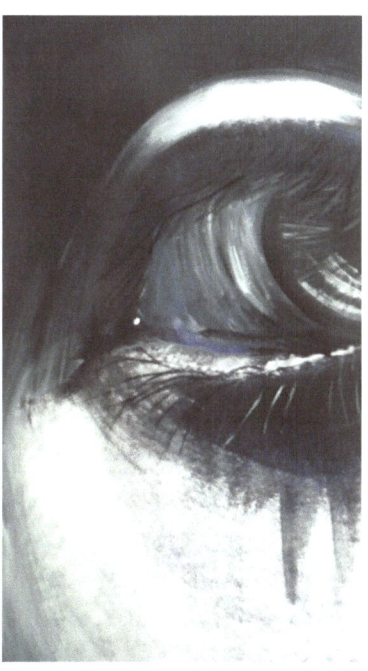

Ultimately we become these preconditioned stereotypes and judge ourselves alongside these classic ideals. This judgement on ourselves causes us constant conflict with our identity and self worth. If we can challenge these stereotypes and develop independent confident identities as a society we would be fulfilled.

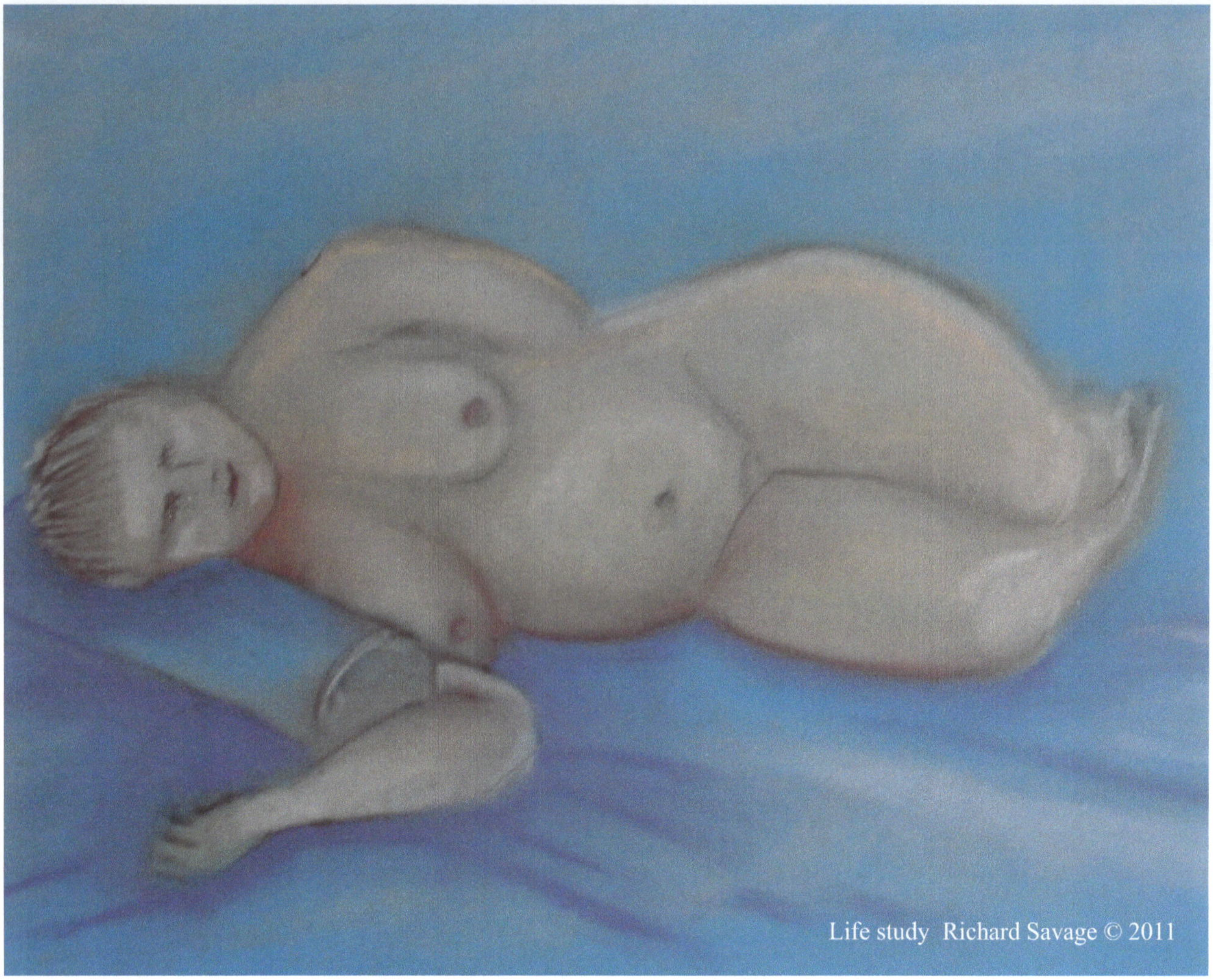

Life study Richard Savage © 2011

Tabby, one of my regular life models.
The sketch is in soft pastels and watercolor pencils.

Riga
From The Social Networking Group Fetlife

Beauty is instinct. Like sexual attraction, beauty can be found without any warning and can come from anywhere. It may even surprise you when it appears. For me, beauty is little speckles of something that appear out of nowhere. They build up until the beauty is prominent. Sometimes it happens when having a conversation with a person. The longer I talk to them, I begin to notice speckles of beauty around them, little things, like the way their freckles are formed or the way they shift their weight when nervous. I don't look for these aspects, they just appear. And it doesn't have to be just in people. Objects or locations are filled with surprising beauty. You just need to take the time to look.

Hollis Cartwright Blume
Co-Creator, WaterMeWell Inc. *Inner Healing Apparel* Inspiring Unconditional Love

Listen To Beauty

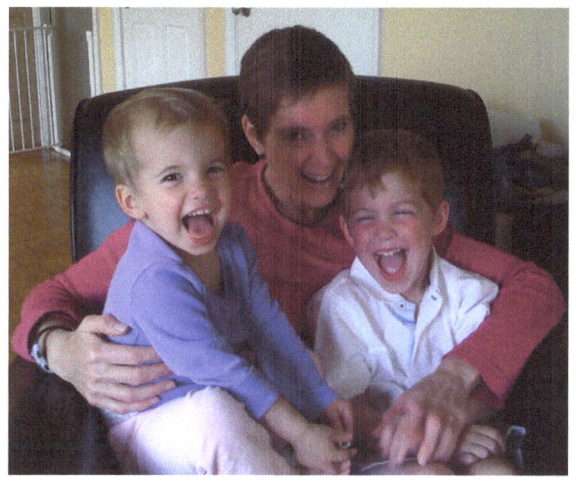

Beauty is infinite, as it grows it's roots in love. If we are willing to try on different lenses to experience beauty, I think we are then able to see that it is limitless in its forms and expressions. One such expression of beauty is illustrated in a person's voice. If you really think about one's voice, it does so many things and serves so many purposes.

It can sing. It can shout. A voice can laugh and can cry. It can be soft and soothing, velvety and alluring, high-pitched, low-pitched and everywhere in between. It expresses infinite emotions and changes with a person throughout his or her lifetime. Voice is inherently beautiful simply because of its ability to change, express and elicit just about any mood, feeling or emotion, depending on how it is used. Voice gives beauty expression.

Next time you think of it, stop and really listen to a person's voice and the beauty it contains. And never forget the silence there is when its presence is gone.

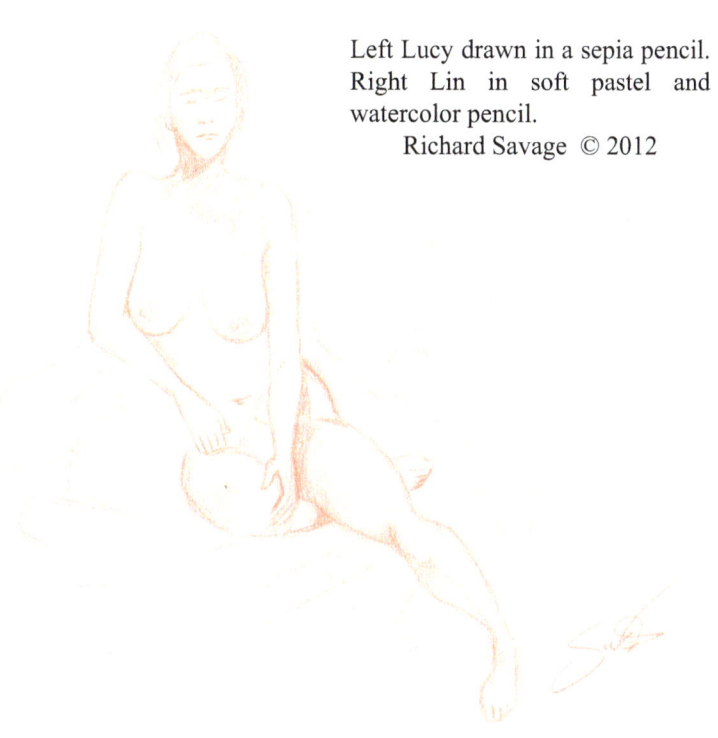

Left Lucy drawn in a sepia pencil. Right Lin in soft pastel and watercolor pencil.
Richard Savage © 2012

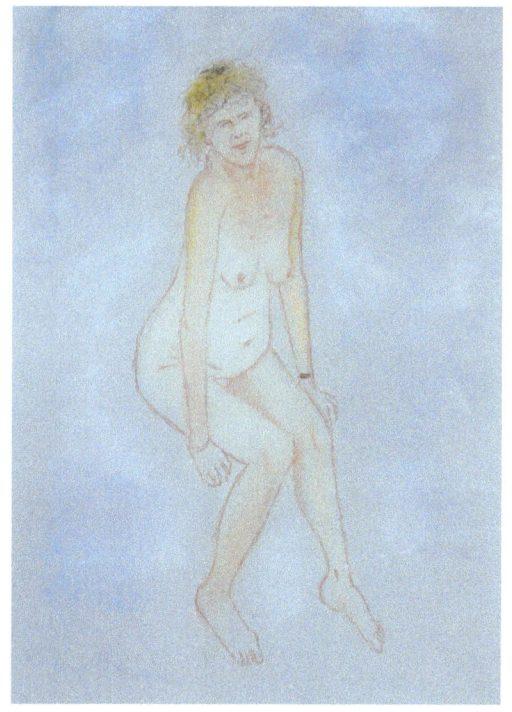

Alex Cowen
Contributor From London UK

Can I Be Attractive?

Beauty and attractiveness are things I took for granted. I don't mean that I thought I was really beautiful because I didn't, but I always thought of myself as attractive. I had days when I woke, looked in the mirror, thought "Uurgh!" and didn't like the face that was looking back at me, but those are days I think we all have; bad hair days, bad face days, and they are only momentary.

I have always had my fair share of boyfriends and all the usual teenage and early 20s angst about them, but nothing major. I never was a person who went on diets. I liked my body. I always had a bit of a tummy which I thought was attractive in a woman. I have always been small; 5 foot. That never bothered me. I loved it.

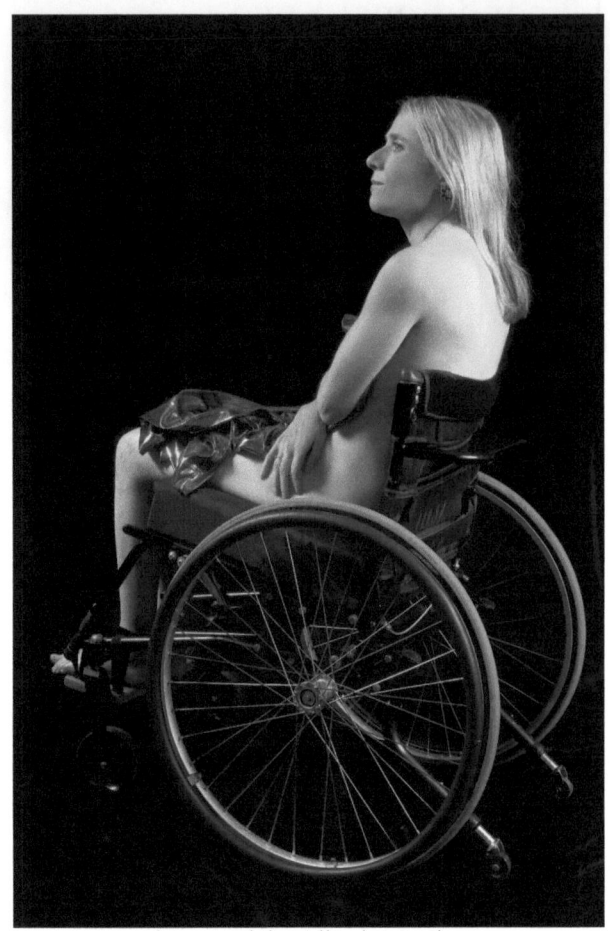
Photograph by Alistair Morrison

I loved the way I was.

When I became disabled it really crushed my feelings for how I was as a woman. Was I attractive? Was I still sexy? Was I still desirable? Even though I had a husband who loved me and found me attractive and we had a good sex life, I began to shrink away from myself as a sexual woman, as a sexual being.

Society is constantly surrounding us with pictures of women with perfect, thin bodies but with these large, voluptuous tits. I came to regard them as melons with skin. They didn't move! I didn't see them as attractive but so many men seemed to think they were.

There I was, my body changing from sitting in a wheelchair. I was losing muscle tone and for the first time I began to dislike the way my body looked and I wanted to hide it. On the outside, friends, and possibly even my husband, wouldn't describe me like that. I still liked wearing nice clothes and, when I went out, I wasn't exactly a shrinking violet. But inside me something was shrinking.

My confidence had been squashed and knocked by my disability. The fact that I still had an attractive face but my body was not what you would call stereotypically attractive or sexy cut me to the quick.

I knew I had to do something about it but I didn't really know what. I mean, what more could I do? I had a husband who loved me, a handsome, gorgeous husband, and my face still looked lovely but I just couldn't reconcile what was happening to my body, the fact that I no longer seemed to be noticed as a sexy attractive woman. I felt that, in a way, men paid lip-service to the fact that I was attractive but if you scratched the surface, would they have sex with me? Probably not. I knew it shouldn't have been preoccupying me at all. I had so many other things in my life that I was passionate about but this was a growing, creeping unease, a discomfort and unhappiness.

The first thing I decided to do was to pursue an idea I had to turn an iconic picture on its head. I wanted to have my picture taken, in the nude, in the style of Christine Keeler using my wheelchair to sit astride.

This picture was the personification of sexiness. I wanted to challenge people's ideas and perceptions of what is beautiful.

I kept this idea to myself for about two years. I was worried about telling anybody in case they stole my idea, but I was also worried people would say, "What a ridiculous idea! Who on earth would think you could look sexy in the nude on your wheelchair?"

Then, one evening, I went to a dinner and was seated next to two very nice men from a well known advertising agency. We were having such a good conversation and I thought to myself that it was time to put my head above the parapet because otherwise nothing would happen, and I wanted something to happen. I wanted to challenge myself, to push myself to the boundaries to see if I could get back some of that feeling of sexiness and attractiveness that I'd had before I became disabled, before my body began to show the signs of my disability in a way that changed the shape of my body and what I was able to do with it. I so loved being able to move in a sexy way. I missed the simple feeling of walking when I felt good about myself and the way I looked. Since I couldn't walk I didn't have that and I didn't feel the way I moved in my wheelchair was sexy and attractive.

When I told the advertising men about my idea they were so keen they wanted to get hold of the original photographer who was still alive and living in Australia. However, somebody from the PR department of the charity giving the dinner was also listening and she too thought it was a great idea. Her colleague contacted a well-known UK photographer and he said, "I'll meet with her and see if she interests me and then I'll think about doing the photo." He had taken photos of so many famous people and beautiful women, Bette Davis, Kate Winslet, Helen Mirren, Sir Laurence Olivier, Sir John Gielgud, Tom Cruise... and then me! So, no pressure then!

I went to see him and was surprised to meet someone who was so young looking. I was nervous and actually told him that I thought I would be meeting somebody with more gravitas. Thankfully, that made him laugh rather than offend him! He really understood me. We got on really well, I really liked and trusted him. He said he would take the photo but he asked me to go and do some homework, to practice some positions on my wheelchair, with my husband's help, to see how I thought I looked and which positions were the best. So, I went home.

We have a long mirror in the bedroom. I got my husband, Lionel, to take my clothes off because I can't take them off myself. I asked him to leave me on my own and when I looked in the mirror and saw my body, I cried. It was the first time I had seen my body fully in the mirror in about five years.

The way I saw my body was part reality, part imagination. When I had looked at my body previously I hadn't thought it was that thin. I hadn't realized it had changed that much, but the reality of seeing how thin some parts of my body had become made me cry. I didn't know whether I would be able to do the photograph despite really, really wanting to. I really wanted to have the courage. I really wanted to stop shrinking away. I really wanted to get back some of the confidence I had lost. I really wanted to believe in myself as a sexy, attractive woman. I really didn't want to buy into the perfect body fascism.

I hate hospitals, they are my total phobia and yet I was considering having a boob job because sitting in the wheelchair had made my body change in such a way that my breasts were no longer prominent. My breasts have always been smallish, but lovely, and men seemed to love them. Now for the first time I felt that my beloved breasts weren't good enough.

I can remember, at the age of nine, my friend's older sister, who was about sixteen, had really nice breasts. I remembered thinking, "She really takes those breasts for granted, she doesn't appreciate how lovely they are and when I get breasts I'm never going to do that." And I hadn't. When I got breasts I loved and enjoyed them and I'd felt happy to have the breasts I had, but now, for the first time, I wanted to have a boob job. I was shocked at myself but that's what the disability and my impairment had done to my body and my confidence. I knew that this couldn't go on.

So, I did the photograph and it was an amazing, liberating, enjoyable experience. I know that's a weird thing to say. There I was, sitting in the nude, my catheter showing, with a handsome photographer, who had seen some of the most gorgeous, interesting and attractive people in the world but somehow I felt in safe hands.

I thought to myself, "What is it that makes me feel sexy? What is being sexy?" Then I realized I will never be an Elle McPherson type. I would never have had a perfect body even if I wasn't disabled. But my body is amazing, with all it has had to go through, and all it has put up with. It's still there, it still wants to be in there, in the mix, wants to look good, wants to go out, wants to look sexy, be sexy. I still want all those things. I still want to have sex, to be attractive, to look nice and that's what makes me sexy. That I still want to be out there in the world, out there in the mix, interested in people, interested in life is what makes me sexy.

I would say that, for me, it is still a work in progress, in that on the outside I can look attractive and sexy but I still have this nagging kernel which is something, I need to get rid of, this feeling that men might say, "Oooh, you look attractive and sexy," but if you scratch the surface they'd run a mile. Now, I know I shouldn't be thinking like this. I'm in a relationship and, anyway, sex isn't the be all and end all but I would just like to know that it's possible. I would like to know that the opportunity is still out there for me if I ever chose it. I want to know it's there.

Never underestimate, judging a book by its cover. The cover can be absolutely beautiful but inside lots may be going on.

Since the photograph, I've done other great things, but that was such an important step. It began to heal a vital part of me, beginning to repair how I felt about the physicality of my body. I still need to keep reinforcing how I see, and feel, about myself. I dress up and go out. I go to sexy events and clubs, perform, do exciting things. I am lucky. I am supported and encouraged to go for these things by some wonderful friends. And of course I eat lots of trifle and get my highlights done. Fun, laughter and mischievousness! And I love my breasts now. I'm smiling because, after some long months of struggling, I really love myself again. I still have my bad days when I don't feel like that. I am still surrounded by media portrayals which invade my self-perception but the more I do for myself, the more lasting and sustaining and sure are my old feelings of sexual attractiveness. If people don't find me sexy then that's their problem. My confidence is inextricably linked to how I feel about my face and my body, not necessarily whether others would have sex with me, as important as that sometimes is. It's about whether I feel I am sexy and attractive. It's about, it's always been about, how I behold myself.

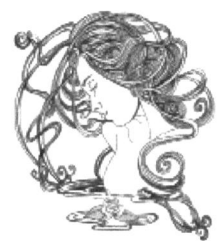

Beauty in Every Form

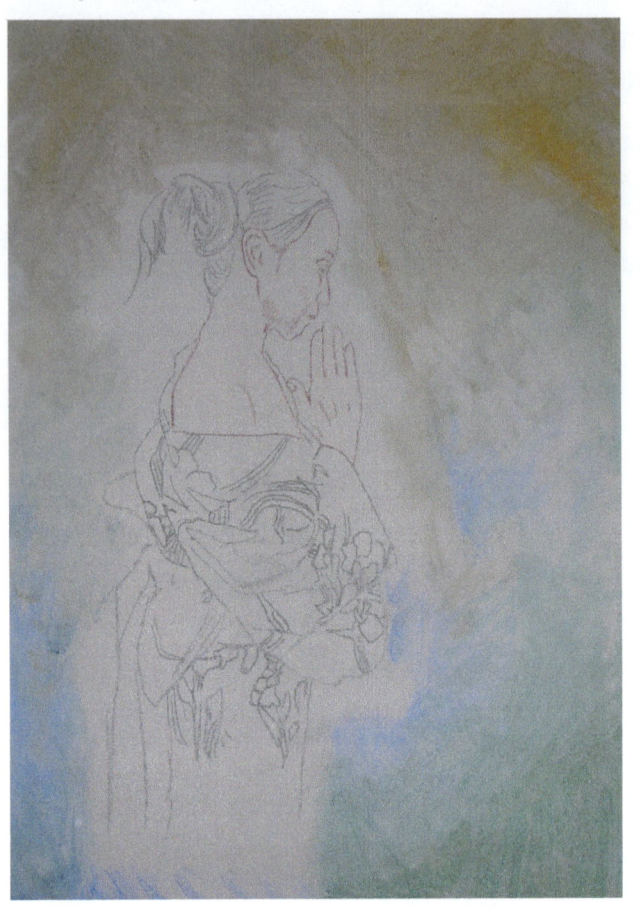
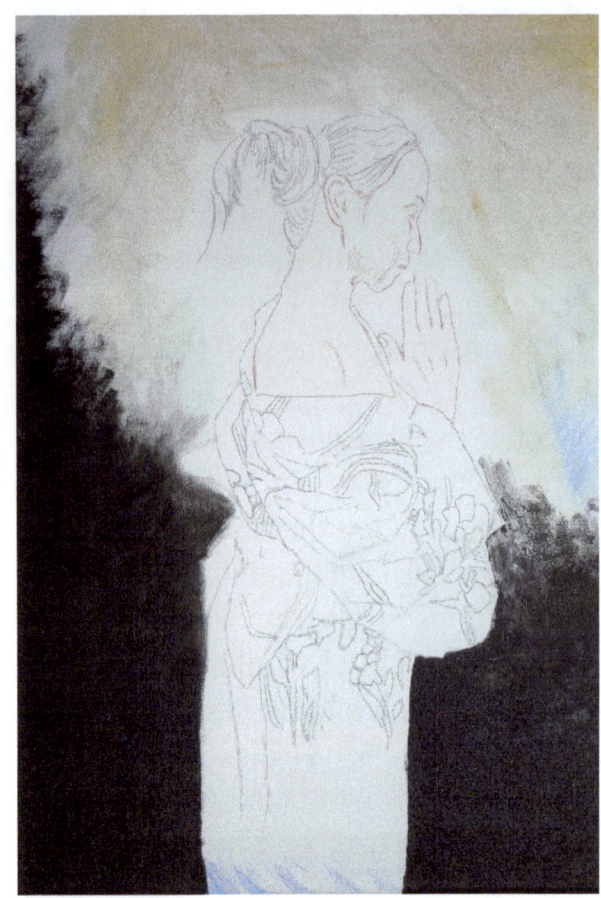
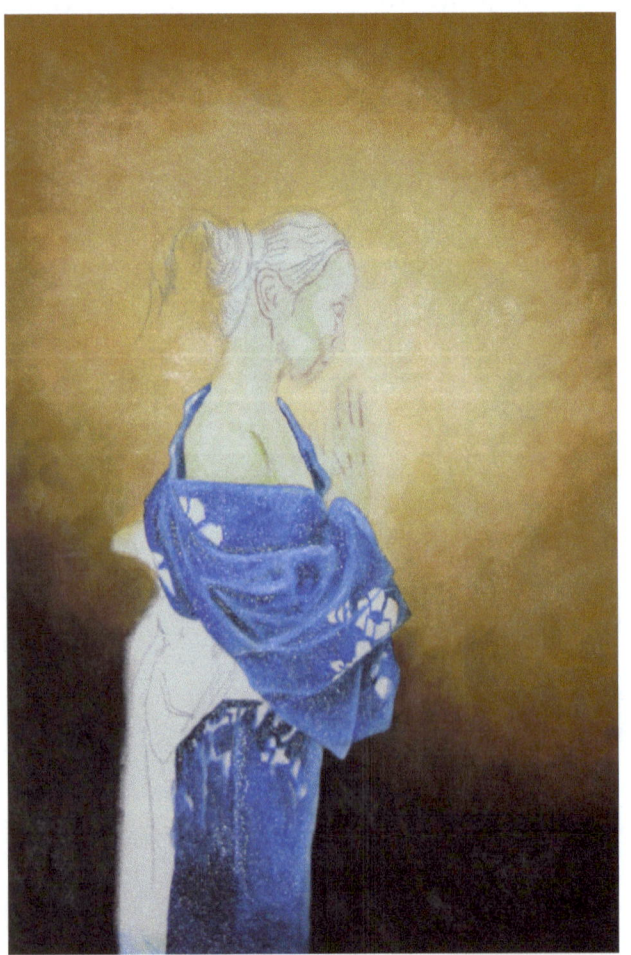
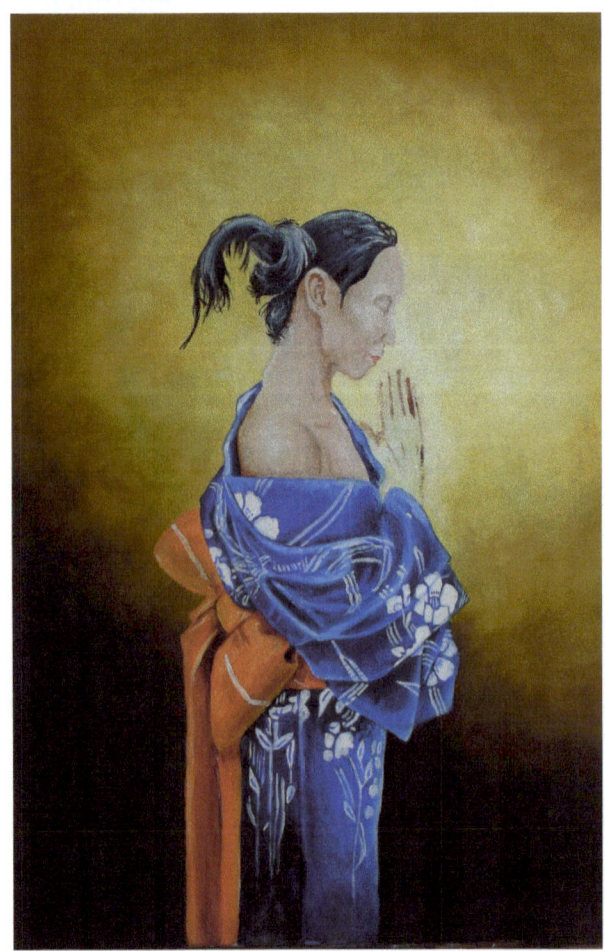

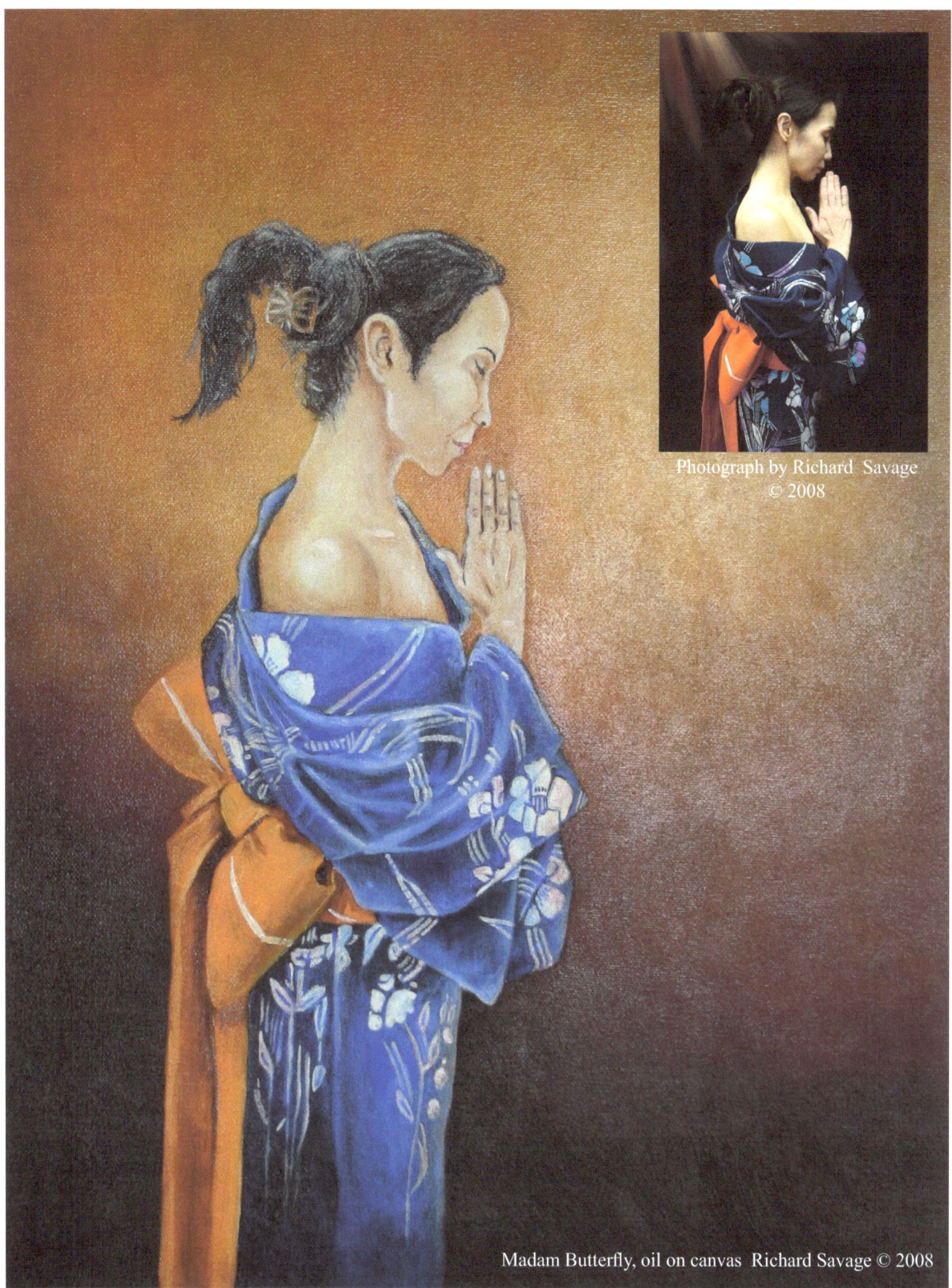

Madam Butterfly, oil on canvas Richard Savage © 2008

Above is the picture I titled Madam Butterfly. The pictures on these two pages show the development of the image, from the sketch, through various stages to the finished painting. The model is Aya I'Anson.

Beauty in Every Form

Aya I'Anson
Model From Japan Currently Living in the UK

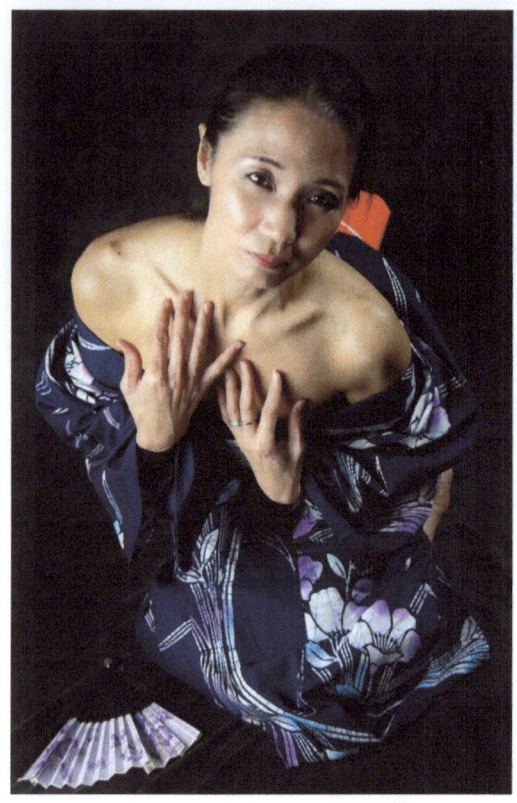

Photographer Mike Crawley
© Mike Crawley www.photofrenetic.com

What is Beauty?

Flowers are beautiful, a rainbow after a heavy rain is also beautiful. Scenery covered with pure white snow is beautiful. A red burning sunset is beautiful, and of course, a young lady with a pretty face and a nice body is beautiful.

Basically, I think beauty is something that impresses people. It's something that produces feelings of relaxation, happiness and warmth in people.

However, there are differences between natural and human beauty. Flowers, rainbows, snow scenes and sunsets just exist and we can analyze them in any way we want to. When they are beautiful, they are simply beautiful.

On the contrary, human beings behave and act.

How many people think a really beautiful looking lady is still beautiful when she speaks in a bad manner or when she puts her legs on the seat in the tube?

In my country, Japan, we put more importance on how people behave than how they look. For instance, in the ladies powder room, lots of ladies brush their hair over the sink after they do their make up. Unfortunately many ladies do not clean their hair out of the sink after brushing. So, Japanese people do not find these ladies beautiful, even if they *look* beautiful with their immaculate make up and brushed hair. Real beauty in human life needs not only physical beauty but also mental beauty, which I believe is more important.

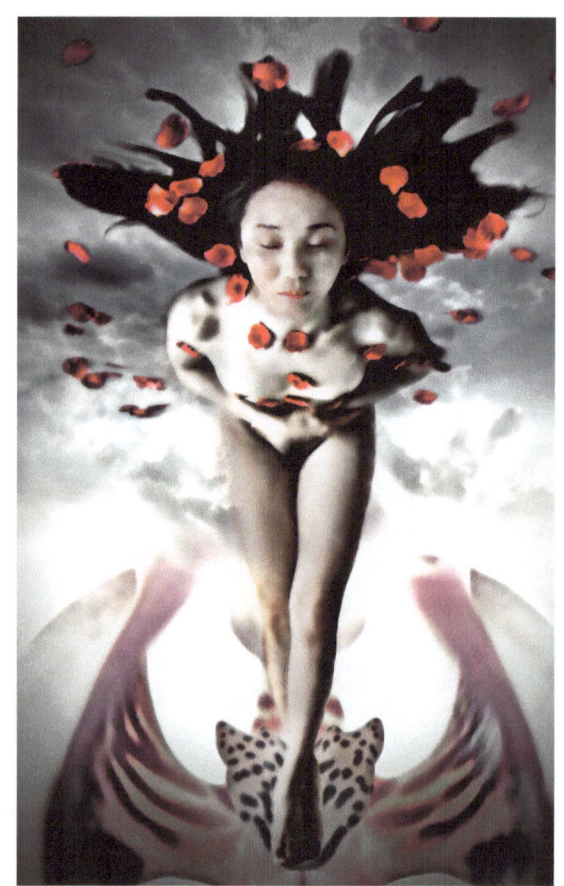

Grey Photography - Copyright 2009

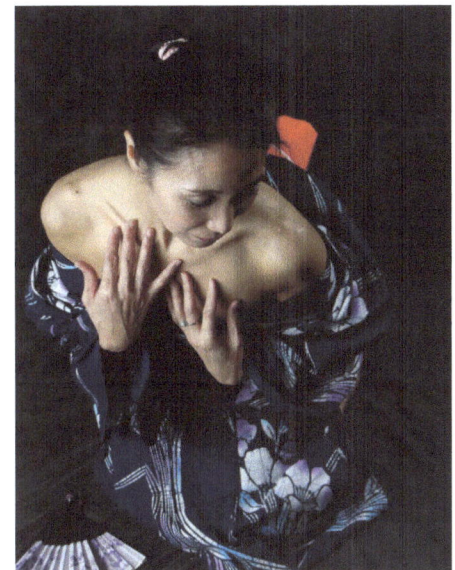

Photographer Mike Crawley
© Mike Crawley
www.photofrenetic.com

When I model, I am often asked how old I am. Some photographers explain this by saying that they need to prove that I am over 18 years old. Good excuse, but it is not credible to consider that I am a teenager, or even in my early twenties. I know that they are asking how *old* I am and not how young I am. I think these people are only interested in youth and solely seeking surface beauty.

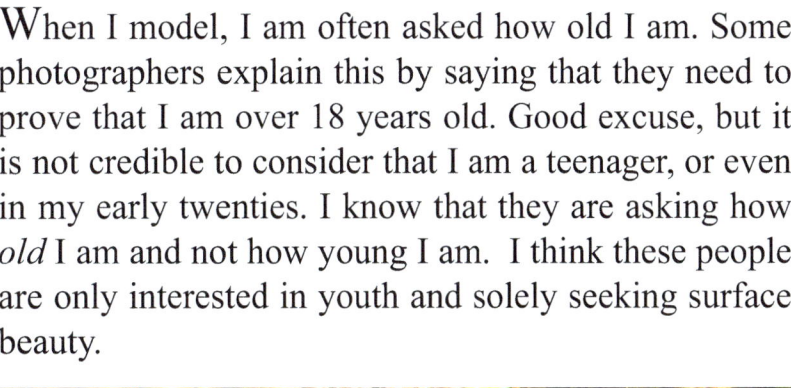

Grey Photography - Copyright 2009

The mother who is feeding her baby in her arms is beautiful because of her love for her baby. Sweaty marathon runners are beautiful because of their sweat and effort. A bride's mum at a wedding is beautiful because she is confidently thinking that she brought up her daughter well.

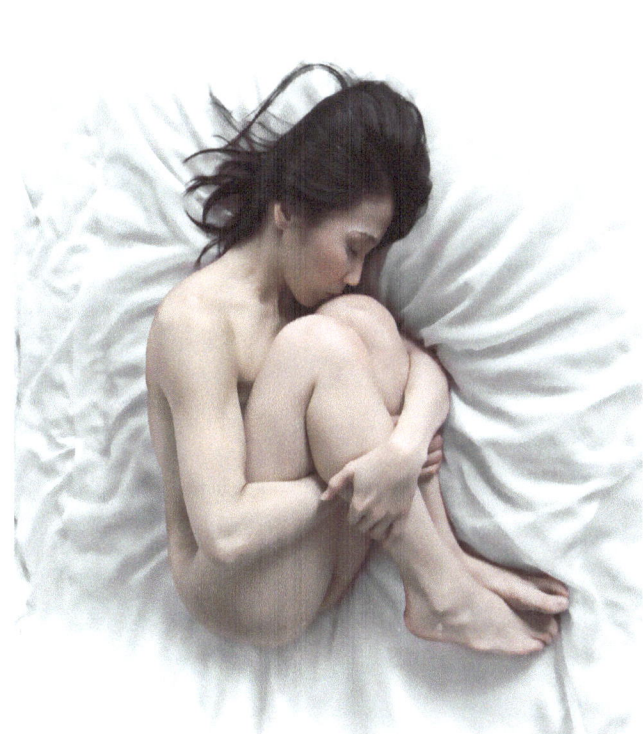

Lots of experiences, with both tears and laughter, make people more beautiful. There is a proverb in Japan, "There are two ladies, younger is beautiful and the older is more beautiful."

Grey Photography - Copyright 2009

So when I model I try to let my experiences and my personal qualities supplement whatever natural beauty I have.

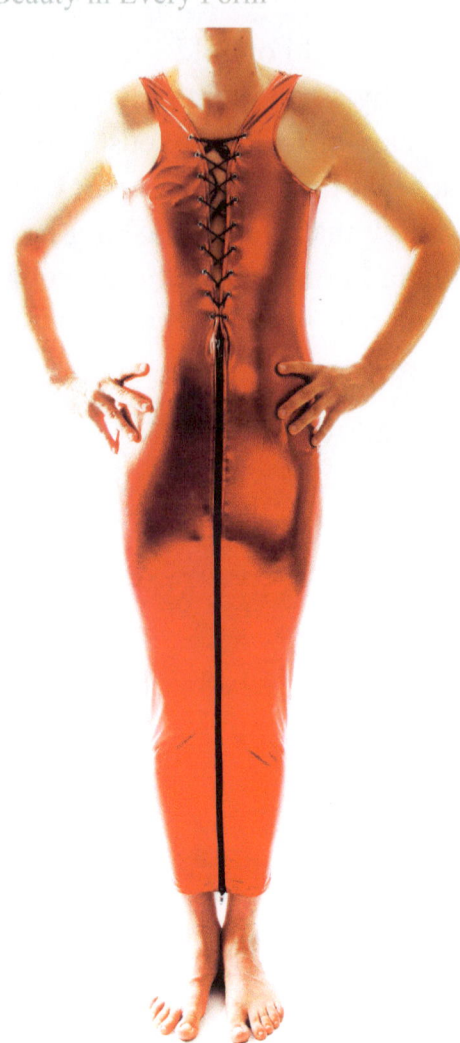

Chris
A Fetish Model From The UK

I have only just recently taken up modeling, although I have been into wearing Lycra for nearly ten years. For the last five years I have been taking photos of myself and putting them online. Rubber is still fairly new to me, I have been into that for about two years. I don't own much as it's so expensive but it would be great to model some more.

I started wearing Lycra when I was about 14, I'm 23 now. I remember my first time modeling, I was told to put on a Lycra dress and to wear nothing underneath. I was quite nervous at first, but after the dress was on to keep my modesty, I was at ease.

I like to think of myself as a subject for the camera rather than a 23 year old guy in front of a person who is taking his picture. As I have progressed as a model, I have learned to do more and have felt more at ease going ahead with what I've been asked to do.

Photograph by Rob Morris

I think the clothing helps with this. If I was just naked then I would feel self-conscious, but the emphasis is not on the naughty bits or my slightly podgy belly, it's on the whole me. It is how I look and how I feel in the clothing that I am told to wear. When I am in my fetish wear there are a lot more things I am happy to do because everyday restraints are lifted.

My greatest pleasure in modeling is being under the control of the cameraman and his assistant. Being told what poses to take, what clothing to wear and what to do. I do get a little say, but I am happy for the decisions to be made for me. It makes me feel very submissive, but without the physical and verbal elements that would go with a typical D/s relationship. I have not been a model for long but I have had some great experiences and hopefully there are many more to come.

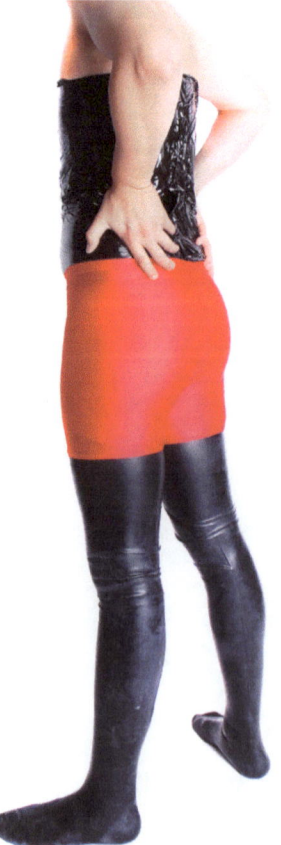

Photograph by Rob Morris

Left Carol in soft pastel and watercolor pencil.

Below two images of Tabby in soft pastel and watercolor pencil.

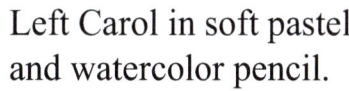

Life study Richard Savage © 2012

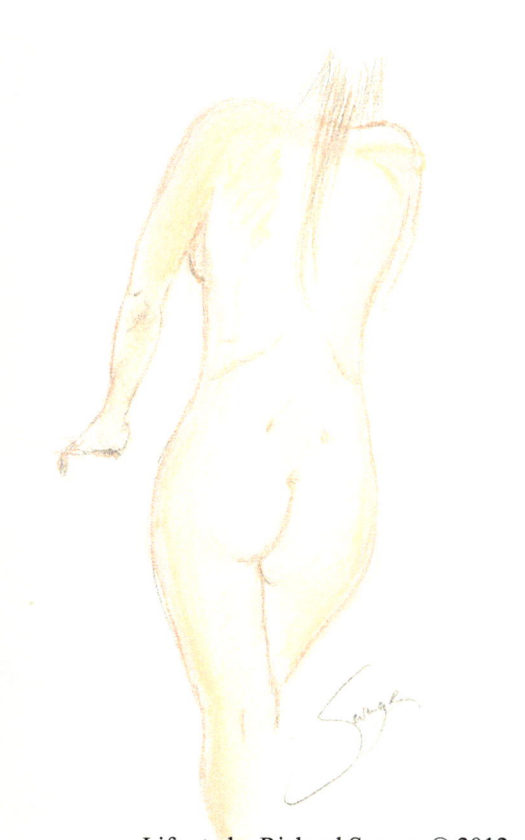

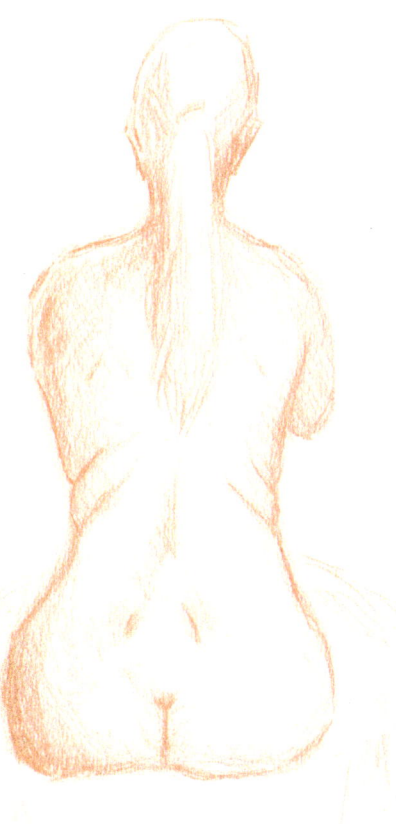

Life study Richard Savage © 2012   Life study Richard Savage © 2012

Tina
Life Model From Norwich UK

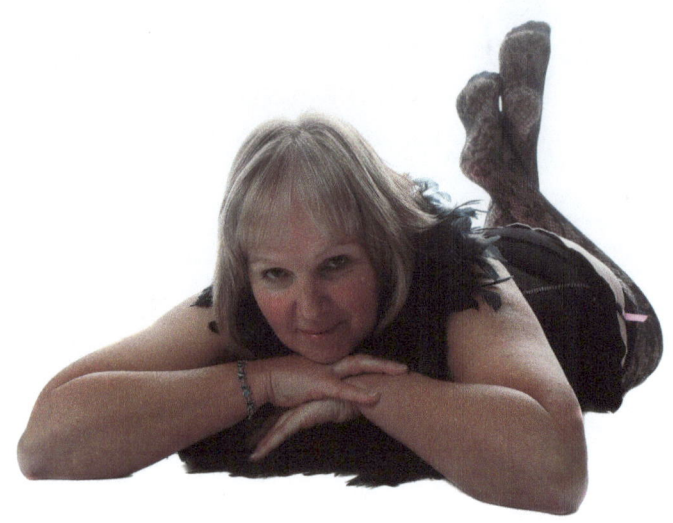

Photograph by Rob Morris

I am 53, divorced, a mum and nana. I am very comfortable in my body. It is not a size 12, look closely and you will see the stretch marks, scars and blemishes, something to be proud of, it shows an interesting life!

I am a vegetarian which was a lifestyle choice a few years ago. I love to laugh and I am always happy.

My hobbies are interesting and crafty, ranging from lace making and watercolour flower painting to puppet making and wood carving.

Naturism plays a big part in my life. There is nothing nicer than feeling the warmth of the sun on my body. Skinny dipping is lovely.

A back operation left me unable to walk any distance and with limited movement. Walking with a stick people perceive me as nobody. They see the stick and nothing else. However it doesn't affect my life modeling. When a tutor saw me walking with a stick she was very questioning about my ability to do modeling. I assured her I would be fine. We had a great session and subsequently I was booked for more classes.

My modeling started 3 years ago. I started modeling because I needed the money after my divorce. To my surprise I enjoyed the experience. Not bad for someone who was camera shy and was not fond of being looked at.

My first modeling job was a portrait class. The group was friendly and made me feel welcome. It was great to sit and do nothing but meditate. I was lucky I sat facing a huge mirror which the artists were in front of. It was great to see the pictures emerge from a blank canvas. It felt strange yet exhilarating to see how the artists had painted me. The first life class was lovely. I had no trouble removing my robe and taking up a pose for the artists. However I remember it being a really cold day. There were convector heaters blowing warm air onto me. Sadly they only took the chill off the room! One drawback of modeling is that most studios have high ceilings and are cold!

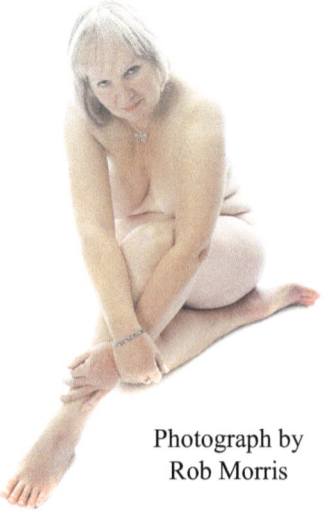

Photograph by Rob Morris

The one thing about modeling that gives me pleasure is time to meditate and think. It is chill out time. I have an ability to switch off and sit rock still, something the artists love. It is always lovely seeing the finished pictures. Everyone sees something different in me. I am always amazed at the skill of the artists. Over 3 years I have been very lucky to be given two portraits.

My thoughts on body image; *be proud of who you are*. It is really only since I turned 50 I realised this is me. My body has been with me all through my life I deserve to enjoy it. I am not perfect but in my eyes I am!

I now embrace my shape, flaws and all, and project it in positive way. I have been told I enchant people and ooze sex! Now you can't get a better compliment than that.

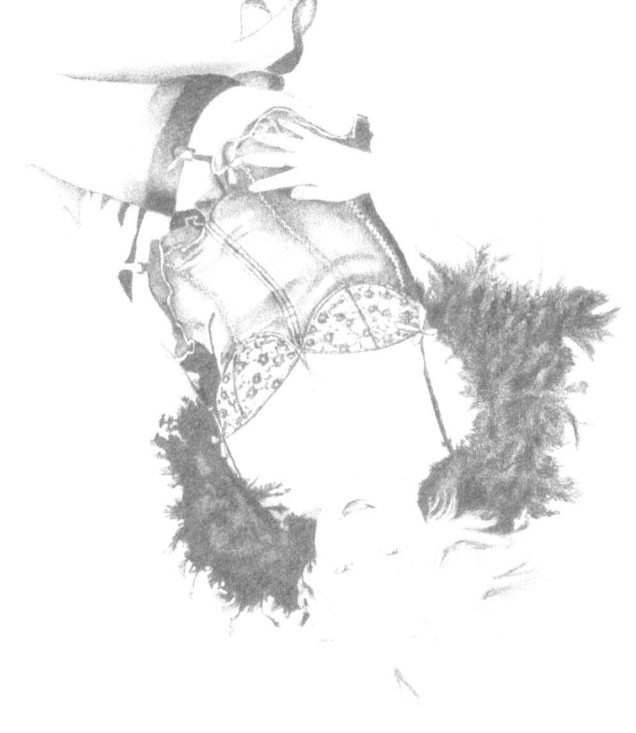

Diva's Repose, pencil on Bristol Board   Richard Savage © 2010

The best experience was an Access to Art class. It was a giggle from start to finish. I was depicted in clay, sewn, made in wire, painted, written in poetry and drawn in charcoal.

The students set the scene. It was like a crime scene, blue police tape all around the *bed*. Lots of random objects were strewn across the sealed off area. Amazingly not one of the students painted the scene, they only painted me! That certainly was the best one so far.

My inspiration is that this is my baby. It is my business. I really enjoy doing the modeling. I love life classes more than portrait ones.

Something to encourage others, that is a tough one. Just go for it! Be proud of what and who you are! And above all, enjoy!

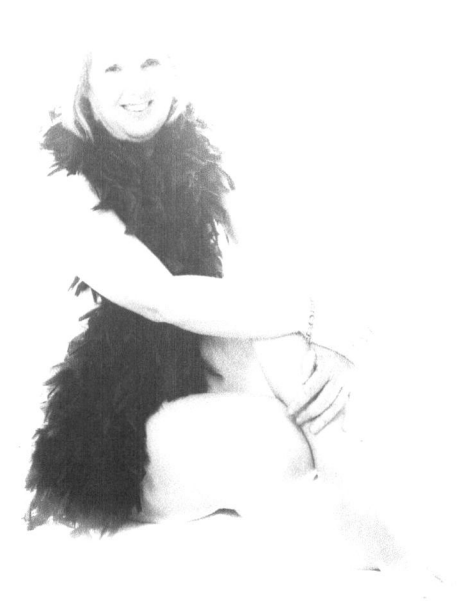

Photograph by Rob Morris

Christie Mawer
Author, Public Speaker And International Expert On Authentic Female Sensuality Based In Edmonton, Canada

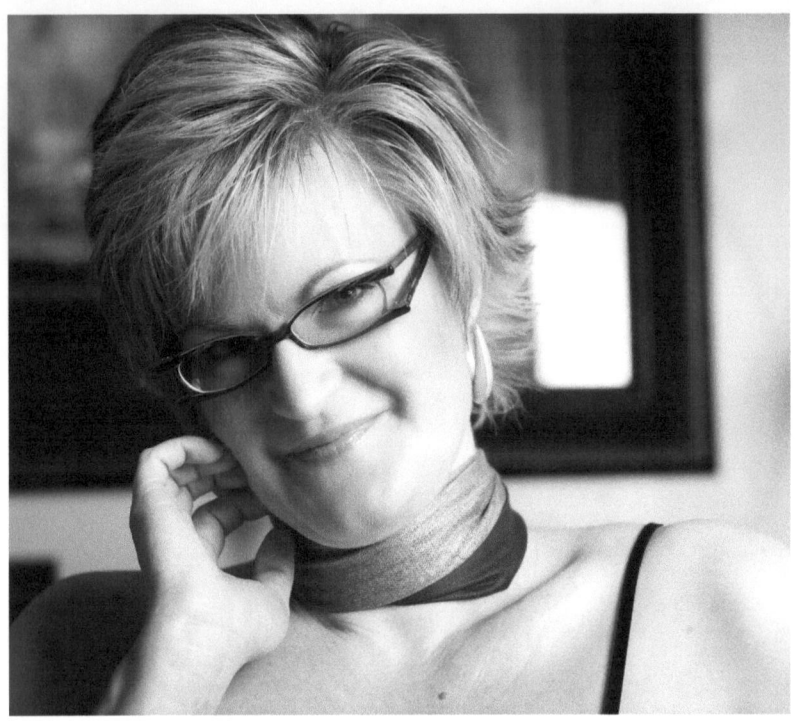

Be Beautiful, Be You!

Beauty. Yikes. How many times have you asked yourself if you were beautiful? How many times have you judged yourself on your level of perceived beauty?

How often have you not believed someone when they said you were beautiful? Such a short word which brings up so many opinions and thoughts. The insecurities it can create are ridiculous.

From a young age, people are categorized as attractive or unattractive. That category can have an incredible effect on the way we view ourselves in society.

When I was young, my mom had labels for my sister and myself. She was the pretty one, I was the strong one. I compared myself to my sister. She was the supreme example of what beauty meant in my family, and I fell short. Her lips were larger, her eyes were bigger, her face was rounder, and her nose had a cute upward turn. She was shorter than I, although we are both tall and, as we grew, her breasts were perkier.

This all led to great insecurities about my own beauty or, as I felt, lack thereof. I identified strongly with characters like The Ugly Duckling, The Elephant Man and Cyrano de Bergerac. They were ugly but underneath they were actually beautiful if you took the time to find out. I felt that was me; overlooked, unseen as I really was and judged by my inferior looks.

To make it even more obvious that I wasn't up to snuff in the looks department, my younger and, I believed, prettier sister not only started dating before I did but also got engaged before I'd even had a proper date let alone a boyfriend! My belief that I was ugly only compounded with all this evidence.

Jump ahead 20 years and things have changed remarkably. I now embrace my personal beauty. I see what I love about the way I look rather than what I don't love. I still have a hook nose and a protruding chin and my stomach isn't flat but I also have beautiful green eyes, a great smile, beautiful hands, incredible long legs and, I'm told, a great ass and perfect breasts. I may be 6 feet tall but thankfully I'm well proportioned and am no longer afraid to wear heels even if it makes me the tallest person in most rooms. Actually, that's fun!

So, how did the change occur? It certainly wasn't overnight.

The thing is, the beauty was always there. My face hasn't changed. My body is essentially the same. The secret is in accepting who I am as I am. That secret works for everyone. There are many people out there who don't subscribe to the accepted standard of beauty. Very few of us look like Miss America or the models on the runway or in the magazines. When we compare ourselves to them, we will inevitably fall short. Based on the number of them that have eating disorders and drug addictions, I'd venture that most of them feel that they fall short as well!

So why is it that there are hundreds and thousands of women that are considered beautiful in their everyday lives even if they are overweight, don't have $200 haircuts, may not be wearing the most flattering clothes or have acne? It's because they believe in themselves. They carry themselves with a confidence and self love that is unmistakable and attractive. Think about it. How often have you met someone that if you only saw a picture of them you may have gone, *meh, nothing special*, but meeting them, and getting to know them, you see something very special and are immediately attracted? I'm not talking sexual or romantic attraction necessarily. I'm talking about being drawn to them. Wanting to get to know them, to have what they have, that you are inspired by their presence.

The simple truth is, when you love yourself and are true to yourself it doesn't matter what you look like, you are beautiful.

My biggest struggle was not really with what I looked like but with how I presented myself to the world. People could tell that I was not comfortable in my own skin. I was constantly trying to adjust and figure out what was expected of me in any given situation. I was trying to fit in, to do the right thing, to not say anything stupid. Inevitably I ended up doing the exact opposite; being an outsider, constantly doing the wrong thing and putting both feet in my mouth up to the ankle.

Once I understood who I really was and owned it without apology, things completely changed for me. I was able to see myself in a true light rather than the light of suspicion and fear. I was able to speak my truth in any situation without fear and in a way that people could hear and understand. I found my calling in life. Things started to fall together.

There is something in the universe called congruence. Congruence is symmetry or agreement. When your inner life and your outer expression are in congruence, you are authentic. Authenticity is being genuine. When these concepts are present in your life, it's like a miracle.

I said earlier that I found my calling. My personal struggles have brought me to a business that helps women embrace their Authentic Beauty. I do this by unleashing their sensuality.

To me, there is nothing more beautiful than a woman who is truly herself and willing to express herself fully in all areas of her life. Sensuality is part of that. Actually, it's the key to all of it. Sensuality is your senses. It's how you live your life. It's how you interact with the world. It's being present in the moment and truly experiencing everything around you. When you are able to do that, you are authentic and you are beautiful.

Sensuality is a funny concept. It's often confused with sexuality. They are not interchangeable. They overlap, yes, but they are far from the same. Put simply; sensuality is experiencing the world – especially pleasure – through all 5 senses. Sexuality is genital contact. Basically, you can be sensual without any sex and you can have sex without being sensual. Once we all start living a truly sensual life and fully understand that it is separate from our sexuality and that it is natural, healthy and *fun*, our lives will be so much different. So much of our personal negativity and so many of our judgments will disintegrate and we can have a healthy love for ourselves as well as a healthy expression of who we really are. At least that's how it happened for me.

I encourage women everywhere to live by a simple, yet sometimes hard to get to motto: *be beautiful, be you!* No matter what your shape, size, skin condition or similarity to manufactured perfection, you are *amazing!*

Join the beauty revolution and know without a doubt that you are beautiful just as you are.

www.thebadkitty.com
www.blog.thebadkitty.com

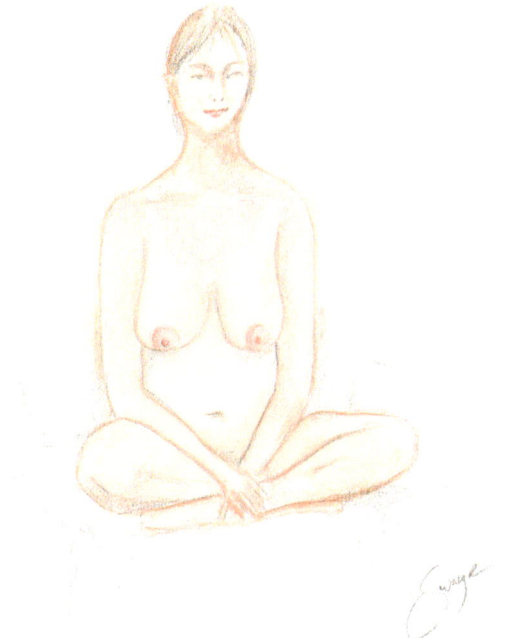

Life study Richard Savage © 2012

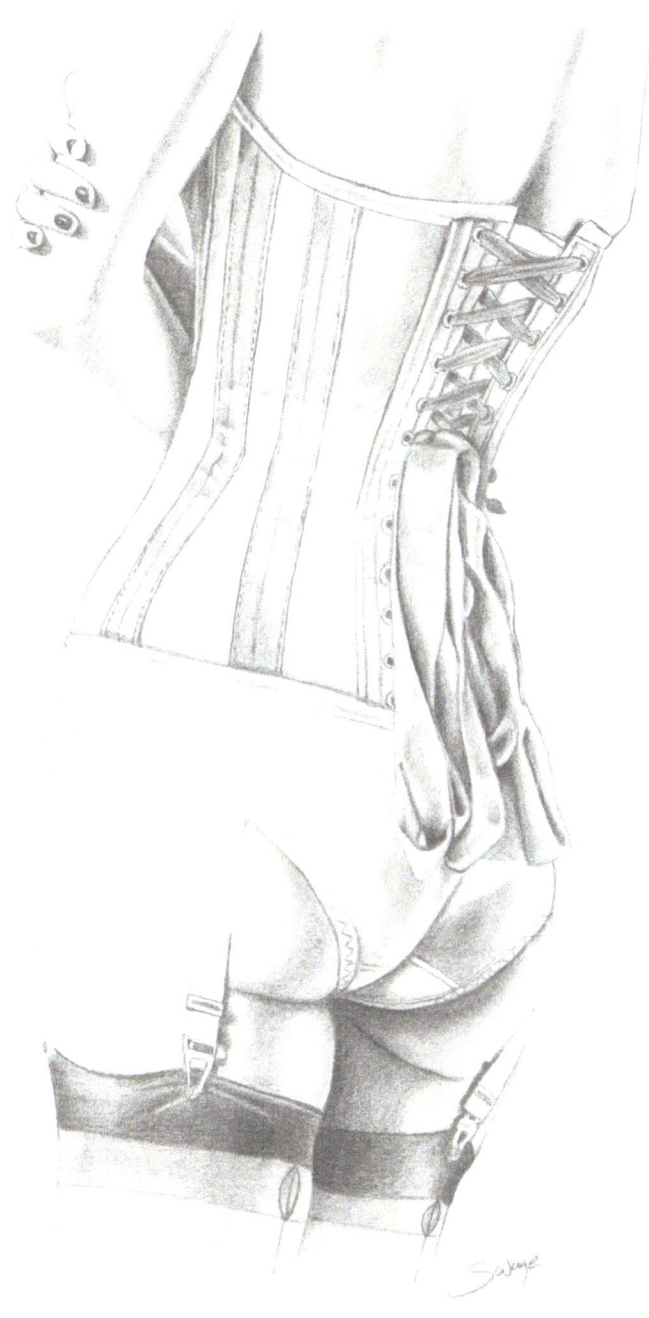

Patiently Waiting, pencil on Bristol Board Richard Savage © 2011

Above is a drawing of one of my life models, Lucy, drawn in 2011. We have been lucky with models who come to our group. The great majority of models I have worked with have been very easy going, which suits our studio style. We have a very laid back policy which in my opinion brings out the best in both model and artist.

I was once asked in an interview, what quality I prize above all from models. I would say that the quality I admire more than any other is a nice personality and tolerant nature. Nobody wants to hear the model complaining, but on the other hand I would also like to think I never give the model anything to complain about. Having said that my thanks go out to my life models who have gone above and beyond the call of duty. On two occasions, during Life Casting, the Plaster of Paris failed to set in a timely fashion, leaving my model in an uncomfortable position for an extended period of time. Not once during that time did either model complain. In fact they seemed more concerned with the quality of the final casting rather than their own comfort.

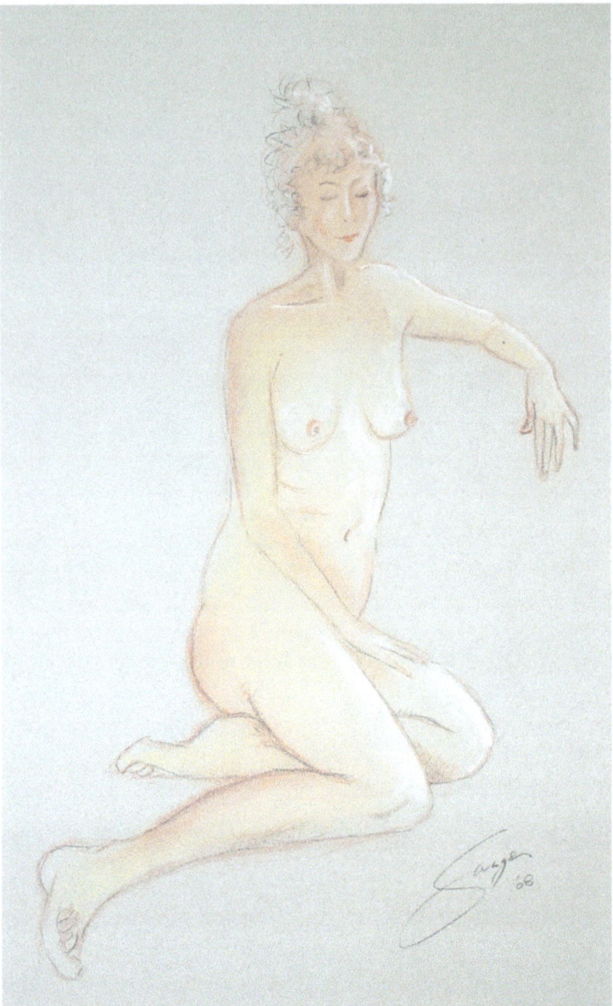

Life study Richard Savage © 2008 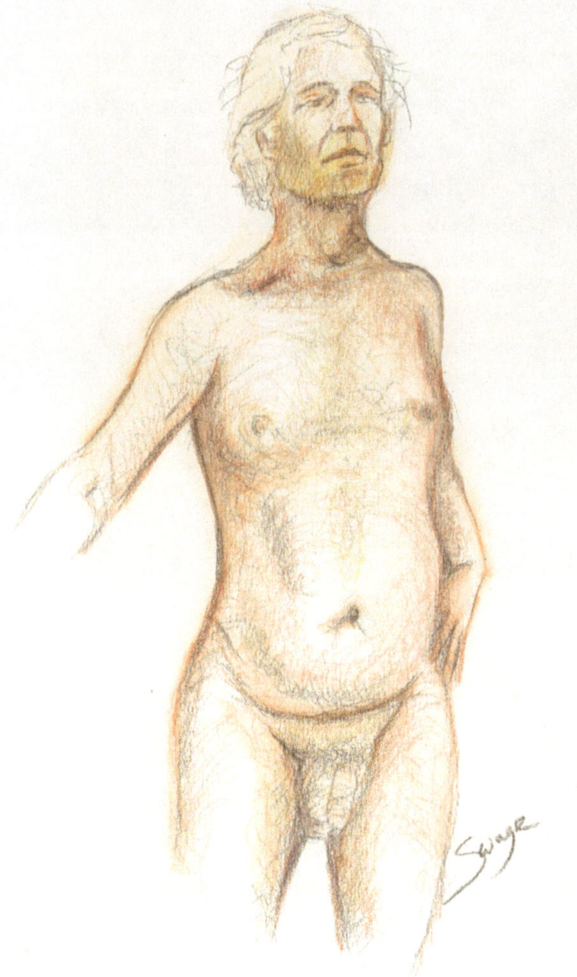   Life study Richard Savage © 2012

Pictured above left, Lin and right, Clifford in watercolor pencil and soft pastel.

Lin

When drawing from life most artists do not pay much attention to facial features. Faces are usually left with just the shape and lightly filled in features. In my opinion this approach is much more effective when looking at the overall impression.

Hair is of great interest to most artists particularly if it has an unusual appearance e.g. long, wild or curly.

Beauty is only skin deep, but ugly goes clean to the bone.

Dorothy Parker

Elizabeth N. Spire
Publisher At Unseenwords.com, Author, Performance Poet

Beauty

Should short or tall, or fat or thin,
Define all that lies within?
Does color of eyes or hue of hair,
Make one more desirable or rare?
Should race, religion or basic creed,
Dictate our love, our life, our need?
Is not beauty in all that's found;
Above, below and all around?
Is a rose less sweet to smell,
If a petal rips, do tell!
Time is what makes landscapes change,
Be they wild sea shore or mountain range,
Is beauty only seen with eyes?
When brain is where the passion lies.
Cannot the blind, or deaf or dumb,
Have their heart beat like a drum?
Does twisted limb or lack of one,
Preclude one from a life of fun?
Should we not look beyond the gloss,
To see true beauty or it's our loss,
Our curse to be put off by scars,
When beauty is found in burning stars!
Are amazing canyons wide and deep,
Not formed by waters that more than seep?
Is not weathered rock more sublime,
When bells are hit do they not chime?
If we cannot look in the eyes of others,
And see new friends, companions, lovers,
Are we not then the ugly ones,
To see creations daughters or fine sons,
As less deserving of our hearts,
Because they have a few missing parts?
Are only the tall, slim, tanned and fair,
To been seen as touched by beauty's share,
Of rich endowments and kind words,
If so then is beauty only found in cloned herds?

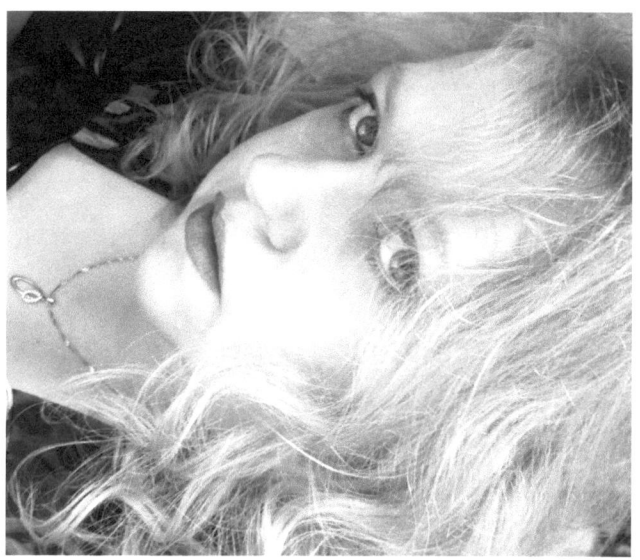

To me great beauty is unique,
An algorithm of more than just physique!
It has intelligence and art,
Soft, strong, hands, amazing heart,
It's short, it's tall, it's fat, it's thin,
For it is the beauty that lies within,
Not changed by time, decayed with age,
It's full of passion and righteous rage!
It looks beyond my moral shell,
And sees the soul in which I dwell.

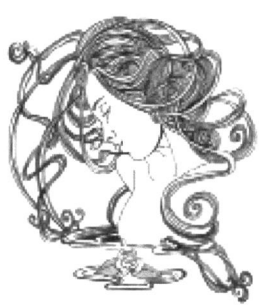

Pentyn's Pet
Writer, Artist And Management Professional Living In England

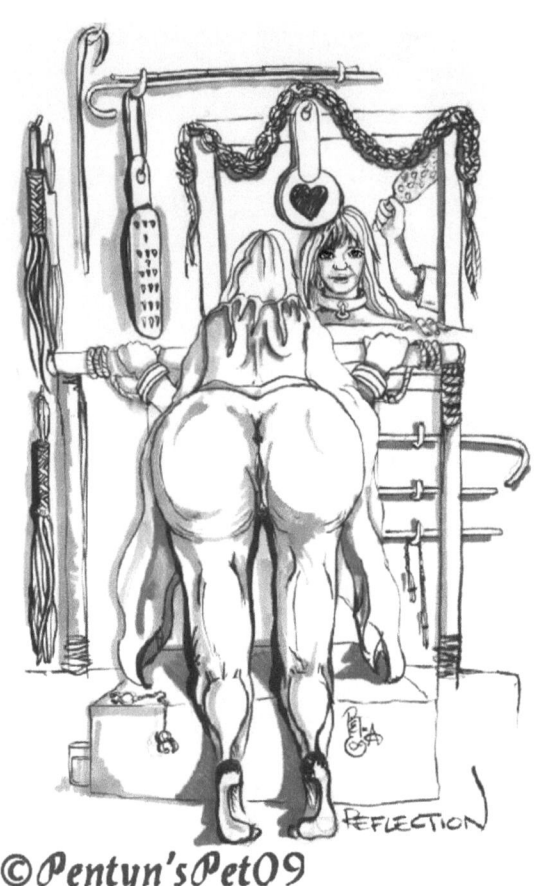

As a child of 8, I barely lived through a sadistic, evil rape. The rapist said I deserved it because I was pretty. I decided being fat would prevent me from ever being pretty. So instead of being a prisoner of someone who would hurt me I became a prisoner of my size.

I became drawn to the lifestyle of domination and submission. The first time I played in front of others and the dominant told me to strip no one fell dead with disgust or laughter at the sight of my grotesque form. The only comments I got were complimentary about the size of my nipples, breasts and bum. It was a miraculous moment of liberation and self-acceptance.

For the most part, BDSM is less what you look like than how you respond. It is using your brain as a sex toy. It was really in bondage that I found freedom to be who I am.

I'm still fat, but now I'm only a prisoner by my free choice. I have an adoring and loving Master who I serve as a 24/7 slave. He enjoys and celebrates my nearly 50 year old body, accepting and loving me unconditionally. And they call us perverts!

He gave me the online name honeyslave, just one of many names I have. I should explain, I write an online journal, writing about my life story, about my size and our relationship within our BDSM lifestyle.

I am a size 30 and beautiful. Beautiful because Master says I am. My master is my husband too. He adores me, and he is in complete control of every element of our lives. As the submissive I surrender, accepting his will over mine, giving up not just my consent in the bedroom and dungeon, but also my shame and fears.

It's not just in the bedroom scenes, but what I think, feel and do every day. Every day he expects me to surrender my will and daily he reminds me that I am his adored girl, I am absolutely loved and desired, beautiful and everything I need to be.

He doesn't judge my appearance, but how well I obey, how much I work to please him and how hard I work towards the success of our relationship. It's not about breaking me down or belittling me. I am willingly his property and he invests in me, refurbishes me, maintains me, makes use of my strengths and *period features* to enhance my value, comfort and appeal so in me we both find the woman we need me to be.

Our relationship is braided with both vanilla and leather elements; it is not a single dimensional cartoon, but a fully rounded and exceptionally strong relationship where we both strive to provide what the other needs.

We regularly discuss our dreams, needs and feelings; we actively play and enjoy each other's bodies, and we are both absolutely open and truthful knowing there is nothing to lose through truth. There are no grudges or pettiness. If he says I am forgiven, then it is forgotten. If he is wrong, he says he is sorry and asks if there is anything I need to accept his apology. I believe these aspects are essential for the absolute level of trust we experience. We each work to provide what is best for the other. For the twelve years of our relationship I have, without fail, been secure, content, fulfilled, satisfied and loved.

I would like to say to anyone reading this, before they think I am ignorant or easily manipulated, I have an advanced degree and I am a qualified professional with a senior level managerial post. I spent 16 years trying to love an abusive man enough to heal him. I know the difference between being abused and being nurtured.

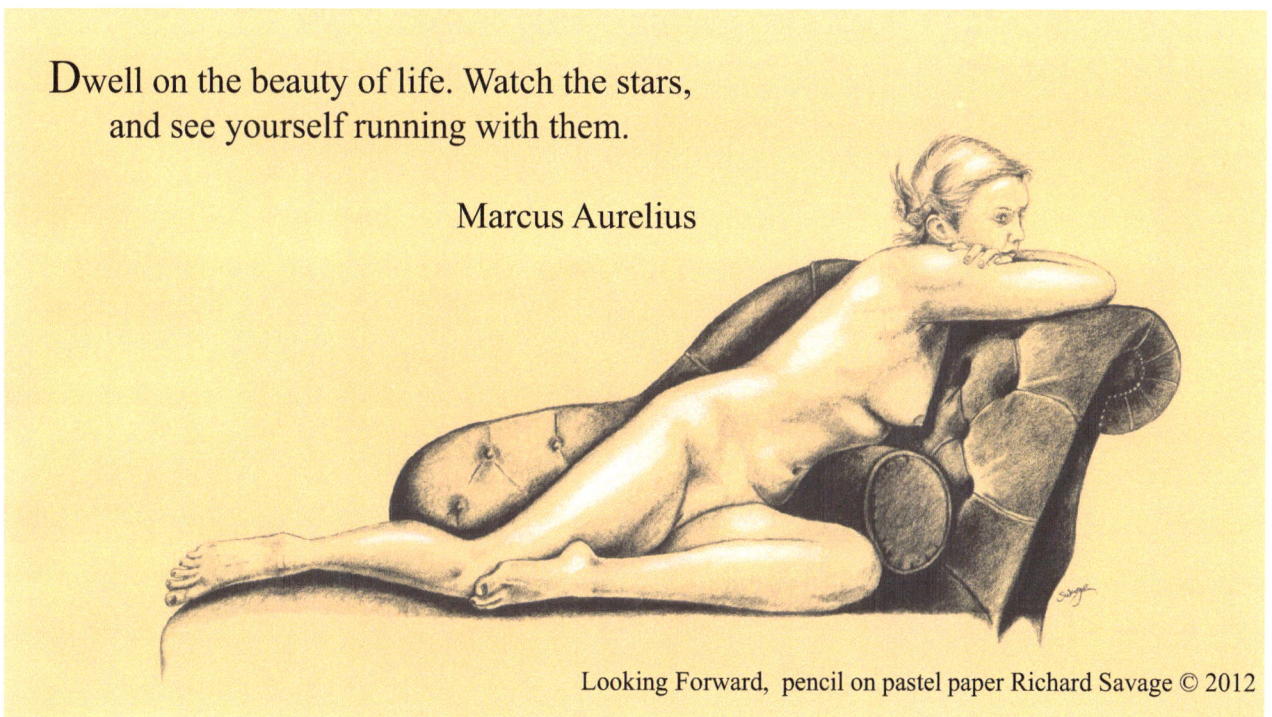

Dwell on the beauty of life. Watch the stars, and see yourself running with them.

Marcus Aurelius

Looking Forward, pencil on pastel paper Richard Savage © 2012

Carol Tierney
Model, Writer And Chain Mail Artist From The UK

It's no revelation that what is publicly hailed as beauty is totally arbitrary. Anyone looking at pictures from a few decades past is more likely to laugh at the strange attire that we all wore back then, than to think that we looked a million dollars. Look back over a longer period of time and through various cultures and it's clear that beauty can't be defined by whether someone is fat or thin, tall or short, dark or fair, colorful or sombre. However much the glossy magazines would like us to think otherwise, beauty's not an industry, it's not even physical.

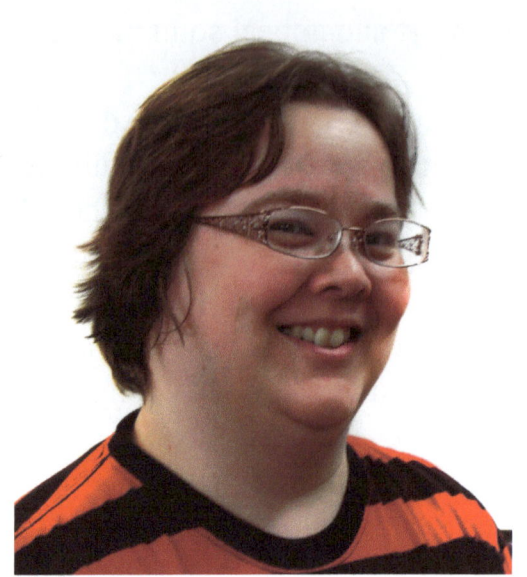

What does seem to persist over the centuries is the idea of inner beauty – that being a good, kind, and noble soul is where true beauty lies. Logically however, that doesn't work either. However much of a saint someone is there will be those who don't see them that way. A man's inner beauty can quickly translate to him being the powerless victim of bullying and being seen as a weak pitiful do-gooder. Even the most famous humanitarians of our time are political figures with haters as well as admirers. Politics is everywhere, and there are two or more sides to every story. All the reports of ambulance crews being assaulted show that helping and caring for people isn't necessarily always appreciated. So, that can't be real beauty either.

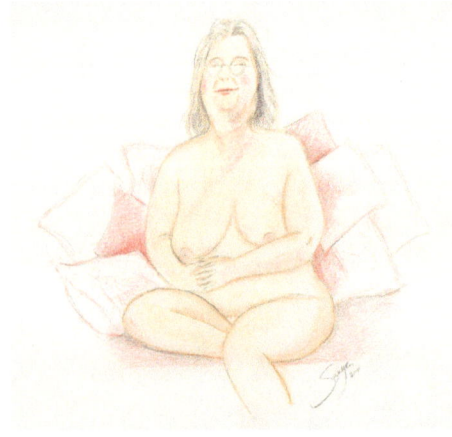

Life study Richard Savage © 2012

When I started thinking about beauty I did what I often do and went and browsed the various quotes on the subject to see if anyone famous had said it better than I could. I found a couple that came close. Confucius said, "Everything has beauty, but not everyone sees it." More recently Conrad Hall said, "There is a kind of beauty in imperfection." Both of those I'd agree with, but the quote that really captured my thoughts on the subject comes from H G Wells. "Beauty is in the heart of the beholder." That makes sense. Beauty isn't something you see or something that is possessed in limited supply by a few privileged people or things – it's something you feel. I'd go beyond that and say that it is something you can actively choose to feel. Beauty is quite simply an act of love.

The pictures in those glossy magazines are beautiful because the people who buy the magazines look at them, admire them and love them. It doesn't matter that fashions move on and times change.

The person being given a hard time for trying to help is beautiful because someone sees what they are doing, admires them and loves them. It doesn't matter that not everyone sees the same thing. If their actions touch a few hearts and make a few people feel happier about the world, that is beauty.

Life study Richard Savage © 2012

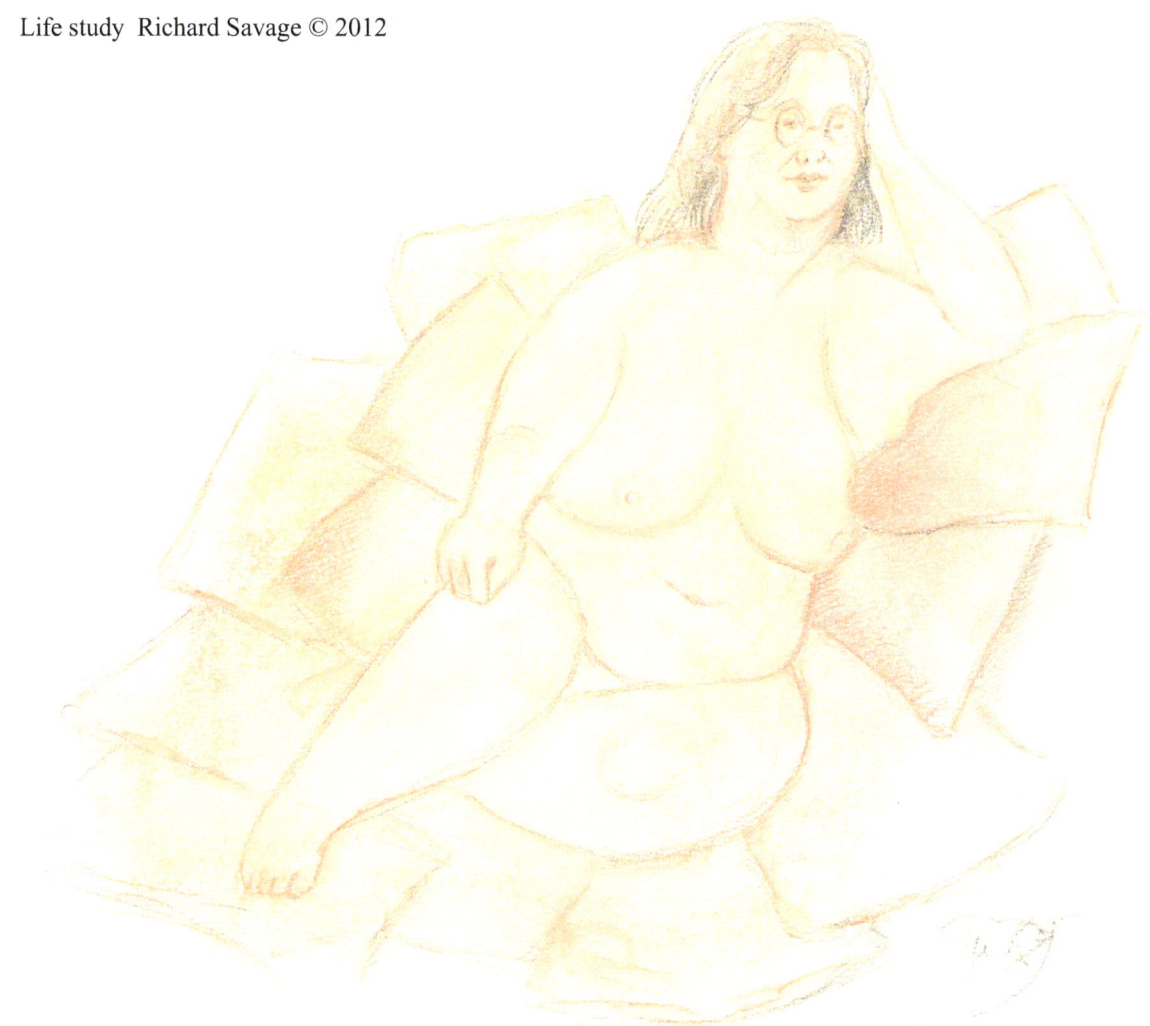

Whether it's a painting in an art gallery that has been admired by millions, or a delicate spider's web that no-one else has noticed, if you look at it and let it touch your heart that is beauty.

Once you realize that beauty is something you can choose to feel, it really is everywhere. Simply taking the time to stop and look for it is an act of love, and if you love beauty you will always find it. Whatever you admire, whatever you appreciate, whatever you love, whatever you value, whatever makes you happy, that is beauty.

Beauty in Every Form

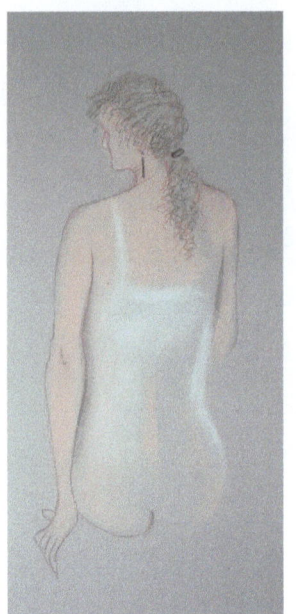 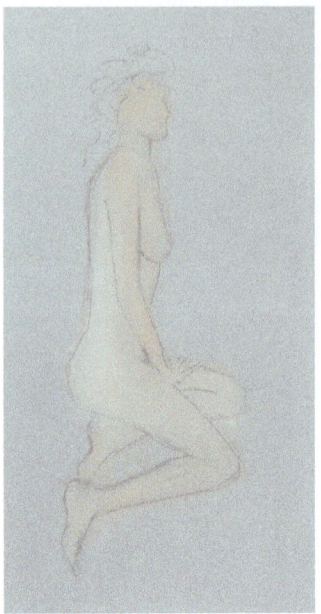 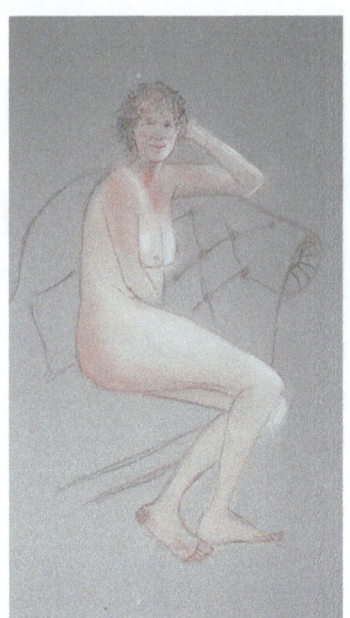 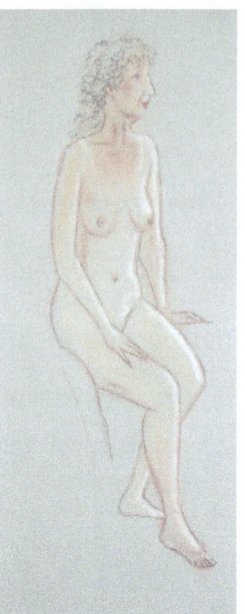

Life drawing studies of Lin in soft pastel and watercolor pencil Richard Savage © 2009

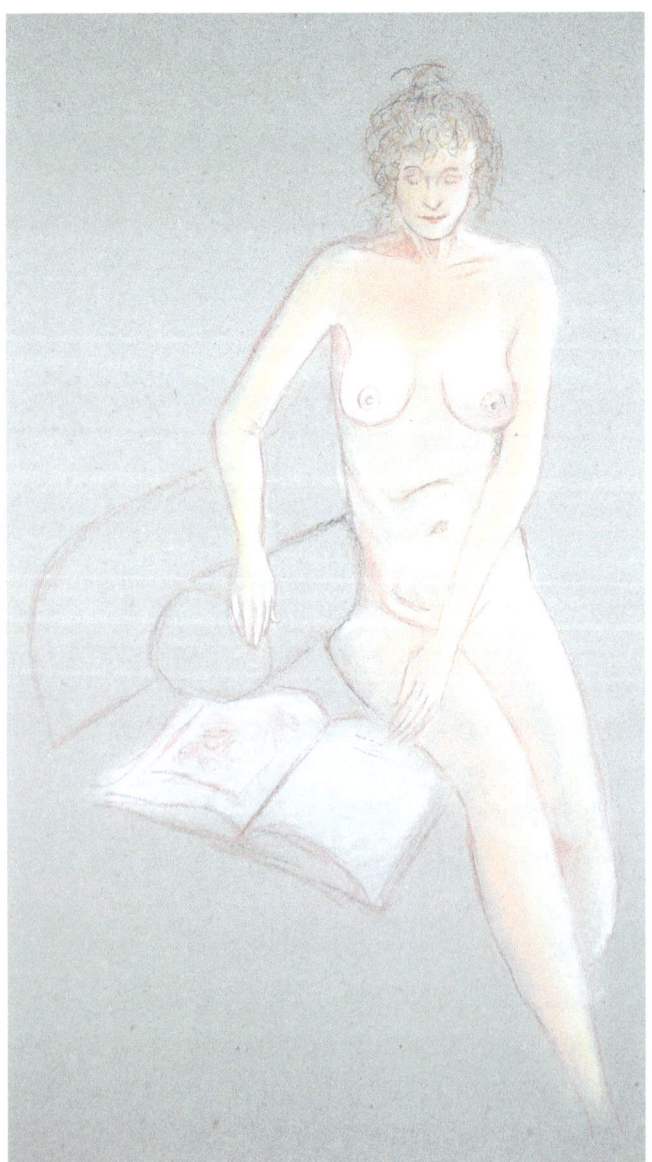

Lin

Life modeling can attract models who are exhibitionists, those who love to show off their physique, tattoos or body piercings, it's a perfect stage for them.

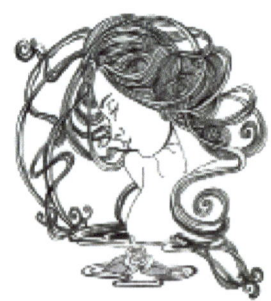

Beauty?...
To me it is a word without sense
because I do not know where its
meaning comes from
nor where it leads to.

Pablo Picasso

Lee Rush
Author With Black Velvet Seductions

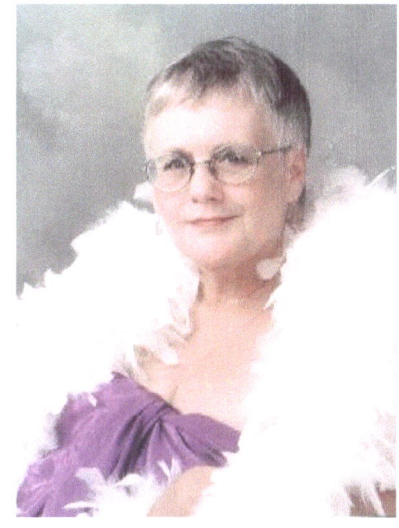

In contemplating why I write, I suppose it takes me away from the daily life. The words that bring out feelings and ideas do not conform to daily life. There is a need to get some of the ideas and words out of my head. There is something about it that makes me smile when I've finally gotten it down right.

When considering body shape, I usually make the man taller, but it's more important to me to show what's inside than outside. What drives the characters, what makes them feel, is more important than whether or not they have a great tan or big muscles!

A tall, dark, handsome hero and thin, blond, long legged heroine, is a nice fantasy, but is hardly realistic. My characters are usually older, perhaps because I'm older and like to think that there's still romance between older people.

The most beautiful body can contain an insipid soul. It's what's inside that makes beauty. We don't see ourselves as others see us. So, what we see in the mirror might make us frown or shake our heads, but to that special person we are glowing with youth and love and all things lovely and beautiful.

Many years ago I was told, by a salesman trying to make time with a much younger me, that just because there was snow on the roof it didn't mean the fire was out in the furnace. Just because you get older doesn't mean you stop loving or needing love or searching for it. And just because you have loved and lost doesn't mean you can't love again.

Sometimes people are beautiful.
Not in looks.
Not in what they say.
Just in what they are.

Markus Zusak

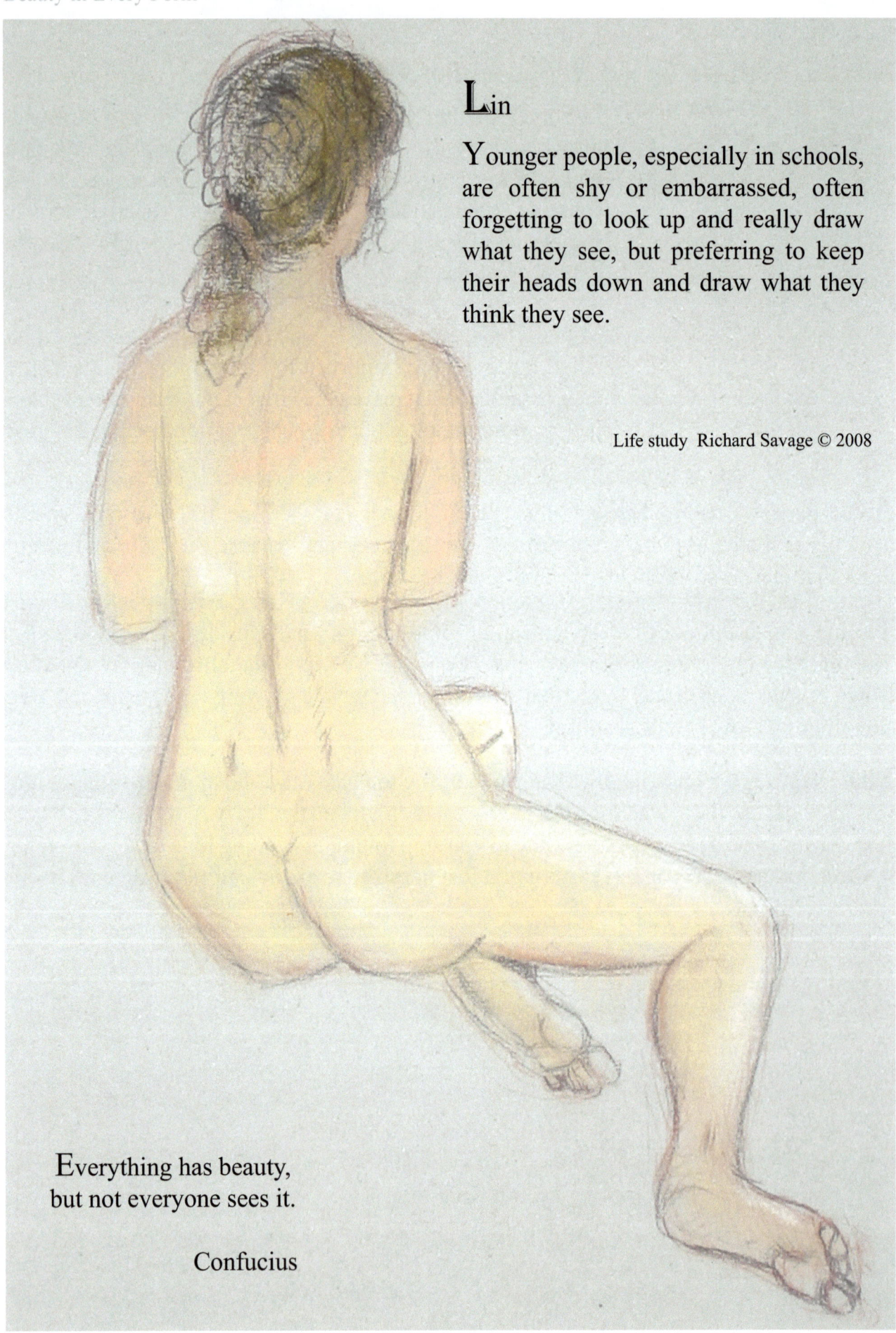

Lin

Younger people, especially in schools, are often shy or embarrassed, often forgetting to look up and really draw what they see, but preferring to keep their heads down and draw what they think they see.

Life study Richard Savage © 2008

Everything has beauty,
but not everyone sees it.

Confucius

AJ Best
Writer Northern NY, USA

Beauty Is In The Liking Of Oneself

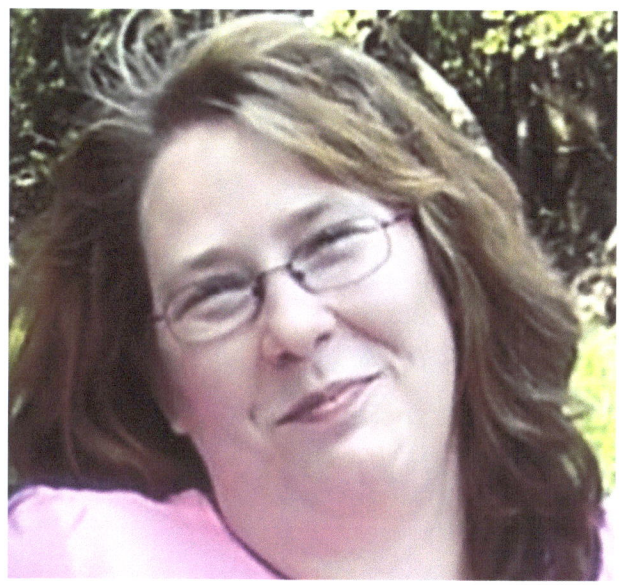

Beauty. Just the word gives me the creeps. I've never had it, just ask my dad. When I was in 5th or 6th grade my father made sure to tell me that I was fat and ugly. You have to understand that hit home from more angles than one. When your father, the man who knows everything in your life, tells you that you are not only fat, but ugly as well, your world crumbles.

It didn't matter that, at the time my father said it, I was nearly six feet tall and barely 150 pounds. I only saw what my father told me.

It took many years and many men telling me how beautiful I was, mostly through sex, to believe in myself. It wasn't the sex that made me believe I was beautiful. It was realizing that my father was a bitter man that helped me to see that he was wrong. He didn't want anyone to be happy. Yes, there were tons of therapy sessions in those years and they soaked in, but I remember the sex more. I needed a male to tell me I was beautiful. I hated myself for that.

I wanted to know I was beautiful for myself not because of someone else. It's taken 35 years to get to the point I am at now. I am fatter than I was then, but I like myself; and that makes me beautiful. Not my father, not sex from random men, not therapy. I needed to like myself. It's taken a long time, but it was worth every second. And I'm worth it.

Beauty...
When you look into a woman's eyes and see what is in her heart.

Nate Dircks

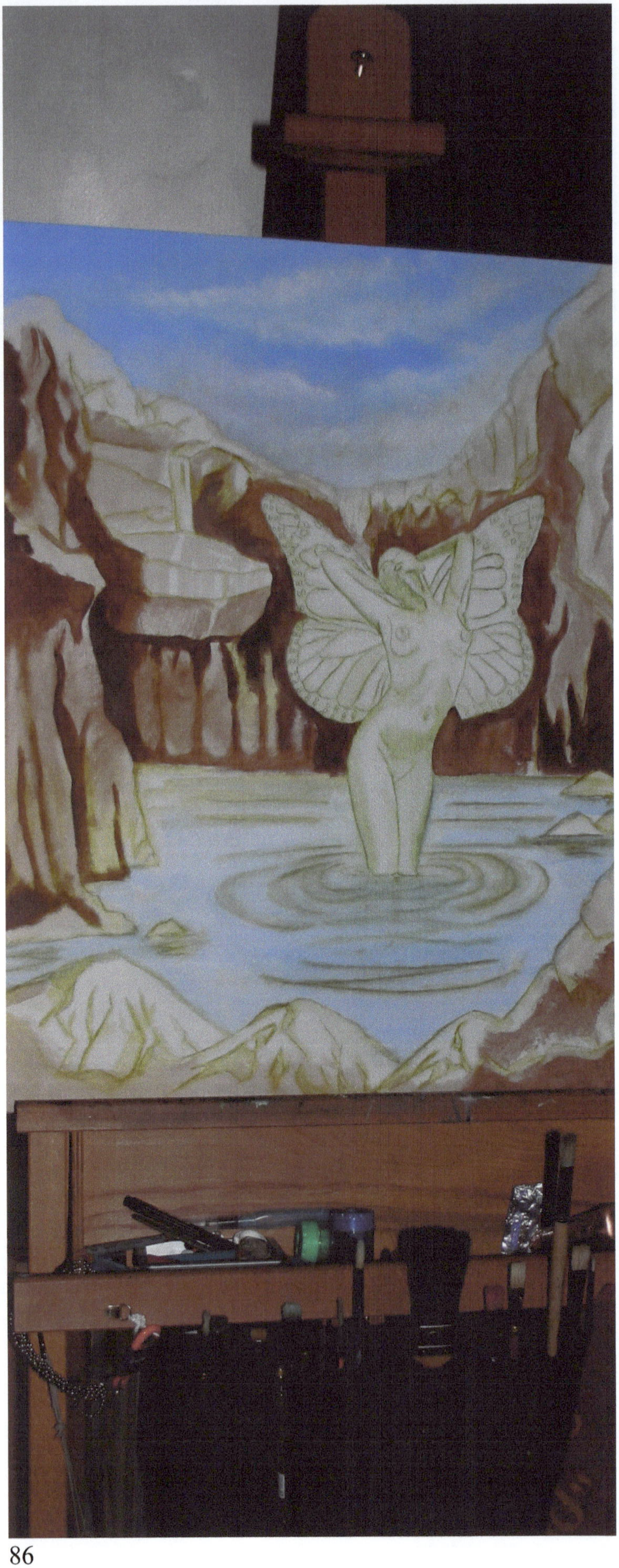

Beauty in Every Form

Beauty is such a personal and subjective topic. I offer this as just a view. When picking a topic to paint, my choice is driven by the eventual use for the picture. The picture here was suggested to me by a fellow artist. It was done as a practice piece in oils and was intended as a piece for my portfolio although it is now part of a private collection.

Shown here are three stages of this picture. Left, the first sketch on the canvas with the primary areas blocked in. Below, shows the picture in development, although I was unhappy with the detail in the water and I considered there were problems with the composition. Eventually I cut it from the stretcher to make it a smaller much more focused image, seen right.

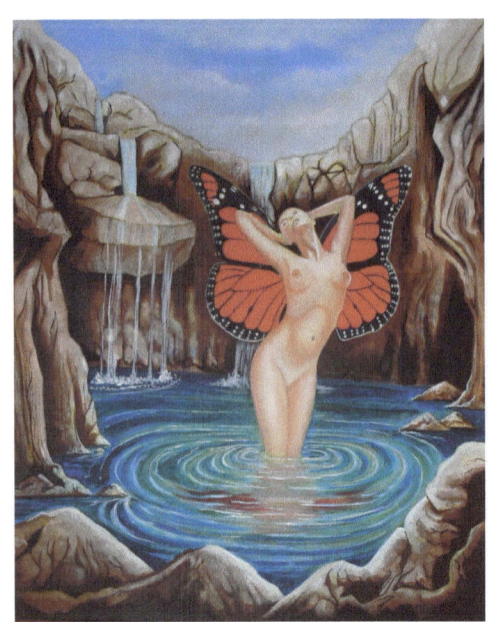

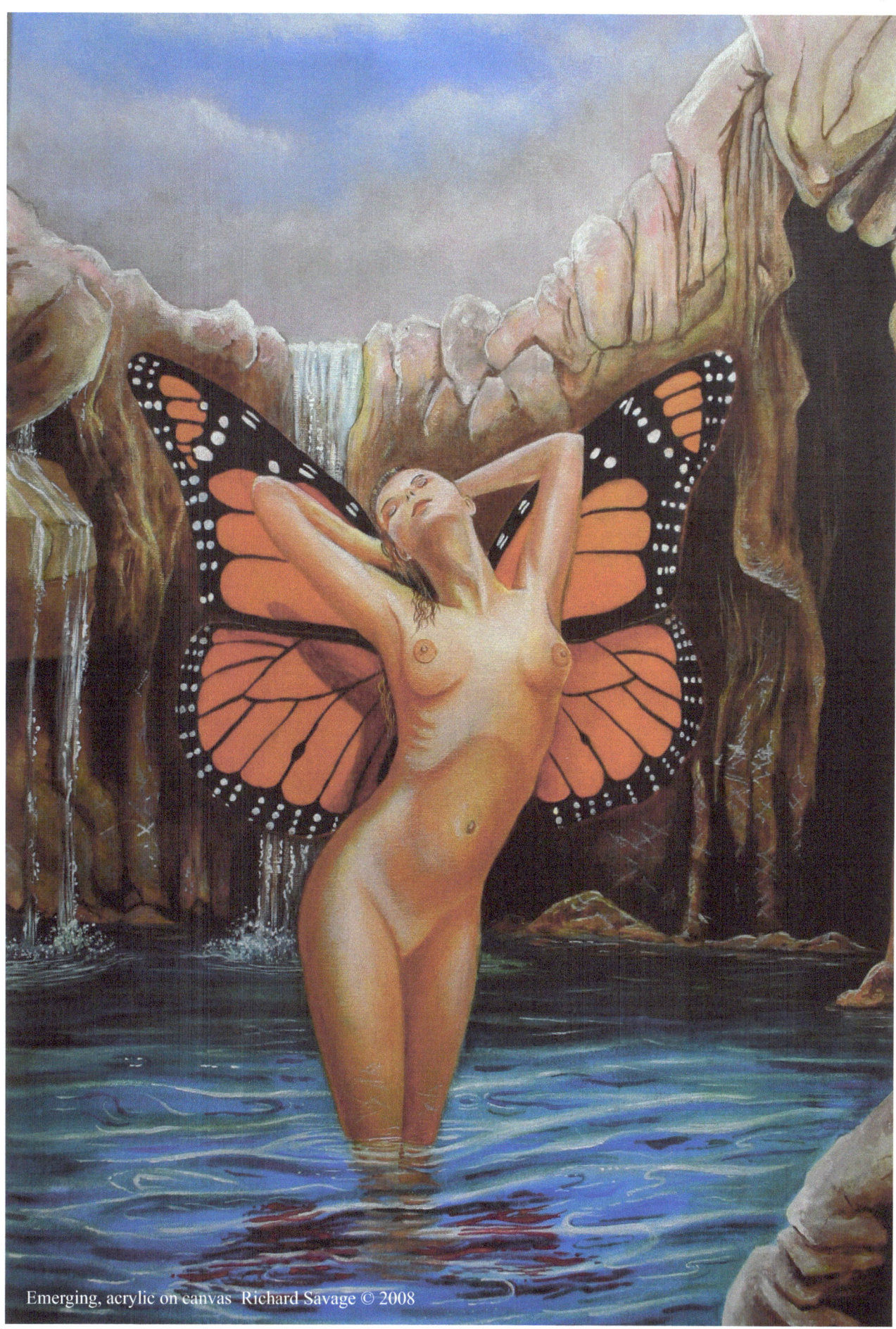
Emerging, acrylic on canvas Richard Savage © 2008

Beauty in Every Form

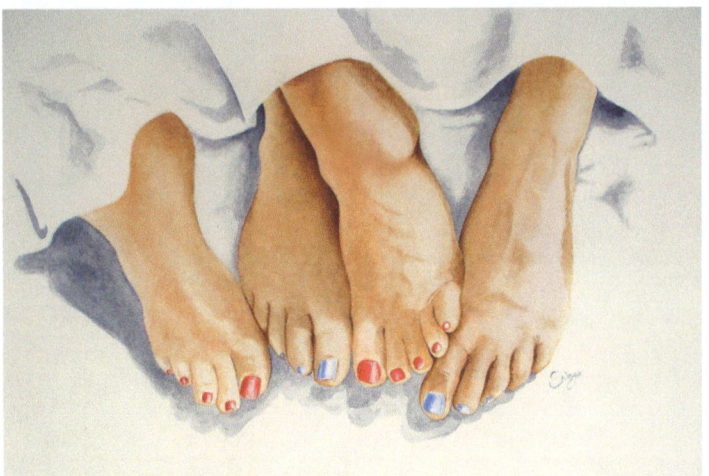
Lazy Sunday Morning, acrylic on paper Richard Savage © 2005

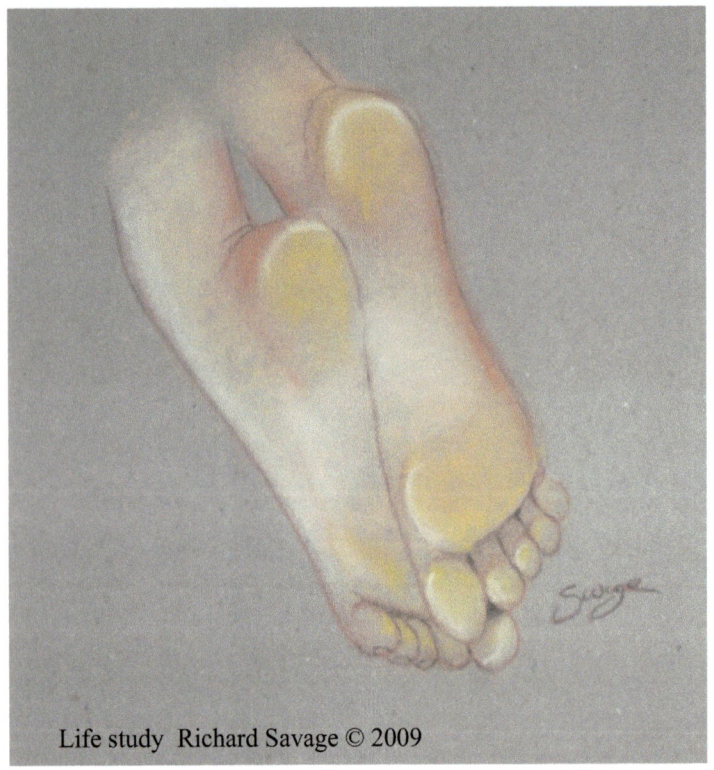
Life study Richard Savage © 2009

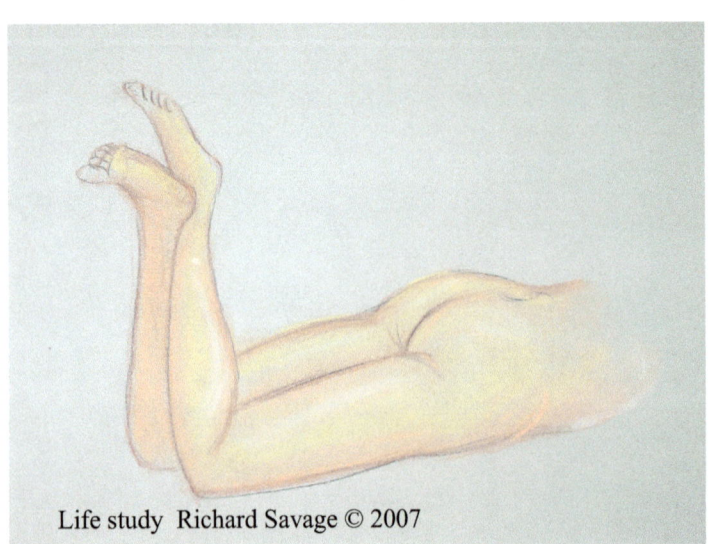
Life study Richard Savage © 2007

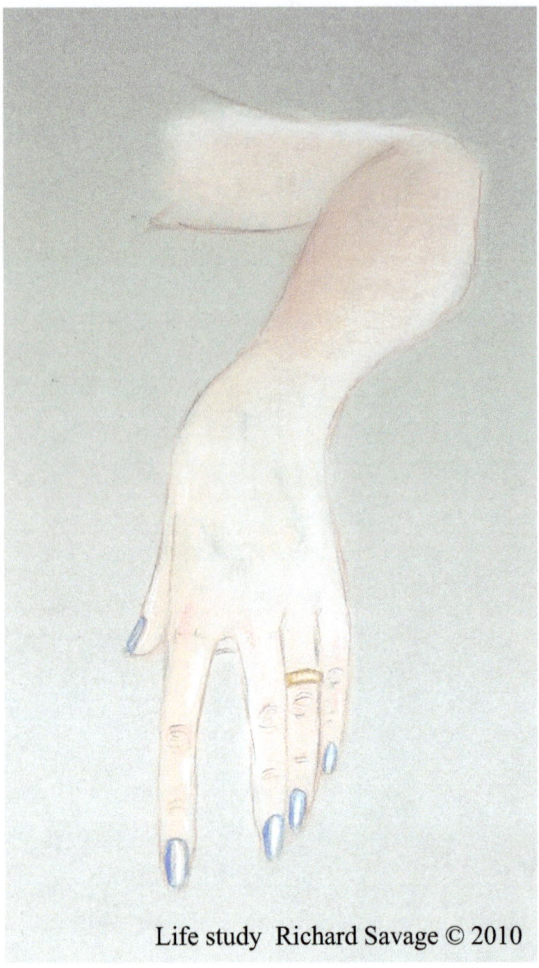
Life study Richard Savage © 2010

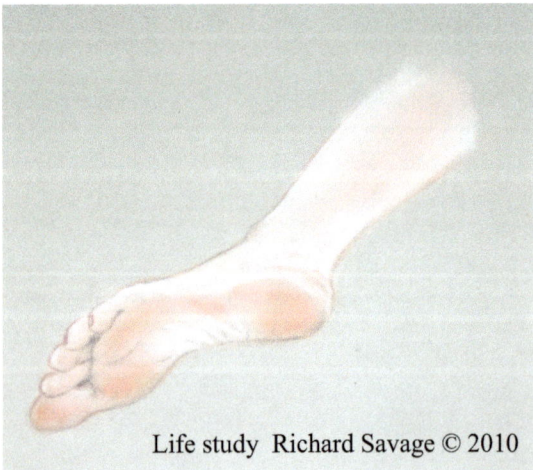
Life study Richard Savage © 2010

I might be a little strange but I take pleasure in drawing individual body parts. During a life class where typically we get 15 - 20 minutes to draw a pose I can find myself lost in the details of a hand or a pair of feet, maybe I am a little odd but I do see beauty in the strangest of places.

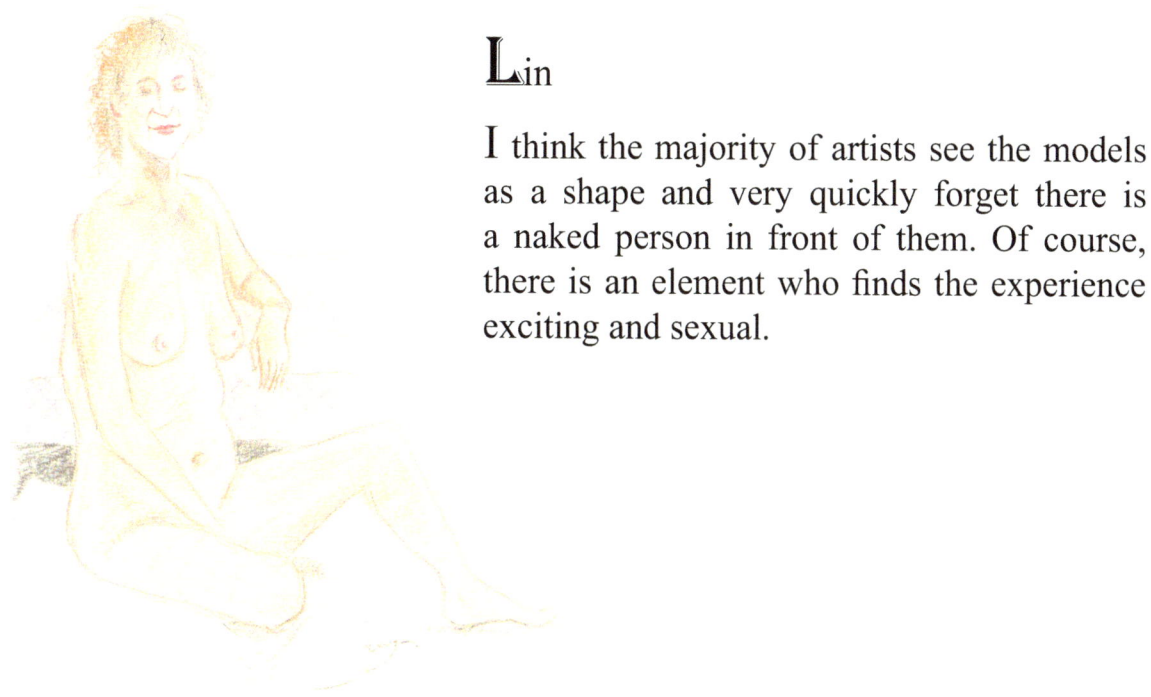

Lin

I think the majority of artists see the models as a shape and very quickly forget there is a naked person in front of them. Of course, there is an element who finds the experience exciting and sexual.

Life study Richard Savage © 2010

In some ways there is a fine line between the erotic and life drawing. In other ways they are poles apart.

I have been asked many times to define what makes a picture erotic. For me it is much more about what a picture makes you think than what you can actually see.

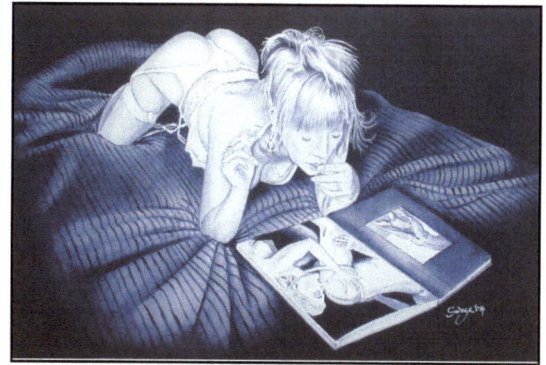

Bedtime Reading, acrylic on paper
Richard Savage © 2004

In life drawing class it is anything but erotic to my eye. All is there, all in the open. Regardless of how good looking a model is I don't think it is an erotic environment.

I think of my life group as a very honest environment. I did have an artist that asked about coming to my life class. He was worried about becoming sexually aroused during the class. I explained that it was just not like that.

I enjoy my erotic art but it is distinct from my life drawing.

The thing I like about my picture, Bedtime Reading, seen above, is the scene of a woman enjoying her own sexuality. It is all about her. The picture is about a woman as consumer of images rather than being the object in the image. I love the irony that in my picture she is both.

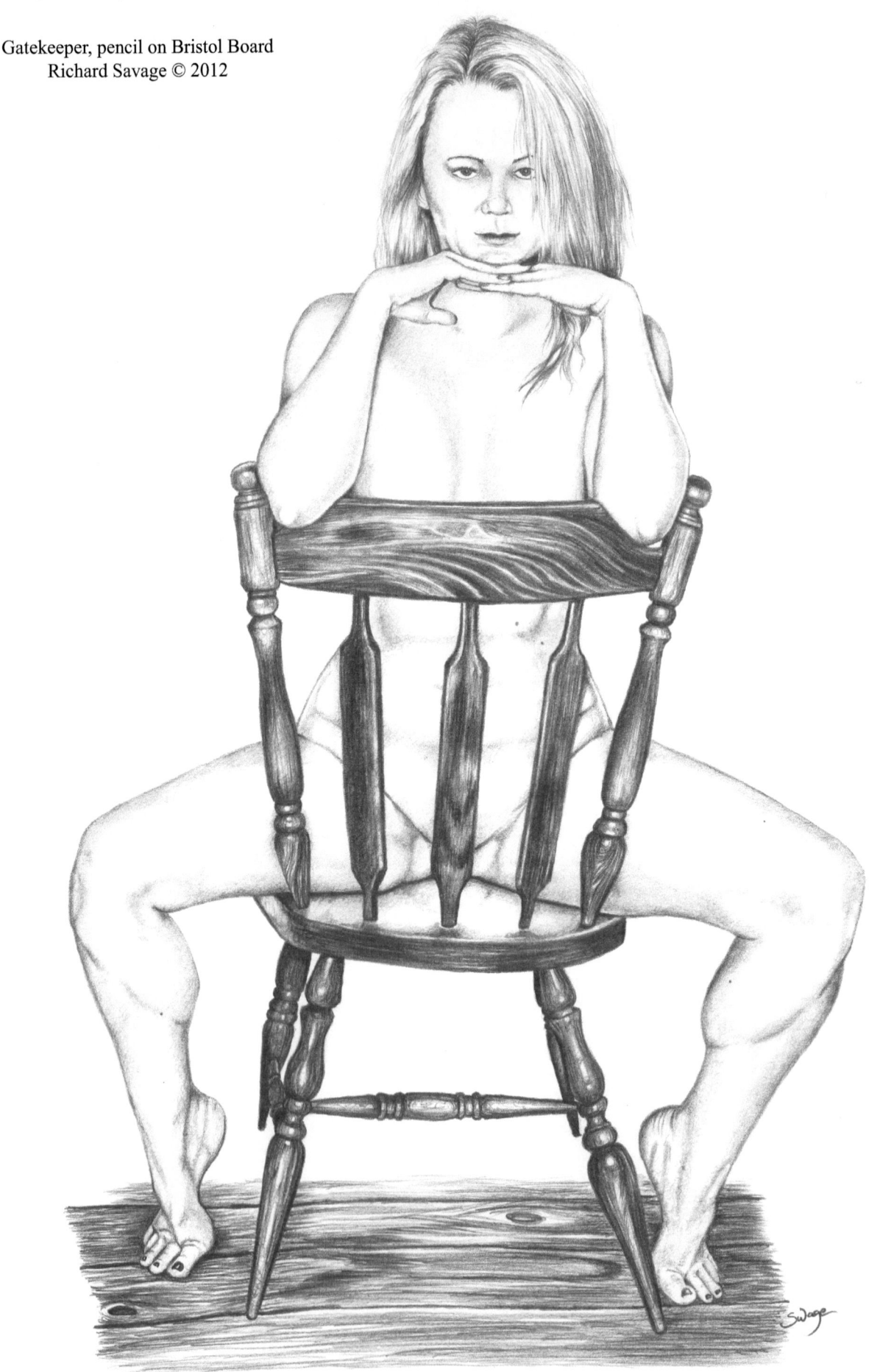

Gatekeeper, pencil on Bristol Board
Richard Savage © 2012

Liz Wright
Writer From The UK

I heard that the cat walk clothes are designed mainly by gay men for boyish figures. This makes perfect sense to me. Clothes are designed for a flat, tall man's body instead of for the shorter, fuller body of a woman. Given that all fashion starts on the cat walk, there is little hope for real women at this rate.

Beauty is often in function. A woman's body is utterly functional, not only in her physical make up for reproduction but in the stockiness of the hard worker, the strength of her arms, the layer of fat that is there in case food gets short, the stocky legs for holding weight and walking and so on.

Beauty as fragility is something connected with a rich person's view. As average people we cannot be or appear fragile. It is the strength of coping with our everyday lives that makes women beautiful.

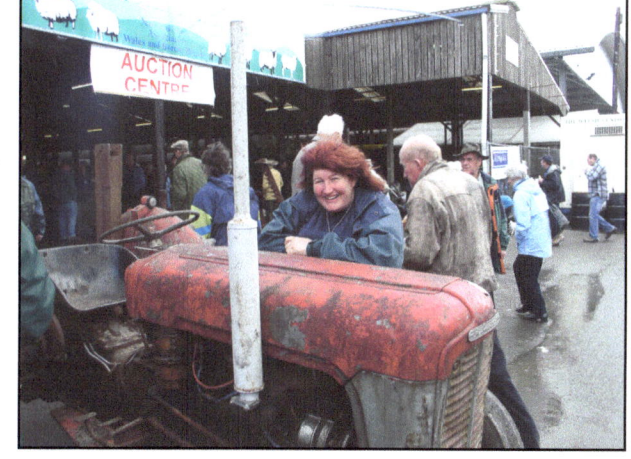

I always think that all of us that came from peasant stock have survived because we had to. We lived off bad diets and too much work. Then suddenly life improved but our metabolism remained stuck back a few generations ago when we had to live off not much food. The result is we all put on weight.

I love Africa. There people think fat women are good because being fat means you are not ill, you can work and you have money. People in Africa would feel sorry for Victoria Beckham.

I tried to explain the concept of bulimia to some Zimbabwean friends, but they really didn't get it. "So, you eat it and then you throw it up, so what do you live off?" They asked.

When the oil runs out all us traditionally built good doers will rule the world again!

Beauty comes in all sizes, not just size 5.

Roseanne Barr

Beauty in Every Form

Roxy Vandiver
Model From Houston, Texas

A twist of fate started me on the path to becoming a model. In a world where *models* are usually thought of as very tall, thin and extraordinarily beautiful, I didn't think that a girl of 5'6", with a crooked nose, who's covered in tattoos would stand a chance.

One of my very close friends is an extremely talented photographer. One night after gaining some liquid confidence in the form of several margaritas, I asked him to photograph me. I started fully clothed and ended up completely naked. We had so much fun and took such amazing photos that we decided to shoot more and more.

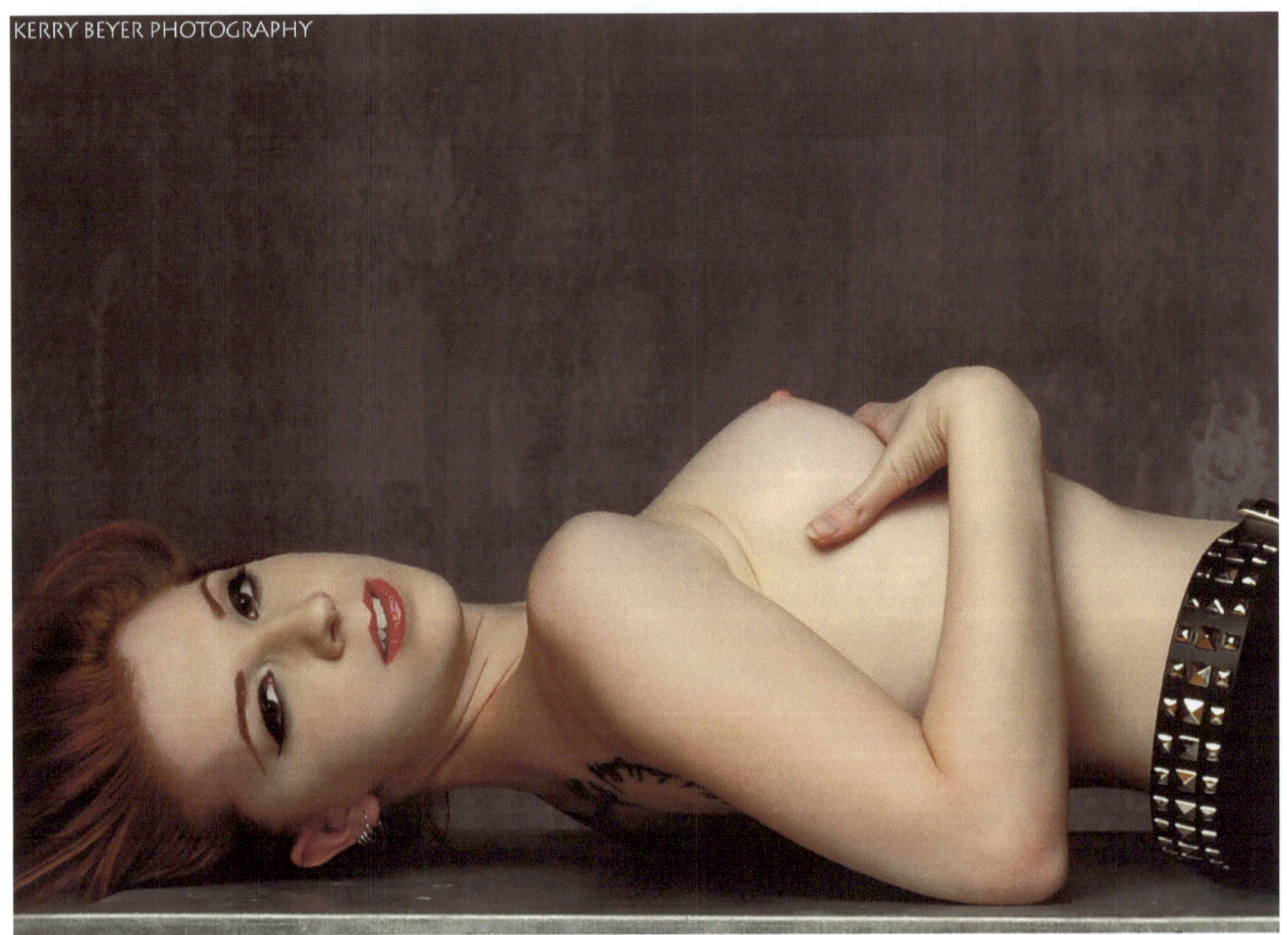

Photograph by Kerry Beyer

Over the course of 2 years we shot thousands of photos and it became an artist/muse relationship. It wasn't until another photographer approached me wanting to photograph me that I realized I might be able to model professionally. I started my website and blog and before I knew it photographers from all over the country were requesting to work with me.

At first, I was terrified to work with new photographers. I felt like my body wasn't perfect enough and, at 25, I was too old to start modeling. I have cellulite. I have stretch marks. My nose was broken when I was 14 and has definitely had an impact on my self-esteem. But through working with many photographers and meeting other models I have found that no one is perfect. Everyone has flaws and the pictures we see in magazines are lies and illusions created in Photoshop. Nobody looks like that.

My best experience of modeling has been the realization that no matter how easy it is to look in the mirror and tear yourself apart, other people aren't nearly as critical of you. That bump on my nose, most photographers don't even notice it until I point it out. After 10 years of punishing myself for not having the perfect body or face, I have finally forgiven myself. And I know now that everyone else forgave me a long time ago.

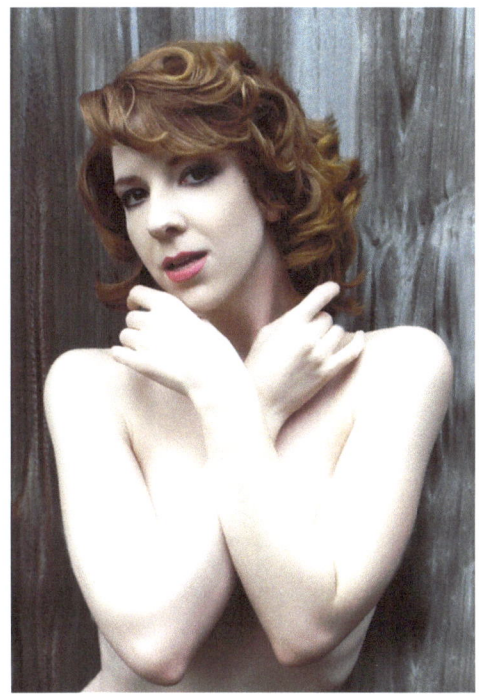

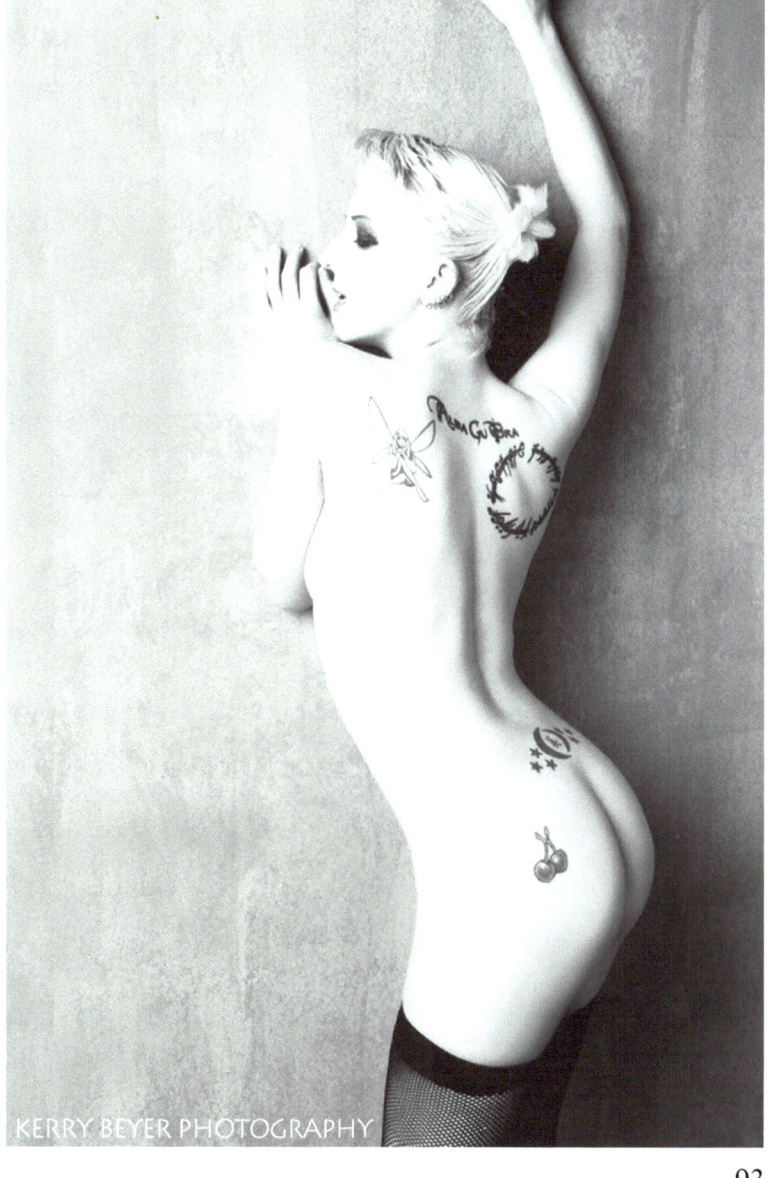

It is my belief that every woman should treat herself to the experience of having a professional photographer take beautiful, sexy photographs of her. It did wonders for my confidence and made me feel beautiful in a way that a freckle-faced, red-headed child never thought she could.

Photograph by Kerry Beyer

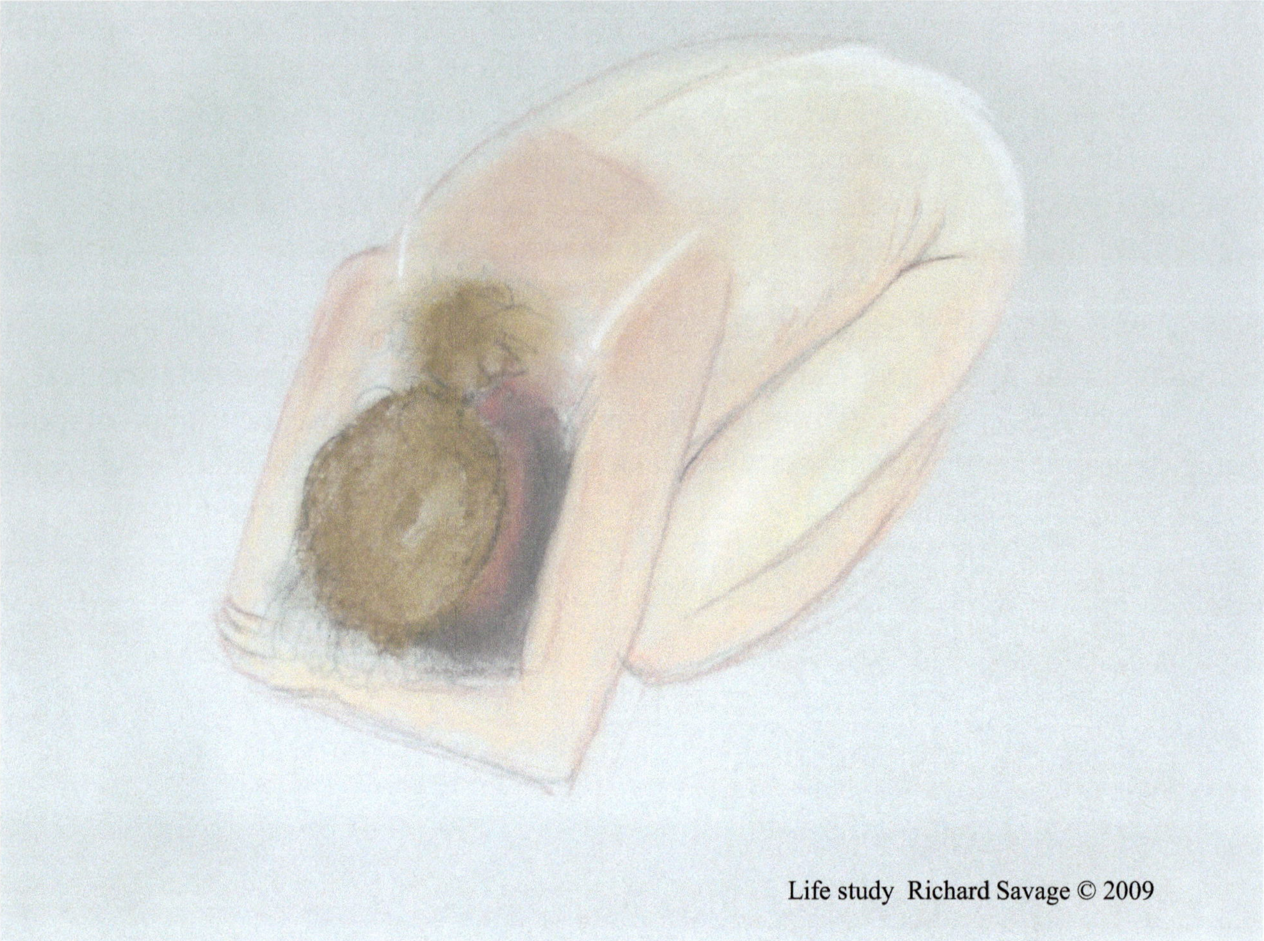

Beauty in Every Form

Life study Richard Savage © 2009

Lin

Most artists prefer natural bodies without any enhancements but some men seem to like breasts, whether real and natural or with implants, that don't move even in a reclining pose.

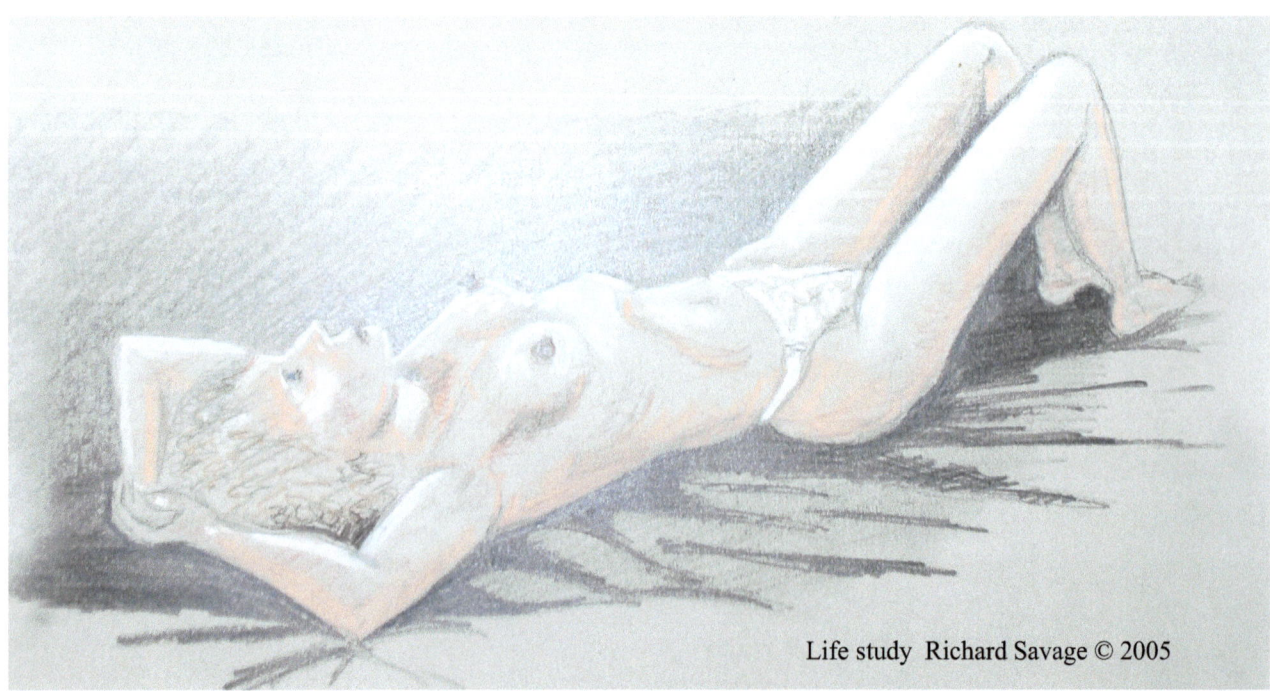

Life study Richard Savage © 2005

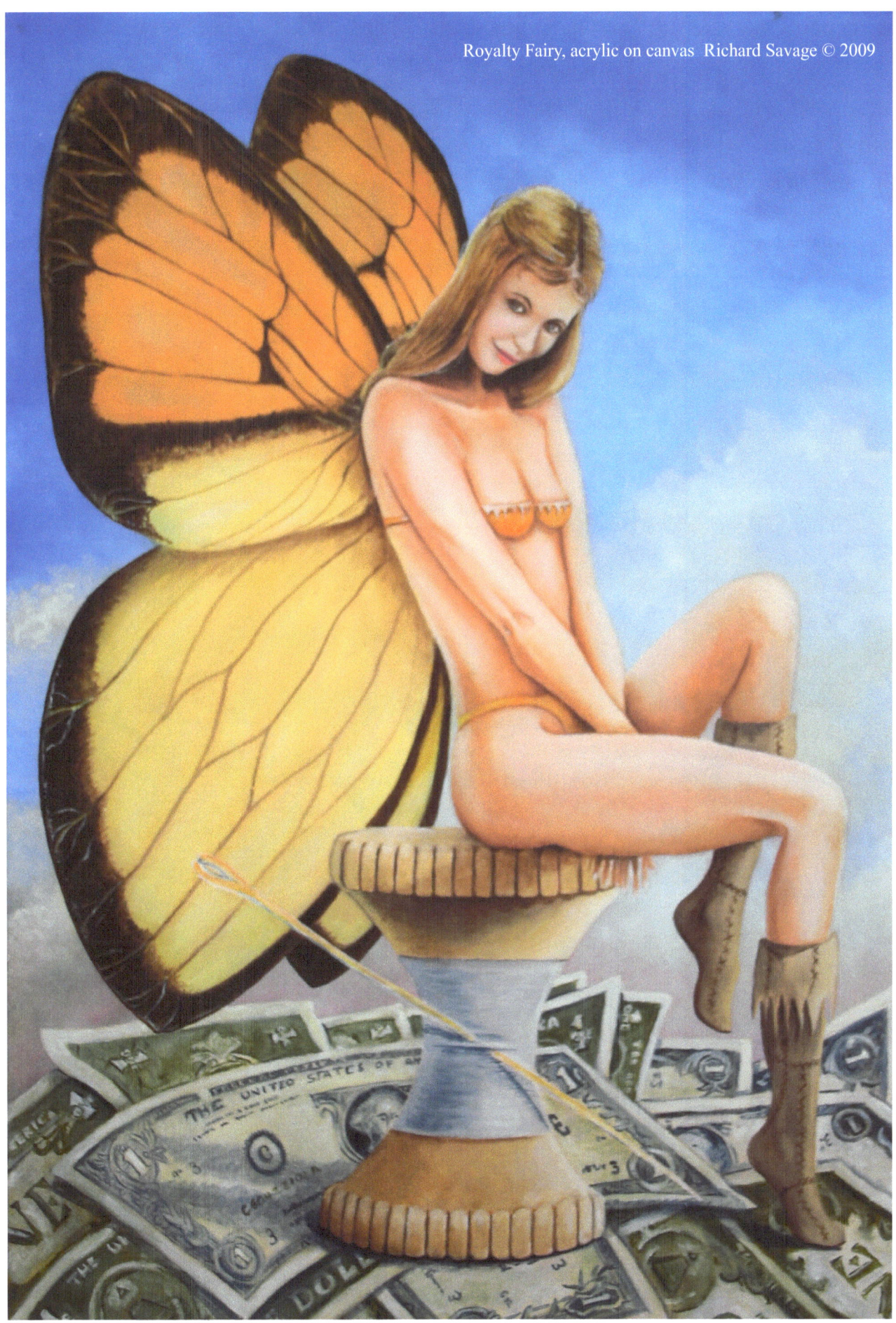
Royalty Fairy, acrylic on canvas Richard Savage © 2009

Richard Savage
Artist And Author From The UK

What I have tried to do with this book is allow people to express their feelings in their own words. That being so, when I asked for comments, not everyone shared my views on beauty. Their thoughts are equally valid and I would be failing if I did not give a voice to an alternative view. I also believe including these opinions gives a degree of depth to the subject. Some of the contributors in this section have asked to remain anonymous and I have respected the request in order to include their views.

Anonymous American Photographer

Sounds more like a cause than a marketing strategy or an artist's vision. I can hear Ray Stevens singing *everyone is beautiful in their own way* in the background right now. There is something too Politically Correct about all this. I don't trust the idea that says all people are beautiful. Because the truth is, beauty is supposed to mean something exceptional. If everyone is beautiful then really no-one is.

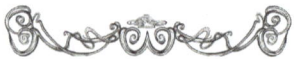

Ayn Amorelli
Author With Black Velvet Seductions

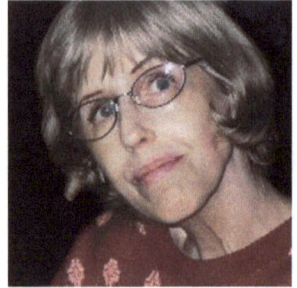

What drives me to write? Well, to tell the truth, writing keeps me sane in what I feel is often an insane world.

When I am writing or developing a character, I try to make her average, sometimes adding a few pounds here and there, so readers can, hopefully easily identify with her.

I find that the little imperfections can often add to the illusion of realism all writers strive for.

Most women want to be as attractive as they possibly can. I don't have an issue with it in fiction, but I do have an issue with the reality. The more attractive a woman is, the higher are her chances of getting married to an upwardly mobile man; she will also usually be granted more promotions in the workplace than someone who's a little homely; she is perceived as smarter, happier, and more well-liked than an average looking woman.

I deal with what I don't like by escaping into reading and writing. I've heard that the mind doesn't know an imagined experience from a real one. I think fiction helps me get what I need.

Anonymous UK Artist

There is only one beauty. As an artist it is my job to bring out the best, the most attractive in a model, the warts and all approach is no mark of beauty. Beauty is a thing you have or you don't. The idea of beauty for all, is just a way of less attractive people feeling better about themselves.

Anonymous German Glamour Model

To say everyone has beauty, devalues professional models. I have had surgery to enhance my body and I am proud of how I look. I get a lot of work because of my looks and I believe it equates to the value of beauty.

Tim Publisher of USA Fetish Magazine

I have spent most of my professional life extolling the virtues of beauty. Not everyone is beautiful and it is naïve to think they are.

While I find some thoughts a little narrow and judgmental for my taste, I feel it is right to give a forum for them. When starting this project the last thing I wanted to do was give the impression that the only view should be mine. During the process of writing and compiling this book, I came across very little negative feeling, rather the opposite. I encountered a large number of people who agree with my feelings on the subject. I stress again, I am not against conventional thoughts on beauty. I just believe rather strongly that beauty is much less confined to just one thing, it can be many things. One of the problems I have with a single definition of beauty is that if there is just one definition, just who exactly sets that definition? I find it interesting that there is no longer a Miss World beauty competition, but even as it came to an end the organizers were looking for some cerebral factors of each contestant to be taken into consideration. I feel sure it is true to say a pretty face won't hinder your chances at a job interview, but there has to be more than that to actually keep the job.

This again is a personal view. On the creative front, either artistic or literary, I like the idea of pushing the creative boundaries a little. I have nothing against the stereotype characters other than the fact I find them a little boringly cliché. Why must all the heroes be tall, dark and handsome, while all heroines are willowy, blue eyed blonds, with ample breasts and legs to die for. Surely life is more interesting than that?

Dr. Talia Witkowski
Clinical Consultant, Heal Your Hunger www.healyourhunger.com

I once worked as a doctor of psychology teaching women to *love their bodies as they were*, all the while hating my own. I tried to convince those around me to settle into bodies that they were not comfortable with to help me become comfortable in my own skin. It did not work.

I was only able to get honest with myself about how much I disliked my own body when I found a way to heal that did not include a diet, exercise regimen, or medication, but rather an emotional and spiritual program and a way of life. It allowed me to heal the deep seated sense of worthlessness that drove me to overeat and try to control my weight and food.

Once I got well, my need to control others fell away and was replaced by a desire to be the best I could be, to attract those who were suffering as I had been.

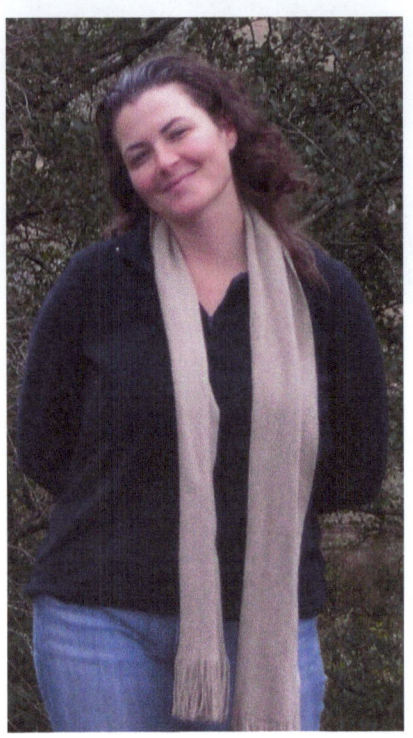
Before

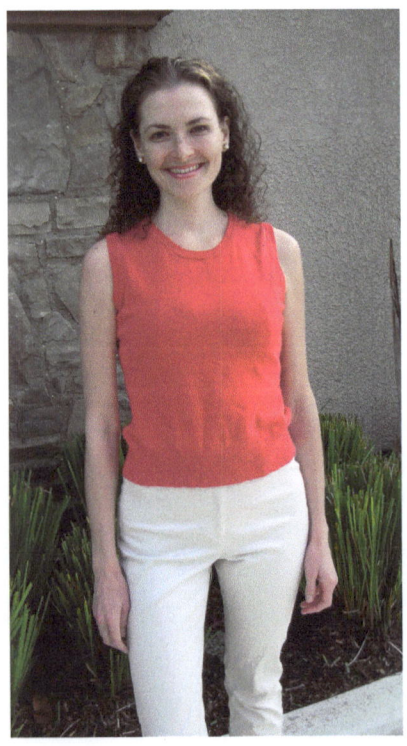
After

Many people live overweight and hide the shame and sadness because they think there is no other way. They are too scared and feel too hopeless to ask for help. They think they have tried everything and failed. I am here to tell anyone who still has a desire to like their body and cannot buy the *love your body as it is* line, that there is a way to be free of the need to hate one's body. This can happen without having to settle into being overweight, without needing to restrict diet, without exercise and without the use of medication or surgery.

I finally got help from Heal Your Hunger, www.healyourhunger.com, a group that taught me, through meditation, writing exercises and personal coaching, how to live differently in order to truly be able to love myself. When I made peace with myself the weight fell away, and stayed away, without having to diet or exercise to do it. This program was truly weight loss *from the inside out*.

After a lifetime of trying to get women to love their bodies as they were, all the while hating my own, it was refreshing to be able to share this message with the world.

Just When Does A Sex Kitten Become The Tigress

Mature..... I really don't like this rather ambiguous term, but just what is mature? Is there an age at which we are no longer beautiful? During the course of writing and compiling this book, I have talked to a great many people with a great number of differing opinions. The people have been from all over the world and take into account a variety of ethnic and cultural ideas. Some have told me how very wrong I am. Some of the views have been rather hard line, that beauty is.... And that there is an undetectable line where things either are or are not beautiful. Age and size struck me as the area where most of these folk seemed to have a problem. I will address my view on size shortly, but first age.

In the discussion forums when the topic of age came up, I invariably asked if they considered their mothers beautiful. Most, understandably, said yes. So, it is the person that matters. I believe that people can take on a beauty as they get older. Certainly, as an artist, I find drawing and painting an older face interesting. With older people does gender matter? You do hear older actresses say the parts become less glamorous as their careers progress, but when you look at the silver screen today I still find actresses such as Helen Mirren and Joanna Lumley stunningly attractive and sexy. With male actors I get the impression that their roles get better with age. Listening to the opinion of ladies, actors such as George Clooney and Sean Connery, seem to have retained their looks. I feel sure you will have your own examples of movie stars, but is it attractiveness? Personality? Charisma? Or do all of these factors roll together to make a person beautiful? And if it works for the stars, why not us mere mortals?

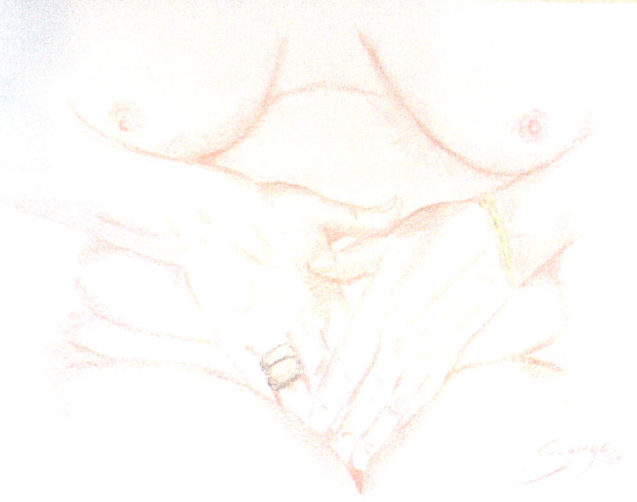

Just Another Personal View

I have known some very attractive people over the years and some have not been the nicest of people. I feel that something of the lack of inner beauty seems to shine through to the surface and I believe the reverse is true. With some people inner beauty shines out.

A Guarded Moment, pencil Richard Savage © 2005

I suppose one of the biggest areas of conflict in the debate about the nature of beauty has been size. My own struggle with weight has been with me from school. I have never really been a creature of moderation so I have yo-yoed in weight over the years.

Over the years, I have had something of a love hate relationship with food. I am a binge eater and a comfort eater. I experience self-loathing due to my own eating habits and it feels like I have this personal conflict with food a lot of the time. My weight over the last 30 years has fluctuated, bouncing between two hundred and two hundred and forty pounds. I currently sit at about two hundred and ten pounds. I know from my personal weight loss and gain that there is a correlation between my eating habits, my mood swings, and my self-esteem. I have owned a restaurant for over twenty-six years which has not helped my relationship with food. It was way too easy to sample tasty snacks or eat food surplus.

Food addiction and eating disorders are dreadful things and I feel our society is rather unsympathetic to those who suffer. I have been touched emotionally by the people that have contacted me on the subject of weight. Some did not want to contribute but wanted to tell me their story, some embrace who they are and shared their stories within these pages. I thank everyone who contacted me. There was one person who contacted me from an Amazon forum, a very intolerant individual, whose opinion was rather set: "Beautiful has nothing at all to do with the beholder. Obesity, for example, is ugly, because it proclaims a selfish chauvinism. An individual with the girth that would suggest that another starved that they could eat is ugly. Slim is essential and efficient, and therefore beautiful whether appreciated or not. Perfection is beautiful, whether that is in human form or in artistic accomplishment."

It just struck me as so very sad that someone should be that blinkered. I am sure that by this stage in the book you will have gathered that, in my opinion, size is no obstacle to beauty.

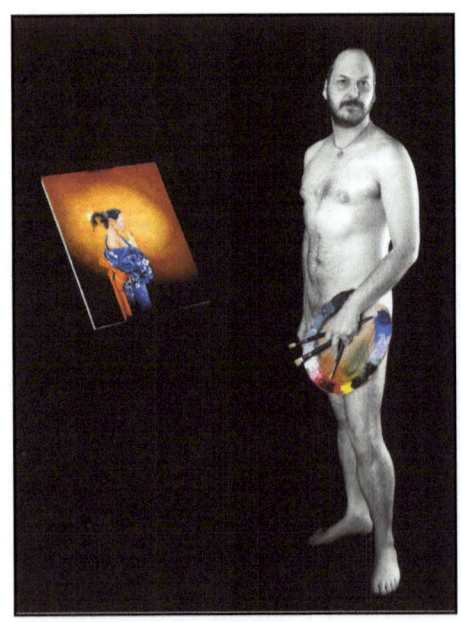

Photograph by Rob Morris

I believe our self image is a fundamental key factor to defining ourselves as people. I feel we owe it to ourselves to love who we are and accept how we look. As an artist I meet a lot of models, and I have not come across many who don't start by telling me about what they perceive as their physical flaws and asking me to be kind.

I had an interesting opportunity in early 2009. I was bullied into a naked calendar shoot. It was interesting to be on the wrong side of camera, the subject rather than the observer. It made me think deeply about my own self image and where I am not particularly ashamed of my body, I do not consider myself as anything more than a slightly overweight, middle aged, balding bloke.

If I am totally honest I didn't really want to take part in the project, but if I had pulled out I felt I would have been letting other people down. Having agreed to do it, I had a series of pictures taken, by a photographer friend and colleague, Rob Morris. I found the experience strangely empowering. Talking to the others in the calendar, I found, without exception, they all felt the same way that I did, that it was a very positive experience.

We have all seen plastic surgery taken to extremes, and for all the money thrown at the surgeon, some still spectacularly fail to hit their perceived goal of perfection. I am reluctant to mention Michael Jackson yet he is a perfect example. I guess the message I would like to leave you with is, be proud of who you are, love who you are as a person, be content with who you are, and if you do want to change what you look like, do it because *you* want to do it for *you*, not because you think the world will consider you a better person for doing it.

I would like to thank you for reading. I hope you have enjoyed the book and that it has made you consider the subject of beauty with new eyes. I would like to thank all of the contributors for so openly sharing their thoughts and feelings. I would also like to mention those who wanted their feelings felt yet didn't want a formal contribution. I hope I have covered their views in my writing. I would like to thank the photographers who allowed me to use their pictures to illustrate sections of this book, a full list of credits follow. More thanks go out to Marian for all her help with research, admin and trying to keep my wayward text and punctuation in check. I would like to thank my wife, Kath, for all her hard work which gave me the time to write and compile this publication. Last and, by no means least, I would like to thank Laurie Sanders, contributor, my editor, publisher and friend. Through all our projects she is a leading light and inspiration. Her hard work and clear vision drives Black Velvet Seductions and inspires me to be the best I can be.

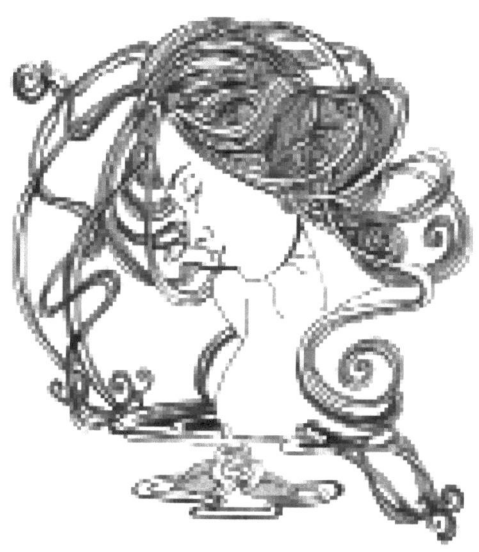

Contributors

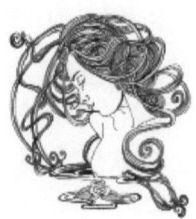

A special thank you to everyone who has contributed to this book listed in the order they appear.

Intro Photography - Rob Morris
Foreword Dr Tuppy Owens
Page 2 Photography - Rob Morris
Page 5 Laurie Sanders, Rob Morris, Lin Reed
Page 7 Lin Reed
Page 8 - 10 Alana Yvonne Wallace, photography - Natalie Perkins, William Frederking, Better Image Studios, Homer's photography
Page 11 Marian Savill
Page 12 Janice, Secretchick
Page 14 - 16 Rob Morris including photography
Page 18 Tabby, photography - Rob Morris
Page 19 Drew Turney
Page 20 - 26 Christopher John Ball including photography www.classicnudes.co.uk
Page 27 Charlotte Hough
Page 32 - 33 Tim Rosier including photography www.venusadonis.co.uk
Page 36 Lin Reed
Page 37 & 38 Andy, photography - Andybelladonna, Drakin
Page 39 Belladonna, photography by Andybelladonna
Page 40 & 41 Nori Zay, photography – Trisha Bowyer, Ka Xiong, Elizabeth May, Liquid Science, Makeup & hair - Viva La Kayleigh, ToriUnicorn MUA, Donna Aguilar, Kittycut. Wardrobe -The Art Farm, Karen von Oppen
Page 42 Lin Reed
Page 43 Becky Vigor including photography
Page 44 & 45 Marian Savill, photography – Rob Morris
Page 46 Katie, Lin Reed
Page 47 Lin Reed, Kat the Leopardess
Page 48 & 49 Tracie, photography – Carsten Dieterich
Page 49 Jill Bickford www.LivingEarthBeauty.com
Page 52 & 53 Bill Clearlake including photography
Page 56 & 57 Nicola Priest
Page 58 Riga
Page 59 Hollis Cartwright Blume
Page 60 – 63 Alex Cowen, photography – Alistair Morrison
Page 66 & 67 Aya I'Anson, photography – Mike Crawley www.photofrenetic.com, Grey Photography

Page 68 Chris, photography – Rob Morris
Page 70 & 71 Tina, photography – Rob Morris
Page 72 - 74 Christie Mawer www.thebadkitty.com
Page 76 Lin Reed
Page 77 Elizabeth N. Spire www.unseenwords.com
Page 78 & 79 Pentyn's Pet
Page 80 & 81 Carol Tierney
Page 82 Lin Reed
Page 83 Lee Rush
Page 84 Lin Reed
Page 85 A J Best
Page 89 Lin Reed
Page 91 Liz Wright
Page 92 & 93 Roxy Vandiver, photography – Kerry Beyer Photography
Page 94 Lin Reed
Page 96 Anonymous American photographer, Ayn Amorelli
Page 97 Anonymous UK artist, anonymous German glamour model, Tim
Page 98 Dr. Talia Witkowski www.healyourhunger.com
Page 100 Photography – Rob Morris

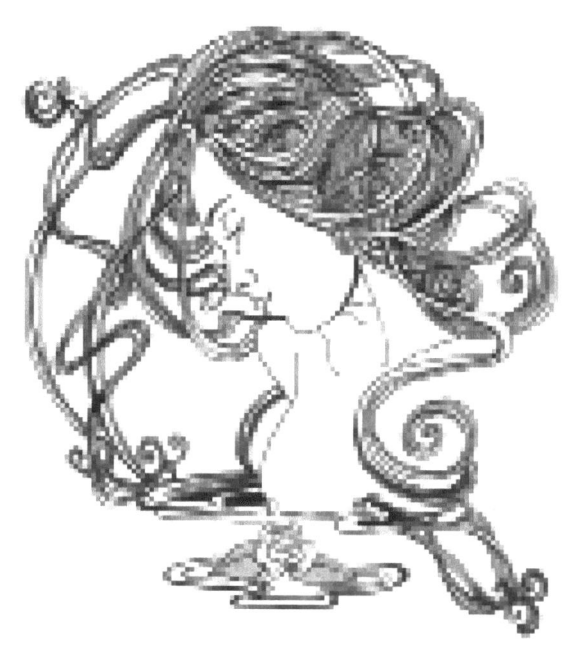

About Richard Savage

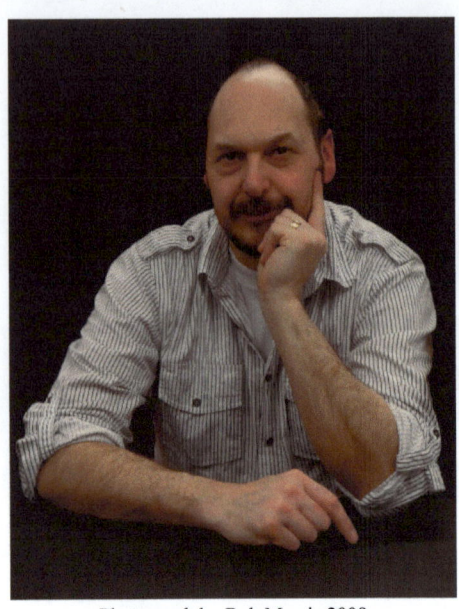

Photograph by Rob Morris 2009

Organizations

Member of The Guild of Erotic Artists
Professional Associate Member of The Society of All Artists
Member of The Association Erotic Artists
The British Museum of Erotic Art
Founding member of the Fenland Visual Arts Collective, chair 2005-6
Member of Fenland Arts Association Executive committee, 2005-6

Published Fiction

First published story, The Anniversary, in the anthology The Crimson Z, Black Velvet Seductions, publication date November 2006
Illustration published in Spiritual Transformation through BDSM: Stories and Submissions from Fellow Travellers, edited by Sensuous Sadie   June 2007
The Key and Temporally Yours, Black Velvet Seductions, publication January 2008
In the Driving Seat, short story, Black Velvet Seductions, publication January 2009.
Spanked! Black Velvet Seductions, publication date October 2010
Beauty in Every Form, Black Velvet Seductions, publication date 2013.

Featured In

Featured artist in Jade Magazine March – April 2007
Featured artist in Scarlet Magazine January 2008
Featured as an artist in The Guild of Erotic Artists Vol. II October 2008
Featured artist in Forum Penthouse March 2009
Featured artist in Scarlet Magazine October 2009
Featured artist in Erotic Knave Magazine April 2010
Featured artist in Fetish Art & Photography 2011 Ltd. Edition FetishCreatives.com

Broadcasts

Music of My Life on the Mark Rumble show BBC Radio Cambridgeshire 10/6/2012
Sue Dougan's Afternoon Show BBC Radio Cambridgeshire 25/2/2013
Sue Dougan's Afternoon Show BBC Radio Cambridgeshire 27/3/2013

Recent exhibitions

The Museum of Contemporary Art, Washington DC, March – May 2005
Cambridge Open Studio Exhibition, Palace House, Newmarket, June 18th - 23rd 2005
Cambridge Open Studio, July 2nd/3rd, 9th/10th, 16th/17th, 23rd/24th 2005
Solo exhibition, March Town Hall, October 5th - 19th 2005
Fenland Visual Arts Collective Open Studios, September 2006
100% pure, The Glass Box, Coventry, September 2006
The Expo, Skin Two, The Barbican Centre, London, October 7th/8th 2006
ETO exhibition, Birmingham NEC, 22nd /23rd July 2007
Erotica, Olympia, London, November 23rd - 25th 2007
Amora, The London Academy of Sex and Relationships, April - October 2008.
Passion, Earls Court, London, May 24th/25th 2008
Excite, Savage Studios, Chatteris, October 24th - 26th 2008
Erotica, Olympia, London, November 21st - 23rd 2008
Excite, Savage Studios, Chatteris, October 22nd - 25th 2009
Erotica, Olympia, London, November 22nd - 25th 2009
100 Square Feet, London, February 2010
Erotica, Olympia, London, November 19th - 21st 2010
Skin Two North, Leeds February 12th 2011
Olympus 2012, 63rd Sci-Fi Convention, London 6th - 9th 2012
The Gallery, Cork Street, Piccadilly London 23rd - 31st August 2012
Menier Gallery, London Monday 7th – 19th January 2013
Currently represented in the British Museum of Erotic Art

Cover illustrations
Covers for Black Velvet Seductions

Toy's Story by Robert Cloud
Rally Fever by Crea Jones
The Stir of Echo by Susan Gabriel
The Crimson Z by Robert Cloud, Lee Rush, Richard Savage, Abby Blythe, Kara Elsberry
Temporally Yours and The Key by Richard Savage
Night Angel by Renee Reeves
Holly's Big Bad Santa by Starla Kaye
Only the Lonely by Susan Gabriel
Spanked by Starla Kaye, Richard Savage, and Cara Bristol
Her Cowboy's Way by Starla Kaye
Their Lady Gloriana by Starla Kaye
Cowboys in Charge by Starla Kaye
Snowed in with Her Cowboy by Starla Kaye
The Bride Wore Red by Starla Kaye
In the Driving Seat by Richard Savage
Trusting Her by Starla Kaye
Intimate Submission by Cara Bristol
Secret Desires by Cara Bristol
Cultural Concession by Anissa Blume
Meredith's First Spanking by Nadia Nautalia

Boredom = Trouble by Starla Kaye
Christmas Crazy by Starla Kaye
Confession Time by Nadia Nautalia
A Special Gift for Her Cowboy
by Starla Kaye
All I Want for Christmas (Biggest Prize Ever) by Starla Kaye
Cowboys and Their Toys by Starla Kaye
For the Love of His Cowgirl
by Starla Kaye
Naughty, Naughty Cowgirl by Starla Kaye
Too Much Red at Christmas Time
by Starla Kaye
A Chocolate Kind of Day by Starla Kaye
Gobble,Gobble...Grumble, Grumble
By Starla Kaye
Naughty in Vegas by Starla Kaye
Needing Her Cowboy by Starla Kaye
The Cattleman's Ball by Starla Kaye
Misbehavin' in Mexico by Starla Kaye
Warm All Over by Starla Kaye
Testing Their Love by Starla Kaye
A Light In The Darkness by various authors, edited by J.S. Wayne
Incorrigible by Abby Blythe
The Anniversary by Richard Savage
Accidental Affair by Leslie McKelvey
A New Way Forward by Nadia Nautalia
Rose's Cowboys by Starla Kaye
Beauty in Every Form
by Richard Savage

Covers for Pink Flamingo

A Shameful Devotion by Ron Kozloff
Capturing Cressida by Imogen Edwards
Convincing Maggie by BJ Wane
Her Submissive by BJ Wane
Crimes & Lovers by Lizbeth Dusseau
Jealousy: Tessa's Submission
by Ophelia
Jordon's Pet by Rose Thornwell
The Velvet Whip by J D Jensen
Sasha's Portrait: The Art of S
by BJ Wane
Swastika Binds: Holly's Sex Mistress
by Eddy Vale
The Handmaiden's Revenge
by Lizbeth Dusseau
The Saga of a Naughty Lady
by Lizbeth Dusseau

Covers for Desdemona

Bras Coup by Anon
Cold Hands Warm Heart
by Vincent Diamond
Forget the Bitch by Anon
In the Stars by Anon
A Visit from the Man in Red
By Jean Roberta
Mr. Johnson and I by Ezra Zane
Over The Limit by Jeremy Spencer
Queremos by Jean Roberta
Rebirth by Scott Allen
Rocky Shoals by Sarah Black
The Rooftop by Faith Bicknell-Brown
Shakespeare by Anon
Stiletto by Anon
Sunny Summer Loving
by Patrick Myers
Blast From The Past by Patrick Myers
The Silent Tutsi by Bradley Stoke
The Lady of the Moon by Anon
The Loan Couch by Jack Pfeffer
The Waterhole by Leonard Waters

Covers for Blue Moon Publications

The Latest Thing in Space Dolls by Sidney Durham
Into The Black by Ally Blue
Night Wolfing by Brenda Williamson
Wicked Women by Pam

Miscellaneous other covers

The Last Days of Thunderchild by Colin A Powell
Zap by Zabeta Manatakis cover and illustrations by Richard Savage
A Very Special Place to Poop by Richard Savage and Laurie Sanders

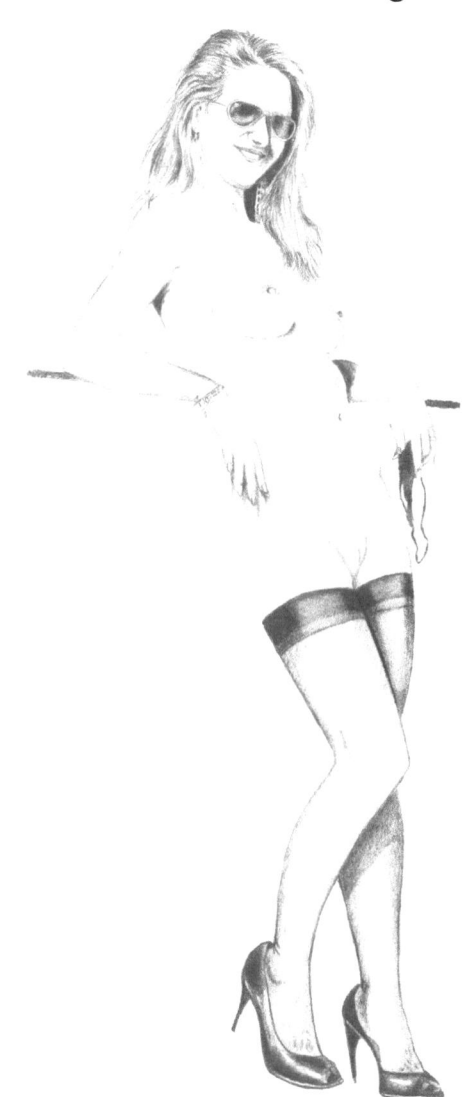

Jennie Shooting the Breeze, pencil on Bristol Board by Richard Savage 2013

To see more of Richard's art visit
www.swage.net and
www.affordable-fineart.com

For further details contact
ric@swage.net

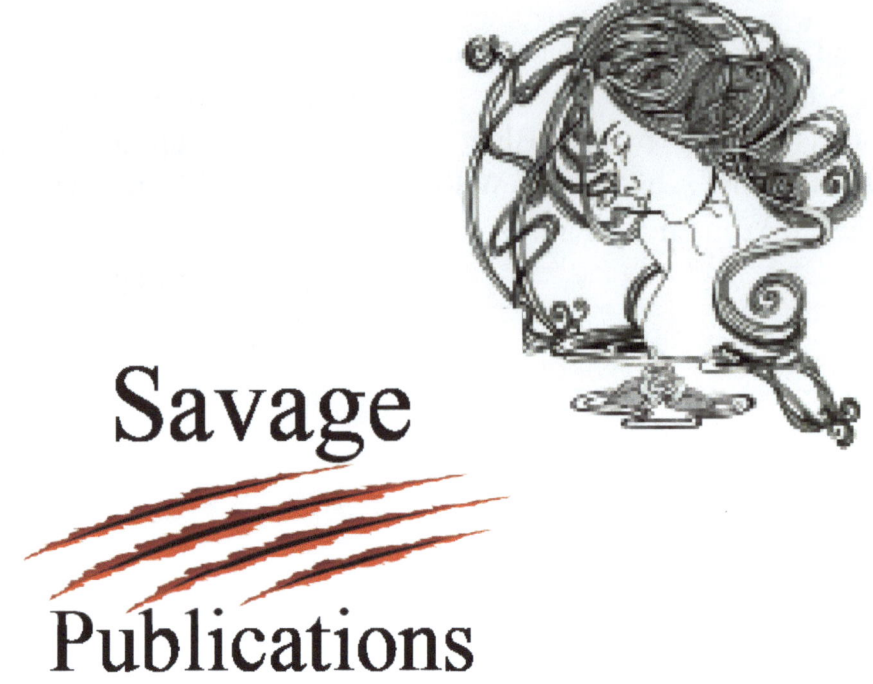

Savage Publications

In Association With

Black Velvet Seductions

Beauty In Every Form

By
Richard J. Savage

www.ingramcontent.com/pod-product-compliance
Lightning Source LLC
Chambersburg PA
CBHW051151220526
45473CB00003B/740